Advance Praise for Lurigancho

"An astonishing true story that has every twist and turn you could imagine. Eddie's is a story that plunges to the bleakest depths and soars to the greatest heights. Guns, drugs, girls, South American hell-holes—it has it all...."

—Nick Green, Director of the National Geographic documentary "The Hippie Mafia"

"Edward Padilla's gritty street prose takes the reader into a desperate Heart of Darkness from which not many could ever emerge. But this gripping narrative turns emergence into a transcendent awakening and genuine rebirth. This is the real stuff, no modifiers required."

—John Kent Harrison, Screenwriter/Director

"Eddie Padilla embodies so much of the promise and peril of post-War Southern California that it makes your head spin: a multiracial child of the New West; schooled by surfers, street fighters, and smugglers; turned on as a '60s seeker; turned out as a '70s nihilist. In Lurigancho Prison, Peru, a Dante-esque catalog of horrors, Padilla paid for California's broken dreams as much as his own. His brave escape and ongoing recovery offer a dagger of redemption and hope in the fight against 21st century cynicism and apathy."

—Joe Donnelly, Co-editor/Founder *Slake: Los Angeles*, author of "The Pirate of Penance"

D1601471

LURIGANCHO

Edward Padilla
and Paul Wood

FLYING RABBIT PRESS
Maui, Hawai'i

Published by Flying Rabbit Press
PO Box 880949
Pukalani, HI 96788
flyingrabbitpress@gmail.com

ISBN-10 0-9706200-5-5
ISBN-13 978-0-9706200-5-7

To contact Edward Padilla for speaking events, email: goldrose108@gmail.com

Cover and book design by Karen Bacon, www.karenannbacon.com
Cover image: BigStockPhoto

"Hope is definitely not the same thing as optimism. It is not the conviction that something will turn out well, but the conviction that something makes sense, no matter how it turns out."

—Vaclav Havel, *Disturbing the Peace*

CONTENTS

Introduction   1

1   Pelone   7

2   Chivo   85

3   Zoila   149

4   Nina   209

5   The Rev   265

6   Lucho   323

7   Reyna   367

Afterword   395

LURIGANCHO

Introduction

I have told this story to thousands of people—to people in jails, in prisons, in high schools and colleges, and I have told it to people in all kinds of recovery programs. But I have never told the story all the way, right down to the terrible bottom and all the way up.

One of the lessons I learned, and reinforced in myself by writing this book, is this: if you want to escape, you can't begin with your feet, or with a ladder, or with a shovel, or with a gun. You have to begin with your own mind and heart. Only then will the necessary assistance come.

Everything in this story is true. I told many lies as I fought for survival, and all of those lies are truthfully recorded in this book. However, I have changed the names of most of the characters. It was my duty to change them. Some people risked their lives to help me. Others—men who are now (I assume) fine upstanding American citizens—would probably be persecuted if I told the whole world that they once spent years in Lurigancho Prison. After all, the mob mentality of the "war on drugs" has given people permission to hate some of the men in this story.

Some names in this story are factual. General Del Gado, for example. Even if he were still alive, I wouldn't see any reason to mask his satanic identity.

In fact, Del Gado died not very long after the events in this story—

gunned down, as he deserved, by a stranger in the dark. The hero of this shooting was an American from Oregon, a young man who had just returned from combat in Vietnam only to discover that his own father had been seized by the Peruvian police. The vet traveled alone to Peru with the intent to rescue his father, but he arrived too late. His father had already been executed by a shot to the head, delivered by Del Gado himself. The young American confronted Del Gado as the General was exiting a police station. Del Gado took aim and shot at the stranger. The vet emptied the clip of his nine-millimeter pistol into Del Gado's chest then made his escape back to the U.S. I found this story reported in a popular pictorial magazine, and now, twenty-five years later, I sincerely wish I had kept a copy of that article—proof of my experience. For Del Gado himself has faded from history, replaced by any number of equally capable sadists.

The events described in this account are all true. For storytelling purposes, my co-writer and I did shift the actual timing of certain events. After all, most of the time spent in prison is intensely boring.

In a sense, Lurigancho is not on the map, not on any map that tells the truth. Lurigancho is a psychosis, an invention of our insane times. It is a poisonous jellyfish with tentacles that reach all the way to the U.S. border and into the mind. Peruvians call it "la casa del Diablo," the house of the devil, suggesting that the reality of Lurigancho is in part metaphysical.

And yet it is also physical and it does exist, and it exists today pretty much as I experienced it thirty years ago. Amnesty International has ranked it as the worst prison in the world.

Lurigancho is Peru's largest prison. It was built to hold sixteen hundred prisoners. But in the year 2000, by the prisoners' own count, it was housing about seven thousand people.

The structure consists of twelve "pabellones" (cellblocks) surrounded by a carefully guarded wall. According to a 2000 report published in the British Medical Journal—the eyewitness account of a doctor volunteering in the prison with Medecinas Sans Frontiers—

only about twenty unarmed warders interact with the prison population, which essentially regulates itself. Prisoners without money have to work for the wealthier ones, doing everything from laundry to sexual services.

Lori Berenson was twenty-six years old when she was arrested for allegedly helping to plan a terrorist attack on Peru's congress. Her real crime, apparently, was an immoderate expression of compassion. In the eighth grade she volunteered to work in a soup kitchen, and then she narrated a commercial for CARE, the international service group. "Over half the children on Earth are hungry and malnourished," she said in that commercial. She attended M.I.T., but left there in 1992 to become more politically active. She traveled to El Salvador and "sided with the search for justice"—which meant joining the guerrilla movement. In 1994 she crossed into Peru, where (she said at the time) "There is a lot of poverty, a lot of social injustice." In '94, Peru's daily climate was explosive. The Alberto Fujimori government's brutal oppression had triggered street fighting and other forms of sabotage by guerrilla forces, groups such as the Marxist movement Tupac Amaru. On November 30, 1995, police raided the house in which Lori was staying, believing it to be the headquarters of the Tupac Amaru.

She was tried at Lurigancho Prison by a military tribunal. The judges wore hoods, and the trial lasted just minutes. Her attorney had done no preparation. There was no cross-examination of witnesses, nor was Lori allowed to make a statement.

Obviously the Peruvian justice system has not improved since my experience.

At this writing she is paroled but still detained in Peru having served most of her twenty-year sentence behind bars. She has circulatory problems and is losing vision in her right eye. Her father Mark Berenson says: "I think the State Department has wronged us by never having taken a stand on [Lori's] innocence or guilt."

On February 28, 2000, four thousand "common" prisoners at Lurigancho staged a protest. They refused to return to their cells.

They started burning mattresses, and they gathered on the rooftops to hang banners calling for better conditions. Authorities sent fifteen hundred riot police to put down the rebellion. Helicopters dropped teargas on the rooftops. The problem is the U.S. complicity in all this. Our country supported the Fujimori regime, promoting it as an example of progress for Latin America. At the same time, the regime was practicing death-squad murders, military massacres, massive police sweeps, and the rape and torture of detainees. The U.S. helped to design and finance courts that were railroading "suspects" through military tribunals with hooded judges. "Fujimori" became synonymous with U.S.-sponsored crimes against the people of Peru.

Since my time in Lurigancho, the suffering of the common people of Peru has been expressed as a "people's war." The Maoist forces of revolution, called Sendero Luminoso or The Shining Path, have proven to be just as violent as their oppressors. Naturally, many of these "Senderistas" now reside in Lurigancho Prison. Their cause has given them the will to resist the prison system's degradation. They have tried to work cooperatively, supported by families outside, to transform the prisons into "shining trenches of combat."

Can prison be a battlefront? Yes, in the nightmare we used to call "Luri World." For instance, on June 19, 1986, inmates in three Peruvian prisons, primarily Lurigancho, staged a protest. In response, the military dynamited its way into Lurigancho, captured 135 protesters, and killed them all. At least a hundred of these men were victims of "extrajudicial execution." In other words, they were killed just because.

Why does the U.S. support such injustice and inhumanity? There must be a pay-off. Could it have something to do with profits to be made with as-yet-untapped oil?

Amazon Watch reports that in 2003 the Peruvian State granted the international oil industry access without restriction to indigenous ancestral lands throughout the Peruvian Amazon. The last refuges of Peru's native people, people living in voluntary isolation by traditional practices such as hunting and fishing—people like Zoila and her family, people like Chivo—these last stands are now in the grip of international oil companies. U.S. companies are leading the race, of course, financed by U.S. government funds.

For example, the Camisea Natural Gas Project has begun to infiltrate the homelands of previously uncontacted peoples in Peru's Nahua-Kugapakori Reserve. Camisea is a project of Texas-based Hunt Oil, a company that has enjoyed excellent White House connections. The destiny of the Nahua-Kugapakori Reserve can be glimpsed by comparing it to a similar situation in the rainforest of Ecuador, where ChevronTexaco operated and left behind more than six hundred toxic waste pits. These pits continue to pollute the area's rivers and streams, the freshwater source for the indigenous people of the region. Cancer, miscarriages, skin ailments, birth defects are rife with the remaining people. The native Cofan people numbered fifteen thousand when Texaco began its operations in the 1970s; today only eight hundred Cofans survive. At the ChevronTexaco Annual Meeting in April 2004, shareholders expressed outrage at the irresponsible behavior of their own company. But ChevronTexaco's CEO David O'Reilly fended off all responsibility. He passed all the blame onto the Ecuadorian government, which he called "inept" and "inadequate."

But if U.S. financial interests are propping up "inadequate" governments, then we clearly have a terrible example of circular buck-passing. This is the spinning of life's water as it circles the drain. Lurigancho is one of those filthy drains, and the angels of my story are the ones being flushed.

Essentially, U.S. tax dollars are financing the destruction of Peru's natural environment and the genocide of Peru's native people. Lurigancho Prison is an important part of the system of genocide—a blotter to soak up the ruined lives.

I say all this in a small attempt to show that the story of my time in Lurigancho is important—not important because of me but important because of the angelic souls who really deserve our caring. I am one of the few people who has ever escaped, and I am still escaping. In writing this book, I have escaped a bit more. But there is no getting away from Lurigancho.

We should destroy it.

1

PELONE

Lurigancho Prison
Peru, South America
1975

Eight thousand men snoring and dying, these are the sounds at night as I lie on my bunk.

I'm lying here thinking about that scream. It came from the first floor, but because it had death in it, it echoed throughout the cellblock. Then I heard a lot of commotion from the other prisoners, all speaking Spanish. About ten minutes later I heard the guard's key open a cell. I thought I could hear sobbing. Then the iron door slammed shut. The snoring resumed—the nightly background music to this nightmare.

I've been awake ever since.

Not a real big deal. A scream in the night is routine.

Now it's first light, and here comes the real wake-up. That fucking fifty-five-gallon steel drum starts rolling down the length of the concrete yard that separates our cellblock from the one across the way. I don't have to look out the window to know the scene—a dark-skinned rag of a man pushing and kicking the drum, the metal barrel bouncing its brutal voice hard against the two brick cellblocks and then off the concrete at each end of our narrow rectangle world. I have heard this mind-grinding barrel every ugly morning of my life for seven long-ass months. I know exactly where we are in the routine. He starts rolling the barrel, and I am suddenly paralyzed by a wave of cold reality. He's at the outside end of our yard, by the gate. He's going to roll that barrel the full length of the yard, all the way up to the wall of the Big Hall. Then he'll stand it up next to our latrine, which is nothing but an exposed hole in the concrete. He'll stand it up next to another barrel just like it, only this one is full of water with a rusty coffee can floating in it. At the end of the day the empty barrel will be full of old yellowed newspaper that six hundred men have used for toilet paper. Then that same rag of a man will drag and scrape the barrel to the opposite end of the yard and torch it, launching an aroma that suits Lurigancho. Smoke will rise into the dead air.

I get up on my elbows. I'm in the middle of a three-bunk stack, so my head is level with the barred window. Looking across the yard, I see the top of the neighboring cellblock backlit by the rising sun. A rat is running across the top of the wall, a rat the size of a dachshund. The bugs around here left for town years ago, but the rats stayed.

Now Rick is out of his bunk and standing at the cell door, jiggling. "Hey you bastards! Come open this fucking gate before I piss on the floor!"

Our cell is crowded with three-tiered bunk beds, seven of them. And we have a couple of Peruvians sleeping on the floor. The guards like to throw Peruvians in here just to irritate us. But soon they'll go back where they belong.

This is the newest of the twelve cellblocks. Money from the American government built it. There are three toilets in here, but they don't work. If you flush them, the cell floods with backed-up sewer water and shit. The place stinks enough without that assistance. We all have acute amebic dysentery. Kaopectate is the drug of choice. We cook our food in the cell—when we have food to cook.

There are reportedly eight thousand men in Lurigancho Prison—built for just over a thousand.

The gringo cell, ours, is at the far end of the hall on the top level of our two-story cellblock. The hall is lined with cells just like ours only more crowded. The clashing of the guard's keys in the locks, that's the sound that men urgently want to hear. Rick is no longer alone at the iron-barred door. The constant human uproar of Lurigancho has done a cross-fade from snoring to hundreds of men waking up in hell, hacking and coughing. I know where the hocks are going—spitting out through the bars into the common hallway. Pretty soon the drumming will start, the insane banging of mental defectives stuck in a hopelessly deep groove.

I roll out of my bunk. Arthur is in front of me. "Mornin'," he says. "You hear that dude scream downstairs?"

"Haven't slept since."

Now everybody's awake and most people are gathering at the cell door—except Kit. "Hey, wake up Kit for count," yells Carlton.

The drill we're all waiting for is this: The guard unlocks the door and we file out and line up in the hall. Then the guard stands at the door and counts us as we march back in. As soon as he gets the count right, we are free to get in line for the latrine.

This is the morning routine on our cellblock, but not on the cellblock across the yard. The guards refuse to enter that one. Lurigancho has several of these locked-up monster pits.

Ivan lives below me in the bunk. Tony lives on top. Right now Ivan's on his back reading a novel. Ivan lays the paperback on his large chest. He is a giant. He says in his buzzing Czechoslovakian accent, very Arnold Schwarzenegger: "What cell do you think that came from?"

Arthur has his old chipped coffee cup in his hand. "Came from the bottom floor. Hope it wasn't my coffee connection." He rattles the cup against the saucer as though his hands are trembling. "Never heard of anybody needing a cup of coffee that bad."

Now Kit is up stumbling around, cussing in his thick Texas accent. He got his foot stuck putting on his pants. He's got that sharp Highway-Patrol haircut. He makes the rest of us look like a bunch of hippies. But at least the rest of us are at the door, dressed and ready.

Most of the gringos are carrying at least three five-gallon trash containers for water. Carlton and a few others have some money, so they pay Peruvian inmates to get their water for them. R.B., Arthur, and me still have a little money, enough to pay a Peruvian prisoner a quarter to get our water. That's why Carlton, the old guy, is standing by his bunk twirling his white handlebar moustache. And that's why R.B., who is standing next to me, has nothing but a paperback novel open in his hands. Stan is in back of us holding his three plastic trashcans. He says: "Fucking water has got to be turned on, man." My observation is that Stan just likes the fight for water. I know he can get downright violent if pushed, and the need for water is a strong push.

Our daily routine of survival begins with the opening of the cell door. Not that we want to leave the cell. But we need the shit-hole and we need water.

The guard wears a blue uniform and a hat with a black plastic bill. His only weapon is a hard rubber club holstered to his hip like a gun. Only his uniform sets him apart from the dark-skinned prisoners. True military personnel, in other words soldiers, carry guns. They are stationed in the gun towers at the four corners of the prison, and foot soldiers surround the place. But they don't come in here. Usually.

Now the hall is filling with men who are pouring out of the six cells on our floor. Once in the hall, I start pushing and shoving harder than everybody else and working my way down to the far end, where the stairway leads down and outside to the yard. The stairway is already packed to a standstill. As usual, fights are breaking out all around me. No one attacks me because Ivan is right behind me carrying five empty five-gallon plastic trashcans and intimidating all who are in his way.

At the moment that I clear the bottom of the stairs, the first men in the yard reach the faucets. They shout to the rest of us: "Viva la aqua!"

A big cheer goes off throughout the cellblock. "Viva la aqua!"

The water-flow from the big tank on the hill has been shut off for the past two days. Drowned rats have plugged the pipes. When that happens, the prison authorities empty the tank. Then it takes a couple days for a crew of prisoners to clean it out.

Our toilet is one hole about four inches across set in the concrete yard. When we have no water to douse the hole, the human waste starts to pile up. Today the pile is about three feet high.

The first sight as I step into the yard is the line of men waiting to shit. The sun hits the west wall. The men squat in the laser spotlight of the morning, caught in that dog-like pose. The smells rip into my small shelter of dignity, but this environment violently demands that I have no privacy ever. The daily routine is survive or die.

The men in the toilet line are cursing the men in the latrine area who, two at a time, shit around the pile, squatted pants around their ankles. Each man donates to the growing circumference. Most are still in boxers and jockeys. As the sun heats the west wall, the odor rises along with the impatience.

Ivan ducks his head through the steel-framed doorway into the yard. The line for the shitter blocks his direct route to the water, but Ivan charges and everyone moves. He goes right to the front of the water line, shoving and pushing. Three of the eight faucets are being guarded by a couple of men who use small steel shanks— knives that they've made from scrap metal—to keep others back while their buddies get water. When they finish, they let the line surge in. The guards never leave the water on more than two hours. The savage and barbarous go first.

Today as always the latrine is the site of urgent dumps with diarrhea flare-ups. Men break out of the line and get as close to the pile as they can, barely getting their pants down before the runny shit squirts onto the stinking pile.

No need to worry about how you look. There are no women around.

Of course some prisoners do care. They have been here longer. They have accepted their lives, and they live in the present—no more whining and trying to find a way out of Lurigancho. Unlike me. I'll be out of here before too long. Six more months at the longest.

Yeah, right.

A few of the guys from my cell are already waiting for the latrine. Others are still coming out of the building. I count twenty-five and get in line at the end; Arthur steps into place behind me, and then quickly another twenty line up in back of him. As I turn to face the head of the line, Arthur says, "You gotta hold my coffee cup while I take a dump, Eddie."

"Yeah, sure. You know what day it is, Arthur?"

"It's Friday."

"It is seven months today we've been here."

"So?"

"What? You don't care how long we've been here?"

"I try not to think about it. Thinking about how long we been here and how long we might be here gives me grief. But I'll be out before you."

What makes you think so?"

"Because it's your fault."

Arthur is a small-built man, five foot seven inches tall, weighs one thirty-five. Eyes are blue, and he has white skin and brown hair. Claims to be a ladies' man and a bad-ass dude. As long as I have known Arthur, I have never seen any evidence of these self-reported claims. His ex and his girlfriends all say he's a gentleman. They like him because he's funny.

"Hold your own cup," I tell him.

Arthur looks past me towards the door we came out of and says, "Look, here comes R.B. I think he found out why that guy screamed last night."

We call him R.B. but his real name is Richard. The PIP—Peruvian Internal Police—arrested the three of us together, me, Richard, and

Arthur. Richard is tall and lean, six-one, and walks with a confident stride. He has hazel eyes and blond hair. I have never seen him
without a full moustache. Unlike Arthur, the ladies report Richard
to be a ladies' man, and grown men call him a bad-ass dude.

He gets to where Arthur and me are standing and he says, "That
guy last night was stabbed. Just through the thigh. He'll live unless
it gets infected."

"Why'd he get stabbed?" I ask.

"That's what everybody was asking the loco that did it. You
know what he said? He said that he kept telling the guy to quit
snoring, but the guy just wouldn't quit. So he had enough. So he
shanked him."

"These people are all nuts."

"The guy said, 'He's lucky I only did his leg.'"

After doing my morning dump and holding Arthur's coffee
cup, I head back inside to get away from the stench. Arthur says,
"I'll see you later. I'm going to see my coffee connection and find out
more about the stabbing."

"Why don't you just go out in the Big Hall? That way you can
actually watch a stabbing."

"Yeah, mine. See you later, asshole."

We both go different directions inside the cellblock. I turn right
to go back to our cell. At the foot of the stairs is the guards' quarters,
and now a guard steps out of the office into the hall. The traffic is
going full tilt, like army ants up and down the concrete stairs. Our
backdrop, the color of every wall, is a pale ugly green. It must be
military surplus paint. After all, we are prisoners of war—captured
by our own country. Three years ago there was no American incar-
cerated in Peru and never had been. The guard sees me looking at
him and says, "Oye, gringo. Un gringo nuevo esta aqui. Espera."

The new American has arrived. We all heard about him through the grapevine. All we know is his first name, Danny, that he was arrested for possessing a baggie with some slight dust of cocaine in it, and that when they searched his suitcase they found a dildo.

The guard motions for me to wait then opens the door that connects our cellblock to the Big Hall. It's a thick iron door that squeaks and creaks like ancient rusted metal then yawns open, exposing us to danger. The noise rises fiercely, as though we've just been dropped into a busy intersection in the worst city on Earth. The Big Hall is Lurigancho's public corridor that runs enclosed through the heart of the prison. All the cellblocks open onto the Big Hall, six on each side, but most cellblocks keep their doors locked tight. The ones that stay open are not nice places to visit, and they release their demons into the Big Hall to stalk and lurk and hunt.

Now the groaning door reveals four Lurigancho guards, all in blue, standing around a white kid wearing a dirty t-shirt. The t-shirt shows a guy on a wave with the words "Surf Hawaii." He's wearing Levi's and Rainbow sandals. Sun-bleached hair, blue eyes, thin build, really scared. He's holding a small suitcase at his side.

The first person Danny sees is me. The way he looks at me, you'd think I was about to cut his throat.

Suddenly I am conscious of my appearance. I haven't cut my hair in nine months, and I haven't shaved in nearly as long. Not that I have a lot of facial hair. But my look seems to scare him. It's true, I've got muscles, and I'm five-ten, which is taller than most here in Lurigancho. I can take care of myself. Maybe he's confused about the fact that I'm pretty tan these days.

"Hey, dude," I say. "Don't worry." I put out my hand. "Here let me take that case."

Danny has his case in his left hand and he keeps it there as he steps inside the cellblock door and takes hold of my hand. He smiles. His grip tells me how grateful he is to see another American.

"Oh man," he says. "This place is too much, man."

"I know your name. Danny. We've got a grapevine. My name is Eddie." As I shake his hand, I pull him inside the door. The guards who escorted him turn away now and march back toward administration. Our guard slams and locks the iron door, and he checks it a couple times. Then he signs with his finger, pointing for Danny to go with me. "Go, gringo. Vayase con su amigo, gringo."

"How long have you been here, Eddie?"

"A lot fucking longer than I thought I would. I thought me, Arthur, and Richard would have gotten out at the PIP palace. On the wall next to my bunk I've marked off seven months. I still want to believe what the police promised—Sergeant Del Gado and Rubio the international cop. Did they bust you?"

"I never met any Del Gado. But that guy Rubio, he was nice to me." The boy speaks with genuine naivete. He's lucky.

"You must have had a woman with you."

"My girlfriend. But I haven't seen or talked to her since they took us to that pink mansion in Lima. Rubio said I would get visits here, and that it's clean and I could swim in the pool and play tennis. I am so fucking dumb."

"Don't feel bad. I swallowed that crap, too. I can hear that fuck Rubio. 'The three of you will be out in no more than six months. And at Lurigancho you will have other American friends. You will play basketball and soccer and swim in the pool.' Fucking liars. Must have laughed their asses off. Yeah, other American friends. Other Americans telling me I won't leave Lurigancho for many, many years—if I live that long."

Danny says, "Do people get out of here, Eddie?" I can see that he's shaking.

"Don't worry, Danny. You'll go home soon. Did the lieutenant do your orientation?"

"Yeah!"

"Did he tell you the trip about how they expect you to escape. And when they catch you trying, they will kill you?"

"Yeah!"

They're not fucking kidding, Dan!"

"Really? How do you mean?"

"That officer who did your orientation, I watched him blow two guys away. One of these dudes got himself caught between the wall and the chain-link fence. He was wounded in the leg. That officer walked up and shot him. Shot the dude trying to escape this fucking hell. Shot him right between the eyes."

While we've been talking other inmates have gathered around Danny and me. "Hey, gringo," says one. "You have American tobacco for me?"

"Ignore these fucks."

"Shot in the head, man? That's insane."

"I know. Just want you to know why you're so full of fear, my man. Be careful and hang with the guys, your fellow Americans. And watch out for a guy named Pelone. We've seen him stab a couple guys over five dollars' worth of cocaine. Don't get into coke, Dan."

"If Pelone stabbed someone, why is he around? Don't they separate us from guys like that?"

"He wasn't committing a crime, Dan. It was just business. Pelone is a businessman. This is the safest cellblock in the whole prison. These people right here are some lowly animals, I agree, but they're not particularly dangerous. They just steal your shit if you get stupid. But mostly our block is filled with educated men with families on the outside who take care of them. Also we've got the Peruvian Mafia guys, some political prisoners, and several legitimate murderers."

I can see the white all the way around the color in Danny's eyes. He says, "What is legitimate murder, for God's sake?"

"Legitimate murder in Luri World is usually over money. Sometimes over honor, but we don't have much of that in here. Come on. I'll show you around the park—your new home for a while."

As soon as we start walking, Dan asks, "What did you do to get in here, Ed?"

We walk down the first-floor hall, the direction Arthur went for his cup of real coffee. The risen sun is lighting up the hall on the left-hand side, casting shadow and sun stripes across the floor. Prisoners begin to settle down. The mood is a lot lighter now that water has begun to flow again.

Dan holds his nose. "What's that smell, Ed?"

"Shit, Dan. Shit."

"Is it always this bad?" He's actually holding his breath.

"No. Sometimes it's worse. Sometimes not. But it always smells like a sewer."

"Are you going to answer my question? What are you here for?"

"For being a stupid fucking idiot."

We slowly walk past the first cell on the bottom floor. A Peruvian prisoner walks up behind us and pats Dan's ass and says, "Oh yes, new gringo. You have a nice ass, gringo."

Danny looks at me like a small dog getting sized up for a bite. The Peruvian leers at him like a drunken sailor checking out a whore. Dan is standing to my right and the Peruvian is on the other side of him, lit by sunshine coming through the bars of the first cell. He's grinning. He grabs his own crotch and says, "Es muy duro por usted, gringo."

Danny asks, "What did he say, Eddie?"

"Dan, he says his dick is hard for you."

"What should I say to him?"

"This!"

I reach across Dan and slap the face of the Peruvian hard enough to knock his grip loose from his water bucket and him down to the floor. He lands hard on his butt.

"I'm not your fucking brother, you scum fuck. No, yo soy un Americano. Este gringo es mi hermano. Y tu eres un animal."

A crowd is building. Men stop for the entertainment. Suddenly Arthur pops out of a cell door midway down the hall and starts walking our way. This could have been a coffee shop anywhere in the free world. Arthur is a strong spirit in a small body.

He steps to my side holding his precious cup.

Dan says, "Man, you did that for me? Aren't you afraid of being stabbed?"

"Dan, we might be in Peru but we are always Americans. One of these motherfuckers fucks with one of us, I take it real personal."

Arthur takes a sip of his strong black coffee. "What happen to him?" he says soberly. We all watch the Peruvian scurry away, his bucket splashing out into the hallway.

"The little bitch was copping a feel off our new guy here. Arthur, this is Danny."

Arthur switches his cup to the other hand and shakes with Danny. "Glad to meet you. Where you from, bro?"

"Huntington Beach. It's a town by the ocean in Southern California."

Dan talks with a bit more ease now. He's crossed over now from the Big Hall, where the vibe is so violent that you feel naked even though you're escorted by guards—even so, you get the notion that the men who roam freely in the Big Hall would murder your guards in a minute and no one would know who did it. And then he met that big dark scary guy on the other side of the door—that was really just me, Eddie Spageddy. Funny how things aren't really what they seem.

"Huntington Beach?" I say. "You mean Surf City? I heard the name was being changed to Surf City."

"I know Huntington," says Arthur. "My mom has a house in Laguna Beach. R.B. lives in Dana Point."

"Who's R.B.?"

Arthur answers, "Richard. He's with us. The three of us were busted together."

"Yeah," I say, "I was telling Dan about our trip when that piece

of garbage interrupted me. Richard, Arthur, and me were busted
because I fucked around with this dude's ol'lady, a guy named Tom
Dawson that we met at the resort where we were staying. It's a short
story. Tom got insanely jealous over me and his girlfriend dancing
and carrying on. So he planted a shitload of cocaine in my room and
then tipped off the PIP."

Arthur says, "Damn, that's the first time I ever heard you admit
it."

"And three of you got arrested for that?" says Dan. "For real?
Man, that's terrible."

"For real, Dan."

"Hey, enough of that," says Arthur. "Let's get the hell out of
here. Go up and show Danny the crib."

Danny shifts his suitcase to his other hand and flexes his fingers.
"Is that where I sleep and stuff?" he says. "Man, it sure smells bad
in this place."

"All us gringos are upstairs," I say. "We have the last cell on the
right, on the sunny side of the building. We can see our prison yard
and the cellblock next door. Over that we can see the only hills on
the horizon. What smell?"

"Don't forget the tank," says Arthur. "We can see our water
tank."

"What do you guys do for food? Is there a cafeteria? You don't
smell that?"

"Cafeteria—" says Arthur, lifting his chipped cup. "You are a
very funny guy, Dan." He sips. "But we have a food truck that gets
here most days. Some days it sells our food to the peasants and
pretends that it broke down or whatever. It comes to the front, to
the administration building, where you had your orientation. Some
of the prisoners go out the door at the end of the hall here, and they
bring in the food. These are all even-numbered cellblocks on this

side. They all do it except twelve."

"What's twelve?"

I say it in Spanish: "Doce."

"Not a good place."

"That's where all the Lifers hang."

"Don't go there."

"Okay," says Dan.

"And don't go to Once either."

"What's own-say?"

"The Hole. Where they kill political prisoners."

"Ever been there?"

"They've never put a gringo in there."

We contemplate that for a moment, then Arthur continues his explanation. "The odd numbers have to bring their prison food through the Big Hall that you just came from. It's the same shit every day. Brown water that's supposed to be coffee and a bread roll that you could use to play baseball. Lunch is white lima beans and white rice, dude."

"Well, that was the bottom floor, Dan. Before we go up, let's look at the yard."

"Sorry to tell you, man, they still haven't put in that swimming pool yet."

"Tony—he's another American—he calls the yard the beach. Tony has been here a bunch of years. You'll meet him and the others up there in our cell."

Now we're standing in front of the guards' quarters again. The door to the yard is just a few feet away, but the corridor is blocked by inmates who have gathered to see the new gringo from the United States. Their brown faces are staring at us like people at a zoo. These fucks all want to go to America.

"Get the fuck out of the way, you assholes," I yell in Spanish.

We push through the bodies and walk out into the sunlit yard. A few men are standing in front of us, their backs to us, laughing and pointing. In front of them is Ballhead, who has come to do his cleaning. He's a black-skinned man who wears a smile on his face and half a soccer ball over his head like a helmet. He is cleaning out the latrine.

As we watch, Ballhead plunges the old rusty coffee can into the newly filled fifty-five-gallon steel barrel. Then he steps onto the mound of excrement, stomping his bare feet. His ragged pants are rolled up above the knees. Stretching his arms out to keep his balance, he gets to the middle of the pile. Then he starts throwing water at the latrine hole and tromping like a Sicilian at harvest time.

"Wow, is that guy crazy?"

"He's just a low-life fuck, Dan. They pay him to do what no one else will."

Arthur says, "He's crazier than anybody you've ever heard of before."

We are still standing just outside the threshold of the cellblock, looking across the barren yard toward the dirt-brick walls of the cellblock across the way, and from that direction we hear furious shouting, and a lot of noise from the men in the yard, and now the screams of a man.

Suddenly at the threshold of the doorway we hear a loud commotion, loud talking and yelling, and the screams of one man above the rest. Being solid cement, the yard amplifies the man's pathetic voice.

"Dame mi vida, por mi madre! Por favor, por favor! Dame mi vida!" Give me my life for my mother's sake.

We go out to see what every man in the yard is witnessing. To our immediate left stands Richard.

"Hey R.B., what the fuck's going on?"

"Look up there."

We look to the end window of the cellblock across the yard. The sunlight is already glaring in the concrete yard, so the window looks dark against the shining filthy wall. But the action that has drawn everyone's attention is happening close to the window. It's like a puppet show.

A man is standing on top of a bunkbed, kicking and dancing. We just see the legs and lower torso. He twirls and hops around. He is screaming as though forced to stand on live coals. Now I can see the arms from below. Two arms flash at one side of the bunk, then another arm flashes at the other side. Each hand holds a long shank. They jab. They hit the lower legs, then one shank hits the thigh, then one seems to hit right up the man's butt. The jabbing isn't wild like people swinging at a piñata. No, it's very sportsman. The shank-men are admiring each other's work. It's an art form. The doomed man falls, of course, and the knife-work that follows makes me think that these butchers are playing to the crowd. They hack open the gut cavity and slash the head halfway off the body, so that it hangs at ninety degrees and you know the man is still seeing and thinking and trying to breathe. A burst of neck-blood splurts against the window. The twitching body slides slowly and somewhat grace-fully off the top of the bunk. I hear Danny, who is right next to me, puking where he stands.

I say, "Hey, don't do that! This is our beach, man! You just threw up on the beach!"

Richard looks at Danny, who is snorting and spitting the flavor out of his mouth. "Every man has a right to puke," he says.

Arthur goes: "That was bad. That was a hard thing to see for the first time. Especially when you just got here."

Danny looks at me. "I'm sorry, really. I couldn't help it."

Richard says, "Just got here? Am I looking at Danny Dildo?"

Danny hacks and spits some more, then says, "Oh man, is that what you guys are calling me? Because of that goddamn dildo the cops found? Shit! That's just great!"

I say, "Hey, it's okay. You gave us some humor in hell, pal. But look over there. That's the bathroom where you do your business. Go to that barrel with the water in it and get some water and flush your puke off the yard and the wall. Then we'll go up to our cell and meet some others. You coming, R.B.?"

"No. I'm going to take a walk on the beach. See you up there later. Glad to meet you, Dan. Too bad it's in here."

"Oh god," says Dan. "I can't believe what I just saw. That poor guy. Do you think he died? What'll happen to those guys for killing him? They didn't say anything about a hospital here. Is there a hospital here? Can that guy get to the hospital?"

Arthur says, "You remind me of when we first got here. When they first put us in the Brigada. I was at least as scared as you are."

Ballhead has been working on his cleaning project right through the killing. By now he has the sewer pipe exposed and he's dousing his feet and scrubbing the cement with them. I hold the suitcase, and Arthur and me watch while Dan goes to get the rusty can from Ballhead.

I say to Arthur: "Didn't know you were scared back at the Brigada. Sorry to hear that."

He says, "I know. You couldn't tell. Not like it was with you."
We both laugh.

Dan returns and tosses a canful of water, dispersing his puke. Then he says in a tone of sheer perplexity, "That's the toilet? A hole in the ground? There's not even any cover or anything!"

"Sometimes we get visitors out here in the yard. If that happens, I don't have to tell you to face the opposite direction, do I? Let's go up and I'll show you our house."

Danny follows close behind me, dragging his suitcase, the natives trying to grab it from his hand. Some actually do want to help, but these will expect sex in return. Without turning around I say, "Danny, hold on with both hands or they'll take it away and it will really cost you to get the fucking thing back."

All day the cement stairway at the end of each tier is a subway station—arriving and leaving, arriving and leaving, but always the same passengers hurrying in a pattern for no reason. At least for no reason apparent to me. I am not at the place of peace gained through the practice of being in the present moment.

Because I'm outta here. I'm not like the rest of these wannabes. Me and R.B. and Arthur will be outta here, just like the cops said. I can't listen to the others telling me different. They just don't know.

Up two flights to the top tier. Someone throws Danny a loud, sucking kiss. "Don't let these animals get to you," I say.

"I guess they don't bother you because you look like one of them, huh?" he says. He's an innocent young guy.

The second floor is a copy of the first, the same ugly pale-green walls and ceiling paint chipping. But here the usual jailhouse writing on the walls is missing. This is very much a neighborhood of true criminals. Criminals in the most respectable sense of the word. Criminals who have dignity and honor. Criminals who will kill your mother and then help you find the person who did that terrible thing.

As soon as we come up out of the stairway we hear behind us, "Oye. My American friends."

Chivo appears out of nowhere looking freshly showered. He is a happy man, and his smile exposes a toothless mouth.

Chivo is a lifer. The Big Hall is his neighborhood. He has lived in the gut of Lurigancho for over ten years and he is a young man born and raised in the Amazon jungle. He once told me that life in Lurigancho is much better than the life he knew as a teenager on the streets of Lima.

A few months ago Chivo said to me, "You are American man, but you are not a gringo. You are one of us. I love you because you have not let the white man beat you down. While you are here in Lurigancho, you will learn who you are, my brother."

I still do not know what the hell Chivo was talking about. I answered him, "My mother is white." To that Chivo replied, "Your father must have been a warrior."

I told Chivo I don't know about any warrior shit. But I do know that when my dad took my mother on a date, he had to send his white friends to the house to pick her up. Chivo loved that story. He laughed as though he'd heard a good joke. I saw nothing funny. My grandfather would have shot my dad if he thought he could get away with it.

I say, "Danny, this is Chivo."

"Como estas Chivo," says Danny. He sounds like he's ordering from a menu. "Yo soy Danny."

"Ah, my American friend." Chivo looks at me. "Es el nuevo gringo, no?" He walks away laughing out loud as though he's just heard a great joke, his buttonless old aloha shirt flying open as he walks, his worn-out khakis rolled up above his ankles. He laughs and laughs.

"What is that about? Is he one of the crazy ones?"

"Chivo? No! Well, he ain't crazy by Lurigancho standards. No, he's probably laughing about your dildo trip."

"Dildo trip? Fuck, man."

"Hey, you made Chivo laugh. He'll be your friend forever."

"Is that good?"

"I hope you never find out how good."

"What does *that* mean?"

Men are clustered at the door of every cell, mostly the men who speak good or bad English. Each of the cells is filled beyond capacity. Laundry hangs on lines of string. People cook on hand-pumped kerosene burners.

"Hey, gringo! How are you?" says Pelone. He just so happens to be here, in the commanding position of his cellmates or gang of slaves, same thing. His long hair is combed straight and oiled and flat against his bony, Anglo-looking face. Pelone knows that the best time to sell coke is when the American first comes to Lurigancho. That's when the American still has money.

"You likee the coca? You say me!"

When it comes to dealing, Pelone is rare because he hates the effects of cocaine on himself. "It make me violent," he said to me once. I almost laughed because Pelone is the most violent person I have ever known.

"Come on," I say to Danny. "Your life has been fucked up enough by coke. But if you disagree, see Pelone here."

Pelone still doesn't know whether to like me or not, and he doesn't speak English well enough to comprehend what I just said.

"Cigarettes?"

"Cigarettes?"

"You have American cigarettes, Dan?"

A dozen natives follow us as we make our way toward the end cell.

"I, I'm really sorry you guys, but I don't smoke and I don't have any cigarettes. I'm sorry!"

"Hey, fuck them!" I shout. "Quit telling them you're sorry for anything. Come on!"

We run into Ivan, my six-foot-four Czech-born bunk-mate. We are just about to go into the cell. "Welcome, this is your house, too," he says. "We will find you space. Only space on floor. But don't worry, come in." Ivan's hand is so big that Dan's hand disappears in his friendly grip.

I step into the cell first. "Hey, you guys!"

The scene is just as I expect it to be. Carlton and a group of four are playing hearts. Carlton sits facing the cell door. He slams down a card, takes the trick, then starts twisting one end of his white handlebar moustache under his large nose. Magnifying eye specs rest halfway down that space between his brow and the end of his nose. He looks over the top of the glasses at us as we enter. His blue eyes have a fierce, piercing quality that I figure comes from years spent in Lurigancho mad as hell.

Hermes yells at Carlton, "You old cocksucker, now you're gonna eat the bitch!" Then he notices us and looks up from his cards to study Danny with detailed attention. Hermes is a fast-talkin' man, very entertaining, always in a good mood, a Puerto Rico native who grew up in New York City. He's a daily visitor, but he won't live here because he has a boyfriend. He insists that the relationship is only sex, nothing long-term. Still, it wouldn't do to bunk with a bunch of heterosexuals.

Most of the other guys are lying in their bunks still talking about the murder on the other side of the yard. There's a lot of speculation going on. But the buzz is easily interrupted.

"Hey listen, this is Dan! He doesn't like being called Danny Dildo!"

In unison every man in the cell sings, "Hey, Danny Dildo!"

That is so damn funny that we laugh like we haven't ever laughed.

"That old guy there is Mr. Carlton."

Carlton says, "Welcome. Don't listen to these idiots. Ask me if you need help or advice, son. These guys wouldn't be here if they knew anything."

I tell Dan, "Mr. Carlton believes that he's not actually here. Oh, and he believes that he's not actually a smuggler, either." Before Carlton can jump in with an explanation, I cut him off, "And this bright, curly-haired gentleman is Hermes."

"Hi, sweetie, how are you?" Hermes says with a sexy wink. He puckers his lips and gives the air a kiss that's aimed at Dan.

I keep introducing around the hearts table. Pointing to Weaver I say, "And this is our very own L.A. cop, Officer Burt."

With his Hollywood grin Weaver says, "Hi. No one ever calls me that. Just Burt. Or Weaver is cool." He flashes a smile from underneath his meticulously trimmed red-brown moustache.

Danny's eyes are wide. "You're a cop? For real?"

The fourth card player cuts in with his thick Texas drawl, "Hey boy, I'm Kit, the other cop. Yip, it's true, Bud. M'full name's Kit Karson. Karson with a K." Kit extends his thin arm and hand to

Danny. He is no longer the big blond highway patrolman of his
pre-Lurigancho life. Dan takes Kit's hand as Carlton leads the next
round with a king of spades. Hermes slaps down the queen, elated.
"Eat that bitch, you old cocksucker! I told you I would get your ass."

The rest of the guys who are in the cell introduce themselves. I
tell Danny, "Not everybody's here. Stan, and Rick, Tony and Hunter,
some of the others are out."

"Where did they go?" asks Dan meekly. "I mean, where can you
go around here?"

"Oh, you know. Visit in other cells. Probably doing some laundry, now that the water is back on."

Kit says, "Soon as we finish this game Weaver and me is going
over to the bowling alley."

"Fuck you, Kit," says Weaver, slapping down a card. "Fucking
bowling alley...."

The Peruvians next door have settled down after the public
execution. In fact, it took less than two minutes for the whole prison
to return to regular routine. The killing, witnessed by hundreds of
men and guards, was just a break in the day, a short bit of entertainment. The guys who were here in the cell watching from higher
up start describing what they saw—crazy fucking Juan and cronies
finishing off the native, stabbing him through the neck and the chest
until he was more than dead. I could tell he was a native. Too trusting.

Later Danny tells us the tale of his own arrest.

Old story, new players.

Bring girlfriend to coca country. Girl likes coca. You get busted.

The actual amount of coca involved in Danny's case was no
more than some residue on a little baggie such as a jeweler would
use to hold a cheap ring. The trip with the dildo was thought up
between Danny and his girlfriend while they were snorting coke
back in L.A. They heard that Playboy magazines are illegal in Peru,

so they came up with the perfect scam—hide the coca inside a dildo with some naughty lingerie, and the customs people will be so shocked they will just pass the suitcases through.

The first night they were in Lima, the girlfriend, Tracy, talked Danny into waiting at the hotel while she went out to find a coke connection. He never saw her again.

He spent two days by himself at the hotel. Then he got a visit from the police, who searched his luggage and found the tiny baggie with the residue. Dan doesn't know where the baggie came from; he thinks Tracy must have brought it with her from L.A. Anyway the cops arrested Danny for trafficking cocaine, and they beat on him a little. He swore he'd never seen the baggie before. The cops believed him but they were mad about the idea that he hadn't bought it from them. They were furious about the idea that someone in Peru might be making and selling coke that they didn't know about.

Through the grapevine of cops and prison guards we already know more about what happened than Danny does. We know that Del Gado raped the girlfriend, and then the PIP robbed her and put her on a plane back to America before they grabbed Danny. Danny is just the PIP's little token trophy to show the DEA that they are arresting Americans.

The conversation ends with Ivan in his thick accent saying, "You know, there is one person I would like to kill." I know who he means because he has said so many times. "Del Gado. If I could get my hands on this Sergeant Del Gado, I would like to kill him." All of us feel the same way—all of us who have violent memories of the Black Knight of Intimidation.

From my bunk I can look out the window. Now Danny and Ivan are down in the yard, pacing east wall to west wall and back, Ivan taking one step to Danny's two. Ivan is explaining something, his arms outstretched, towering over Danny, providing him with a cloud of protection. The big Slovakian voice echoes into my window, which has bars but no panes.

"You are not a smuggler," he's saying. "I am a smuggler. I am in prison for smuggling. You are here because you followed your prick when your brain stopped working. Look at you. You should be getting a surfboard and paddling out in the ocean, not here walking in this fucking prison yard. You know what you have done for the cocaine industry? You have added to the stability of the high prices."

"What?" says Dan. "I added to the price? How?"

"You and that girlfriend, you will go back to your home and tell your family and friends how scary this place is and what happens when you lose at putting your life on the line. After that people will want more cocaine, and they will be more willing to pay the ridiculous prices."

"Are you sorry, Ivan?"

"Do I look fucking sorry? I play the game knowing about these dues. But you were just playing around. And now you end up here with me. You're the one who is sorry."

"You would do this again?"

"Fuck no, not cocaine. Maybe gemstones like diamonds or emeralds. You go surfing, go to college. If I could go to college in America, oh man would I."

"I hope you get out of here soon. All you guys have been here for so long. Meanwhile people out there are partying and wanting more cocaine. They don't want to take the chance, but they want you to do it. And now that you're here, they forget you."

"You are getting it now, kid."

Ivan walks away. Then Carlton takes up stride with Danny. Carlton could be Dan's grandfather—a fifties-hipster grandfather with a long white ponytail. Carlton starts right in. "You know this country would crumble if not for their cocaine trade with the rest of the world."

He goes on for an hour telling Danny that the drug war is propaganda to cover up what the American and Peruvian governments are doing to exploit the natural resources of the Amazon. I can tell from my bunk that Carlton has Danny's full attention. I know what he's saying. The natives of the Amazon are being slaughtered by the Peruvian and Brazilian armies. Many of the natives are forced into the cities, where they cannot survive.

Chivo is one of these displaced souls.

"Danny is going free!" yells Ivan when the news comes down. There's a runner standing just outside our cell. The embassy is here to see Danny. Ivan says it again: "They will set this boy free!"

Suddenly Danny is messing with his suitcase, all flustered, loading up his extra underwear and his five postcards, which are now like sacred artifacts to him.

"Just go, man," says Arthur. "Fuck that shit."

"No, man. My grandma gave me this old suitcase. I have to come back with it. Besides that, dude, you can't get these surf decals anymore. My dad turned me onto them."

So the runner leaves as Danny packs.

Now he'll have to wait for the military escort.

Danny practices closing the suitcase and he says, "Well if I don't come back, I really love you guys." Richard shouts, "Don't tell that shit to René, little man. He'll get the wrong idea."

But Carlton, at the hearts table, stands up. He walks over to Danny and puts his hands on Danny's shoulders. He says, "We have all come to love you too, Danny. You are one of our home bunch. But you've got to go. You are no smuggler. Leave that up to Arthur over there."

Arthur says, "I have never smuggled."

"Aww..." say three or four voices.

"But I've got a couple of overdue library books here. By now there must be a hell of a fine."

Now Carlton gives Danny a pat on the back. "I assume this is goodbye. If you don't come back, we'll know that the embassy took you out."

"Can the U.S. embassy do that?" says Danny.

Richard calls from his bunk, where he's lying with a paperback on his chest: "They can do whatever the fuck they want to, pal!"

"Oh shit howdy," says Kit in his Texas drawl. "Y'all oughta jest let him go. He probly ain't a going nowhere. I ain't wasting my breath saying goodbye." The rest of us look at each other, silently agreeing once again that this former highway patrolman is a true asshole.

The conversation stops altogether.

Now Chivo is at the cell door. Seems that whenever a runner shows up, Chivo is close behind. Chivo with his courteous manners and modest dignity frequently visits the gringos' cell, always wanting to know how he can be of service. He's our volunteer valet. If clothes need mending, he sees that the work gets done. If we need another bunk bed, he can procure it. Today he has a paper bag, which he is carrying tucked under his arm protectively. I say, "Oye, Chivo, que cosas tiene in su bolsa?"

The general attention shifts to the bag. "Tengo fruta, amigo."

Fruit.

Fruit is something none of us has seen since we came to Lurigancho. Suddenly Chivo is holding a big red apple. "Ooh," says Tony. "Can I just smell the bag?" Now the bag is traveling around the cell, and people are dipping their faces in to sniff the apple aroma. "Quanto cuesta?" says Carlton.

In the middle of all this, Danny is ready to go. He has his suitcase in hand and excitement in his bright blue eyes. He looks as though he's holding a brand new surfboard and now his ride to the beach is outside honking its horn. "Okay, you guys," he says, stepping backwards toward the cell door. "I'm going to catch up with that escort. I can't wait. Take care. Maybe we'll see each other back home."

There's a general shout of goodbye, and Danny darts away.

Meanwhile Carlton has started to slice up the apples, and small pieces of fruit are traveling around the cell. Everyone is getting a taste of this delicious rarity. Carlton is offering Chivo a wristwatch that no longer runs. Chivo knows someone who can fix it. They work out a deal, and then Chivo exits the cell and vanishes down the hall.

Just minutes later Hermes arrives for the morning's game of hearts. The first thing he says is: "What's up with that pretty surfer gringo, the one you call Dildo?"

"We think he's going home," says Arthur. "Why?"

"Oh, that's why he's acting so crazy."

Carlton says, "What do you mean crazy?"

"Because he was telling the guard to let him out into the Big Hall. He said he would be okay. He didn't want to wait for the escort."

"Shit," says Carlton.

"That's not crazy," Ivan booms. "That's fucking insane."

Now Chivo is back at the door. He's looking at me, and his eyes are very grim. I jump out of my bunk. I'm right behind him as we exit the cell. Ivan sees that something is up so he says, "Hey, wait for me."

Chivo grabs my arms and says, "No, Eduardo. Only you coming."

"Stay here, Ivan. I'll be right back, man."

I'm on Chivo's heels as we reach the other end of the cellblock and hurry down the cement stairs. The head guard is in his office, talking excitedly on the phone. Next to the office is that huge iron door, closed and locked, that separates us from the animals that roam the Big Hall. There are three guards in the office. All are yelling angrily. The one on the phone is saying, "Si, jefe. Si jefe. Yo no se. Yo no se...."

Suddenly Chivo's voice cuts through the confusion. "Abre la puerta!" he cries. Open the door! The words are commanding. Chivo is emanating an authority that I have not seen in him before. One of the guards jumps in response and starts putting his key to the iron door. Some of the Peruvian prisoners are gathering behind us. "Oje, Chivo," they say. "Que cosas, hombre?" The iron door swings open with its metallic shriek, and now the hellish roar from the Big Hall overwhelms all the little sounds from within our cellblock. Chivo grabs my arm and we step into the Big Hall.

The Hall is as busy as Manhattan's financial district at lunchtime. The air is dark and stagnant and putrid smelling. The iron door slams shut behind us, and right next to the door, as if he's been waiting for us, stands a small, dark native man. His face is very much like Chivo's—chiseled features with prominent, slender nose and dark, glowing eyes, the kind of face that we learned to call "Indian." Chivo says one word: "Dame." The small man reaches under his ragged t-shirt and pulls a shank from his waistband. The steel itself is rusty, but the cutting edge, about seven inches long, is shiny and razor-sharp. Chivo slides the shank under his own shirt, turns to me with his index finger against his lips, and motions for me to follow him. A crowd has already begun to gather around us, but we slide through the crowd. No one wants to get in Chivo's way. No one speaks to him. The flood of prisoners parts for us as we move ahead. Chivo leads me to a part of the Big Hall that is as dark as a bottomless pit.

We are walking fast, and we plunge into the darkness without hesitation. The floor is wet now, a flowing wetness that stinks of piss and shit. The liquid seems to be running toward us from the cellblock door ahead. This particular door, unlike the door that separates our own cellblock from the Big Hall, is wide open. Anyone is welcome here.

Far behind us, at the far end of the Big Hall, we can hear a commotion start up—men shouting orders, boots hitting the pavement, the rattling of rifles. I turn and see about twenty uniformed soldiers, each holding an automatic rifle in front of him, marching toward us quickly. They drive forward in formation, and prisoners scatter to get out of their way.

Now we are reaching the open door. The cellblock ahead is dimly lit with faraway sunlight. A dozen or so prisoners scatter into the darkness at the sudden appearance of Chivo's face.

He grabs my arm and rushes me through the doorway. The waste-water is so deep here that we have to shuffle our feet to keep from slipping. All the shit in Lurigancho must be running down here and backing up out of the plumbing. To keep from puking, I pull my t-shirt up over my nose. Then about ten feet inside the cell block, Chivo stops. He's standing in front of an open cell door. He's blocking my way. I step up to his side and look at what he's looking at. The sound from my mouth is a strangled scream. It says, "Holy fuck. Danny."

Danny is on his knees in front of a brown slimy toilet, his head down inside the bowl. His Levis are down around his ankles. His bare, bleeding ass is pointing at us. The white skin of his body is shining against the red and brown of his blood and the filth. His shoes are gone. His t-shirt is so soaked in blood from the gaping wounds on his back that you can't read "Surf City" any more. The blood around Danny's throat is nearly black, the wound is so deep. Whoever raped him cut his throat so deep that he nearly decapitated him. Danny's face is half in the toilet filth. One blue eye is staring open.

Chivo grabs my arm. "We go! Now!"

The soldiers are close to the cellblock door now. I hear them yelling at the prisoners to get out of the way. We slip into the small crowd that's clustered outside the door, then scatter into the darkness along with everyone else. The soldiers pass us, striking randomly at anyone in their path. Chivo keeps me moving. I'm staggering. I can barely breathe.

Chivo gets me to the iron door of our cellblock. He starts beating on the door. My stomach is churning. I'm thinking of Danny but not thinking of Danny—thinking of myself and the fucking hell I have put myself in. *I left my wife and kids for THIS. Is THIS where I am going to die? Death in here is fucking ugly!*

"Where is that god-damned guard?"

Chivo is standing with his back to my back. Suddenly he raps quickly on my arm and points into the distance. I look to the left, and there in the middle of thirty or forty prisoners stands that crazy motherfucker Juan, the one who took down the dancing man on the bunk. He's holding a suitcase decorated with surf decals. I surge forward, but Chivo has an iron grip on me. "No, Eduardo," he says into my ear. "No, you will die. Not yet. Wait, wait." He is gripping my shoulders and his mouth is right up against my left ear. "Wait. We will kill Juan. Seguramente. Espera. La situación es muy peligrosa."

Now Juan has disappeared in the swarm of prisoners, and now our cellblock door swings open.

About an hour later I get back to the gringos' cell. Chivo and I have been talking all that time, and I've been thinking about where I am and how it operates, and about what people need to know and what they don't need to know. I've been thinking about my own actions and the consequences of those actions for me and for everyone else. So when I come back to the cell, I'm feeling pretty calm.

Of course the hearts game stops for a minute, and people want to know what I've been up to. Ivan says, "We was worried about you, man."

"Chivo took me on a little adventure tour," I say. "But don't worry. When you travel with Chivo, you're traveling with the best security that Luri World has to offer."

Richard says: "Well now, that makes me feel all cozy and safe."

Carlton asks, "What did you discover about Danny? We heard there was some trouble out there."

"Nothing to report," I say. "To the best of my knowledge, the boy is gone, gone, gone. Real gone."

"That's good news," says Carlton. "Whenever anybody gets out of here, that's always good news." And the hearts game resumes.

But that night, when the others are sleeping, I bury my face in the old gray army blanket and sob many times for Danny and for what I saw.

I used to mark the minutes, days, and months on the wall next to my bunk, but now I've covered the marks with a couple pages out of magazines. One's a full page of Farrah Fawcett on a skateboard wearing a pair of tight Levi's. She looks so American. Next to her is Miss America, Jaclyn Smith. And there's a surfing photo out of a surfer magazine. All are secured by toothpaste smeared on the back of the page. I may look Peruvian in color, but I am American through and through.

I've been writing letters to women friends and to Diane.

Diane and I were together for five years before this happened. Now my hope is we can get back together when I'm out. A young gorgeous woman alone.

The American embassy is supposed to bring our mail and our money from home at least once a month. But since I have lived at Lurigancho that little embassy rep has been here only twice. It seems that the purpose of the rep is simply to make sure we are all still here—and of course to give Carlton the chance to vent his intellectual spiel against the United States government.

But today is a surprise. As I sit on my bunk writing a letter to my mom, a runner comes into the cell. He announces that me, Richard, and Arthur have a visit. It is our American lawyer.

Years ago when my brother Dennis began dating the daughter of the infamous George Chula, I never dreamed I would ever be asking for his help. George is a very wealthy lawyer. My brother tells me he is called the Silver Fox and that he usually handles only big-money cases, especially divorce and murder cases. But he believes that Richard, me, and Arthur have been wrongfully imprisoned. He knows that we can't pay him large sums of money, but he has been softened by his daughter's pleading.

"Arthur, wake up," I say. "I think Chula is here to see us."

Arthur mumbles, "Good. Let's get some money from him."

"Coming, R.B.?"

He puts his paperback novel down on his bunk as he gets up and tucks his shirttail in his Levi's. "Yeah, I heard you!"

Stan asks, "Hey, you think your lawyer would mail this letter for me?" He fetches an envelope that he's had stashed for a week waiting for the opportunity to get it out somehow.

"Oh, boy," says Arthur. "Here we go on another scary-ass trip through the building. There better be a couple of guards to escort us. Or three or four. Those fuckers out there in the Big Hall...."

"Shut up, Arthur," grouches Richard. "You're such a little wimp."

I say, "R.B., you crack me up. You're just as scared as Arthur!"

"Oh fuck you, Ed. Mister Bad-ass. Let's go."

Ivan calls from where he is reading in his bunk: "Hey, why don't you guys lighten up on each other, for cripe sake?"

All three of us look at Ivan and kindly say, "Fuck off, Ivan."

Richard is last out the door. Rick calls out to him, "I'm telling you guys, stop wasting your money trying to get out of here. Just pay to get sentenced as quick as possible."

"Yeah right, Rick!"

Each of us has his own reason for being here and his ideas about how he's going to get out. Rick was the connection for a famous rock band. He looks the part, with his long curly Shirley-Temple hair. The rockers are keeping him supplied with cash. So his approach is to just do the time while staying as high as possible the entire time. A humble martyr for rock and roll.

As Richard catches up, Arthur asks, "What'd Rick say?"

"He wants us to spend all our money getting loaded with him."

"All WHAT money?"

"They all think we still have money left," I say.

Richard says, "How much do you think Rick has spent on drugs in the five years he's been here?"

"A lot!"

"He told me that he gave that Peruvian lawyer five grand to get him sentenced to eight years. And in the last five years he's gone through nearly thirty thousand bucks staying on coke and pills."

"Yeah, let's take advice from Smart Rick."

As we descend the stairs, Arthur says, "You think it's Chula?"

"No, it's your mother," says Richard.

Two guards are waiting, and they escort us by way of the outside route. Arthur is visibly relieved that he doesn't have to go through the Big Hall. Instead we walk across the yard to an iron door that opens to the outer walkway. We're in the open air, on a broad concrete sidewalk that runs between the ends of the cell-blocks and the perimeter wall. The wall is twenty feet high. Between us and the wall are two chain link fences, each one twenty feet tall and topped by strands of barbed wire. We are in plain view of two gun towers, one at each end of the wall. I can tell that the guards in the towers are watching us. Other soldiers pass us on the wide walkway. Everyone out here seems to have a rifle. This is the public side of the prison. It's clean and there's even some dead grass along the sidewalk. Not like the other side of the prison, with its trash and stench and chaos.

The guards with us are silent. When we reach the front of the prison, the admin area, we are let through another steel-barred door. Now we are in a walled patio not far from the warden's office. The patio is bare with a few concrete benches, and its expanse is interrupted by columns, very wide columns that support the roof. We spot Chula by the far wall, sitting on a bench. To his side at one end of the bench sits a large cardboard box bearing the bright logo of an American sporting goods manufacturer.

Chula stands and walks toward us, his arms outstretched. He is wearing one of his fine pinstriped suits. With his silver hair the guy looks right out of a Mafia movie. In the past we've had our misgivings about the fact that he represents us, and now as I look at him I remember why. He looks like we have millions. Knowing the priorities of the Peruvian justice system, that perception could keep us here longer. Not only that, the DEA knows Chula because he played the celebrity lawyer role in a well-publicized murder-for-drugs case. Chula's record for winning his cases is very high. So he makes us look guilty as hell.

His manner is soft-spoken. "Good to see you, gentlemen. How is it in there? Are they treating you all right?"

Each of us gives Chula a brotherly hug.

"Yeah, great here," Arthur says.

I say, "Hate to leave."

Richard: "So when *are* we leaving?"

Chula reaches inside his full-length herringbone overcoat and takes out an envelope. He places the envelope in Arthur's hand. "Here, here's a couple hundred bucks for you to split up among you. And Ed, your dad asked me to bring this boxing gear." With his hand he indicates the cardboard box on the bench, but he seems unwilling to walk over toward the bench. "I've got some gloves and head gear and even a few mouth protections."

"They call that a mouthpiece, George. Nothing personal."

"Your dad tells me that you can handle yourself in the ring. Is that so?"

"Yeah. He was Golden Gloves when he was in the Navy. He got me working the speed bag and the heavy bag when I was ten. By the time I was twelve I could get the speed bag to blur. Tell him thanks, will you?"

"Certainly," says Chula. "Anything else?"

"Tell him I love him. And not to worry. But most of all don't fucking tell him or my mom how this place really is."

Chula responds by looking at Richard. "We *are* working on a plan," he says, "and there is every indication you are going to start trial. That's the first step toward going home. We have to go to a lower court first. Then the case will go to the tribunal, a military court. We may be able to get Arthur out at the lower court level."

Arthur is elated to hear that. He hugs Chula. "God bless you, George." He says it several times: "God bless you, George."

With one arm around Arthur's shoulder, holding him close, George looks at me and says, "Ed, turn around. I have a surprise for you."

"What?" I can't imagine what Chula could have.

Arthur seems to spot something and he says, "Oh fuck, just turn around." I'm standing between him and Richard, and the two of them take my shoulders and rotate me, but I turn back. I see her, stepping out from behind one of the large pillars near Chula's bench. She's standing there now in a long cashmere coat, absolutely gorgeous.

Diane. My woman, Diane.

I don't know whether to say, "What are you doing here?" or "Shit! What the hell are you doing here?"

I take three steps toward her. My thoughts explode in my mind. Panic is in the mix. We nearly suck each other's tongues out of their sockets. I whisper in her ear, "I thought I lost you. You are so beautiful. You smell unreal. Just let me breathe your scent. I'm so glad to see you." I pull my head back and look at her face. She has tears running down her cheeks, and so do I. Then we start laughing. For a moment we are not in Lurigancho. It has been almost a year since I have touched a woman or felt any tenderness from anyone. The moment is over quickly.

I can't seem to remember why I haven't tried to escape. Chula is talking about the elaborate process we have to go through, and I am pretending to listen. But standing here with Diane now, all I want to do is find a way out now, right now.

The fatal desire to escape has just been born in my heart. *Maybe we can turn around right now and walk out, arm in arm. Fuck this system.*

Chula carefully spits out a rolled-up piece of tin foil from his cheek and passes it to me by way of a handshake. "Here's something from the fellas back home," he says. "They all love you and want you to hang in there. We're all working to get you out."

"What about me and R.B.?" says Arthur. "You really think they would let me go?"

"I read your original statement," says Chula. "That was good thinking, telling Rubio and Del Gado that you're an artist from Tahiti."

Arthur imitates himself telling the PIP in a scared-shitless voice: "I c-c-came to do p-p-p-paintings of Ma-achu Pi-ichu-u."

Richard wants to know, "Where's MY surprise?"

Diane pulls an envelope from her own coat pocket. "Oh, you have one, Richard. Here, read this letter from Robin."

R.B. reads just the first page. For the first time since I've known him, he has tears in his eyes. He needs to sit down. "I have a daughter," he says, "a baby girl named Amber!"

Several months ago Richard wrote a letter to Robin and told her to forget about him—his life was finished until he got out of Lurigancho. I remember how he looked when he told me about writing that letter—hardened, neutral, enduring. Now here he is sitting on the bench and he shoots me a different look altogether, a look that's probably like the one I have on my own face. Suddenly motivation to get out, one way or another, has awoken.

Richard barks at Chula, "What takes so fucking long with this court system?"

Arthur cuts in, "George, have you heard anything from my ol'lady Debbie?"

"No. But here is a letter to all you guys from Sally, a gal from Dana Point. She's a friend of Richard and Robin."

Arthur cries, "Oh, mail. From a woman!" He smells the envelope.

I take a few steps away from the other men to talk privately with Diane, softly caressing and kissing. "I'll be out of here in just a few more months," I lie.

Diane lets the tears flow. "I never wanted to see you in a place like this!"

I turn to Chula. "George, why did they send Diane? It is so damn good you brought her—but what? Is she going to live alone in Lima? I guess you have a plan, right?"

"Right!" he says with a confidence that matches his appearance.

Richard: "I want to hear this!" Arthur shushes him, "Just listen!"

"As I was saying, you'll no doubt start trial by way of a lower court. If you stick to the original story that the PIP has on record, Arthur should be released with the decision of that lower-court judge."

"Are you going to be at the court with us?" asks Richard.

"No."

"No lawyer?" says Arthur.

"No, you will have counsel. Don't worry about that. I've made arrangements with Tiefilo Ibarra, an attorney in Lima and former judge of the tribunal. He will be in touch with the three of you. He'll be looking out for Diane, too. All three of you will probably go to the first court in a couple weeks."

Richard is not happy. "What the fuck, George? What chance do we have without you there? You have to be there."

Chula's voice becomes grave. "I didn't want to tell you this about me, Richard. But I may need to go in for bypass heart surgery. I can't guarantee I can get down here. I may be in recovery. But don't worry. I will see you guys again. I just hope that I'll see you back home, when you are all free."

Eventually we volunteer to go back inside rather than wait around for Chula and Diane to leave. No one says why. It just seems like the thing to do.

A blue-uniformed guard signals for us to walk in the opposite direction of the way we came. Now there are four guards, all of them smiling and no doubt talking among themselves about the most beautiful girl they have ever seen. One of them says, "Vamos gringos por el Corridor."

This is not the route we were hoping for.

The Big Hall is roaring as though an entire football game had been trapped in a concrete vault, a big crypt with stench and monsters skulking deeper into the shadows. Our guards walk two in back of us, two in front. They carry on their own conversations oblivious to us. We're all shouting to be heard.

Arthur is saying, "You're lucky, man! My ol'lady hasn't even tried to ask how I'm doing, much less write or come down here and visit my ass."

Richard says, "What do you think Eddie and Diane are going to do—go out and party? She's here for all three of us, Arthur."

"Hey listen," I say. "This ain't cool, guys."

Suddenly one of the Big Hall prowlers lunges at Richard, "Hey gringo, un cigaro por favor gringo?" He's a dark man in rags, and he smells like a sewer. Richard shoves him. "Get away from me, you scummy fuck."

Two of our guards rap him with their hard rubber clubs—bap bap—as the peasant runs away.

"What's not cool?" says Arthur. He's leaning toward me as we walk and watching my face.

"Diane likes coke as much as I do. Once I get started on that shit, I don't stop until it's gone. And she's in Peru. Think about it. A gorgeous surfer girl with a habit. In the land of cocaine."

Richard scoffs at me. "What?"

I look at Arthur. "Lucky? I'm fucked!"

Richard does one of his trademark laughs with a face expressing pure disgust. "Oh wow," he says. "You should be the gladdest dude in this whole place, and you're jealous. Are you afraid she'll get it on with one of these Peruvian dudes?"

"No, stupid! I'm talking about catching another case. I'm talking about how much Diane likes cocaine, not sex. I can hardly believe you don't get it! Wait till Del Gado sees her, and Rubio. They'll go nuts trying to set her up. I'm talking about the PIP beating her and raping her and then getting her to sign a false confession for the

DEA. Do you both get it yet? These fucking Peruvians think we're big-time smugglers as it is."

We walk for a while without talking. The crazy hubbub of shouting seems to push against every part of us as though we can hear it with our skin. Then Arthur says, "Right. It's a Danny Dildo situation."

"Potential," says R.B.

"What?"

"Potential!"

"Right. What we have here is a potential Danny Dildo."

In my bunk I lie in deep thought of escape. I was sure until now I'd already lost Diane. But now—regret, overwhelming regret that I haven't busted out of this mess. I had some chances back at the PIP house, the first place they took us. But I never thought it would go this far. It all happened so fast, and I convinced myself that everything would be all right and we would go back home. Now I am consumed with the idea of escaping. But Richard has become so distant that I don't think he can get it together with me. He blames me totally. And his anger is growing because of the newborn baby he may not know until she is a teenager.

So I've been talking with Ivan—quiet, secret talks in which we go over the routine of daily life at Luri, looking for a crack in the system. There has to be one. We want to know the history of escape attempts from this prison. Emphasis on the word "attempts." No one has ever made it. On that score, all the stories agree.

After all, Lurigancho sits like a pencil mark in the middle of a huge canvas of sand. Some hills sprinkled around the canvas offer no apparent assistance to escape.

Suddenly a chill goes through my spine with the thought of failure and of the guards carrying out their promise. And when I imagine myself getting through that, then I face the paper shortage—

paper such as a passport and money.

I'm thinking about talking with Markos, an inmate Peruvian who has lived in Lurigancho going on twenty years. He'll know if the rumor about a tunnel is true. But when I mention the idea to Ivan he says, "Maybe not good idea. As soon as we start asking about escape routes, we will be under suspicion and there are snitches everywhere."

"Just talking like this will make them suspicious."

Ivan and me agree simply to be ready should the opportunity arise. He gives a flicker of his open hand. Later he does it again to make sure I know what it means. It means loyalty.

I'm having a recurring dream. In the dream Ivan and me make it over both fences and then we make it over the wall, and then we race up to the top of a mountain expecting to find freedom on the other side. But all we can see are more mountains, thousands of miles of barren desert mountains, and I wake up slightly more depressed.

When the American government paid for the construction of this part of the prison, at least the part we live in, the purchase was supposed to include a chow hall. So I hear. I hear that the labor force was a crew of inmates who used their tools not to build a chow hall but to dig a tunnel. Story goes they got quite a ways before one prisoner had heart failure. When the guards searched for the missing inmate, they discovered the dig. So the chow hall remains unbuilt. Ditto the gymnasium purchased by U.S. taxpayers but never visited by anyone ever.

The Peruvians do sometimes get a game of soccer going out on the cement yard, the field enclosed by brick cellblock walls. The brick is brutal. Blood is expected.

Walking out of the cell preoccupied, I don't hear the guys at the hearts game asking if I'm okay. My sex drive has gone wild along with my mind. I am having wet dreams. My emotions are completely crazy over how gorgeous Diane is, and she loves to fuck as much as I do.

I see a priest talking to a bunch of natives down the hall. He speaks English.

"Hello, Padre."

He says, "If you're not comfortable with Father, call me Don."

"Okay, Don."

"How are you managing this life? What is your name?"

"I'm not, really."

"Is there something I may be able to help with?"

"Yeah. My girlfriend is here in Lima. She's alone. Do you have a church?"

"Yes, of course. Would you like me to contact your girlfriend?"

"Yes. But also, Father Don, I want to know about getting married in your church. Do you think it's possible?"

"Have you killed anyone? Or hurt children?"

"No!"

"Yes, I think it is possible. Only the warden may give this permission. But it has been done in the past."

"How 'bout my confession, Don?"

"What is your name?"

"Ed, Father Don. Ed."

"Ed, are you sorry for anything?"

"Very."

"You are forgiven."

"Thank you, Father."

"Ed, whatever you have done, life in this place must be more than punishment enough. I wish you well. God bless you."

"Got a card or phone number for my girlfriend, Father?"

"I can call her if she has a phone."

"Well, she's staying above my lawyer's girlfriend's house in a one-room apartment. If you try the phone book you should be able to find Tiefilo Ibarra, attorney."

He doesn't even ask if I'm Catholic.

I begin to put together a plan. *I'm not going to discuss my plan with anyone. Not even Diane. I have got to get out of here.*

The talk with the priest has excited me. I'm full of energy. When I get back to the cell the eternal hearts players are slamming down cards and yelling, but I shout louder: "Hey, all you wimps and wusses! Who wants to box a real man?"

I figure that will get some takers. But only one person bites. And that turns out to be Carlton—who looks like a late survivor of the bare-knuckle days. He cries, "Ha! You couldn't box your way out of a wet paper bag. Where's the gloves? I would be glad to give you kids a lesson or two." And he uses his non-card-holding hand to give his white handlebar moustache a good twist, very Gentleman Jim Corbet.

"Carlton," I say, "that nose looks like a target to me."

Carlton looks at me over the top of his readers, which accent his large nose. "That is about enough," he says. "Let's rumble." That gets a laugh from everyone in the cell.

Richard lays his paperback novel face-down on his chest and says, "Oh, I gotta see this."

Arthur calls from above, cross-legged on his bunk: "I'll be Eddie's corner man."

Ivan shouts, "The gloves are right here under my bunk. They are brand new, too." He pulls out the box of gear that Chula brought. It has been sitting under our bunk.

Hermes starts fanning himself with playing cards. "Oh, this sounds like a little S and M. I'm getting a boner."

Kit stands up from the table. He is the tall ghost of an ignorant highway patrolman. He says, "Hermes, y'all'd get a boner over a bent-over chair. Or anything bent the fuck over."

Hermes says, "Oh yes, right, Mister Texas sheepherder."

Suddenly Stan announces from his seat at the hearts game: "Okay, no one fucks with this hand." He lays his cards face-down on our rickety scrap-wood table. "Come on. I'll be Conkie's corner guy."

I open the box and pull out the bright red gloves. "Oh shit, these are eight ounce."

Carlton is over in the corner at his bunk, taking off his short-sleeve shirt—the one he has sewn in several places because it is so worn. Underneath he wears an old-man-style undershirt. Carlton always complains about not getting to shave with a straight razor. None of the rest of us has ever owned a straight razor.

I slip on the gloves, and while Arthur does up the laces I look over at Carlton. I can see that he has been an athlete all his life. Even now he talks about surfing in the old days and about beating so-and-so in tennis or is it in golf. Must be golf, because he's wearing his purple-striped golf pants. He claims the PIP stole everything he had except his wild golf pants. Carlton is six feet tall. Like all of us he has lost weight, but not as much as Richard.

I say, "You know, with those striped pants and that old-man undershirt you look like John L. Sullivan or something."

"Or maybe his grandfather," says Richard.

Arthur asks, "Who's John L. Sullivan?"

"Some guy who escaped from an Alabama chain gang."

Carlton looks back at Richard and with sympathy for the unedu-cated he says, "Richard, these pants are standard dress code at any golf course in Orange County, California. Where the hell are you from?"

Richard looks over to me. He says, "Don't hurt him. Too much."

We are all about to pile out of the cell and enter the empty room at the east end of our block. Weaver walks in the cell and says, "Hey, what's up?"

Stan says to Weaver as he passes, "Fight."

Over at Carlton's bunk Hermes is helping put on Carlton's gloves. Weaver grins his Hollywood grin and strokes his trim little red-brown moustache. "Between Carlton and Ed?"

The ring is about ten feet across. Somebody used a small rock to scratch a circle into the concrete floor. We're in the big empty room at the end of the cellblock—must have been meant as a rec room of some kind, but it's bare all the time and we generally stay out of it. But now we have attracted an audience, and the room is quickly filling to capacity. The chattering starts right away. A boxing match. A sporting event in Lurigancho.

The Spanish-speaking inmates don't know that this is all in fun. At least I think it's all in fun. But as the crowd pressure builds, I start to feel that I'm in a smaller and smaller minority. Rick the rocker was downstairs when we got going, but now he has picked up on the action and, true to his style, he's placing bets with the Peruvians. Now Weaver has promoted himself to the position of referee. Carlton is in his "corner" with his towel man, Stan, and Arthur is ready in mine. Suddenly the crowd grows tense and quiet, and Weaver yells, "Come out fighting!" To my surprise, Carlton moves quickly across the floor. His arms are longer than mine, and now he's within reach. In fact, he's about to hit me as hard as he can. He's got his fist pulled back to his shoulder.

I tap his forehead with a right jab.

His head snaps back. He looks as though he just ran into a wall. The snap of his head loosens the band holding his hair, and his seven-inch ponytail flares open. A cheer rises from the crowd. Stan grabs Carlton's upper arms and says, "You're okay, champ. Look. How many fingers am I holding up?"

"None, you asshole." Carlton pushes Stan away with his gloves. "Get out of the way."

I stand with my arms down at my sides. Carlton pulls up his gloves and holds them in a defensive pose. Then he wades toward me with a deadly serious look in his eye. I say, "This is just for fun, right? Don't get all carried away, old man."

Carlton's pale face has turned so red that he seems to have a sunburn now, and the spot where I hit him with that stiff jab has started
to swell. Carefully he steps forward, trying to take advantage of his
longer reach. "You were very lucky, son," he says. "Defend yourself."

The first two times that he hits the floor, he's cussin' mad at me.
But after the third time, he sits there on the floor and holds up his
gloves. "That's it. I can't do this. You don't box like a white man."

It feels kind of bad to knock an old man down. But it must be
even worse for him, knowing he didn't even get a single punch to
land.

Visiting someone at Lurigancho is a real adventure, a disgusting adventure.

Ibarra, our new lawyer, acquires a pass from the military for
Diane, a pass that allows her to come to the yard for an hour every
Wednesday—our beautiful yard with our beach and our latrine. The
first visit is very scary for her.

She has come with Ibarra in a taxi. Visitors are not visible to us
prisoners until they enter the yard through the iron door at the far
end, nearest the perimeter walk. Before they arrive, the guards
order all inmates to remain at the opposite end of the yard, near the
latrine, until our names are called.

Ibarra, our lawyer, is first through the door, and this is our first
chance to look at him. He is fat and bald. A ring of white hair, cut
short, circles his head at ear level. He is wearing an outdated brown
suit and a green-and-yellow flowered tie that lies on his white shirt
and protrudes along with his belly from his spread-open suitcoat.

Now Diane steps through the door in back of Ibarra. Her full-
length Alpaca knit dress hangs on every curve of her athletic body.
She has leather boots on her perfect little feet. This is our second
visit, one week later.

A guard tells them where to sit. The guard calls me, Ricardo, and Arturo. The prisoners around us are making comments in Spanish about Diane's body, and we ignore them. Now the yard is crowded with prisoners who are doing the short walk to the east end, where the guards have set up benches for the visitors. As we walk up, Diane breaks away from Ibarra and runs the twenty feet that separate us. She embraces me as though this will be the last time. Her body is a blanket of warm life, her kiss is suddenly sacred, and for an instant we are not in Lurigancho. Then a guard blows his whistle a few feet from us and motions us to stop the kissing and sit down.

"Hi, Arthur. Hi, R.B.," she says. "You guys, this is the man George told you about. He's your lawyer now. Mr. Ibarra, this is Arturo and Ricardo and Eddie."

"Hello boys, how are joo?"

Arthur says, "So when do we get out of here, Mr. Ibarra?"

"Oh boys, please call to me Tiefilo. I am your friend. First we must go to the tribunal. And then freedom, boys."

Richard and Arthur drift off ten feet away, leaving Diane and me to talk alone.

We are on display. All eyes in the cellblock next door are watching us—watching her, rather. We're in a reverse zoo. It's us who are being watched by the animals. No doubt some of the men are jerking off.

Diane is telling me about Richard's baby. I cut her off and softly say, "Will you marry me?"

Her eyes go wide. "Wow! Here, in here? I don't know. Why?"

"No, not in here. I talked to a priest. The priest, did he call you?"

"No."

"Listen. The priest, Father Don—he said it's been done before where someone gets taken out of here for the wedding in a church. We're both Catholic and maybe we could."

"But I love you. We can get married when you get out."

"But it matters to me. I think it will matter when we go to trial. Chula said that we'll be going there soon."

I give her Father Don's number. *Now if she'll just call and carry through, maybe I can get out of here. I'll find a way to slip out even if I have to club Father Don.* I can't tell her that I'm not really looking for a wedding, only for a chance to run. I figure if Diane doesn't know, and no one knows, then no one can snitch me off.

Before the next visit Diane finds out from Father Don that we both need to send home for our baptism certificates and birth certificates. But before the documents arrive, we have a third visit, and that's when things start to get bizarre.

"We don't have to get married," she says. "I love you."

"What's really going on, Diane?"

She breaks down crying. "Ibarra says you'll probably be here for at least twelve years."

"Bullshit, sweetie. I'll be out way before that. How could that son-of-a-bitch tell you that? He's making himself needed so that we'll pay him, that's all. He always tells us the same thing that Chula told us—that we'll be out at trial. Don't worry."

She is crying harder. "I can't wait twelve years. What would I do? Come to hell for twelve years? I can't, I can't, and I can't do it. Oh God I love you but I can't do it. Please forgive me. I'm so sorry."

I am fucked.

The next visit is worse.

Diane tells me, "I made a new friend."

I say, "Oh cool. What's her name?"

"His name. It's a guy. You're okay, aren't you? He's just a friend I can go places with. His name is Ricky. Don't worry. He's like a girlfriend, but more protective. Like the other night he was telling me how much the Peruvian men are into a women's ass. And Ricky says I have the nicest ass in Peru."

I am sick to my stomach. I am dazed to realize this is happening, that Diane is talking to me like this. Without responding to the ass comment I ask her, "Are you using coke out there?"

Diane says, "Yes, but only with Ricky. Don't worry about that either. Ricky only gets the best. You would like him."

This visit ends with a failed marriage plan—consequently, a failed escape plan. But unlike my predecessors in failed escapes from Lurigancho, I am alive to try again.

Something else changes as a result of this visit—right away I go looking for a line of coke and some pills. But not to stop the pain I'm feeling, you understand. I just feel like getting high. That's what I tell myself, anyway.

Man, that shit hurts. Diane is disintegrating. But I can't let anything get in the way. I've got to get out of here.

I find Arthur and Richard in one of the cells downstairs, where they are smoking coke. "Give me a hit of that shit!"

The guy who's getting them the paste is a Colombian named Jimmy. Jimmy is new to us. But he says he's not new to Lurigancho. He served three years here before, he says.

And now he's in for shooting a cop in a shoot-out when the cops raided his cocaine lab. So he says.

He's a thin, tall, light-skinned Colombian who can speak enough English to hold a conversation, with help. He professes to be hooked up with the Colombian Mafia. Seems that we all have experienced not liking another human for no apparent reason. That is the case with me when I meet Jimmy.

Richard and Arthur have been smoking the paste for months. I know how I am once I get started. And they are telling me that this shit is ten times stronger than doing a line. The main thing it does is take over. Smoke it, and then you don't care if you're in Lurigancho or in your own living room. Just as long as there's more paste to smoke. And just as long as the paste is cheaper than the cigarettes you're using to smoke it.

Jimmy the Colombian comes back to the cell with more of the paste. He starts telling us that he knows how to escape when he goes to court. He knows how to escape right from the Justice Palace in downtown Lima.

Here's his plan. Jimmy will get called to court, and his lawyer will be there. He will be placed in the basement of the Justice Palace with all of the other prisoners. His attorney will have the court clerk call him up to court. The attorney will wait in the courtroom while two soldiers escort Jimmy up the four flights of stairs through a chaos of people who are looking for loved ones lost in this so-called system of justice. People will be shouting to their lawyers in huge ancient hallways filled wall to wall with women crying, women with crying babies, and women with crying men. Infiltrating the mob, soldiers will be shoving people and giving orders that no one respects.

"Move where, Señor?"

The break will happen when the upstairs soldiers take control of Jimmy from the downstairs soldiers. The attorney will meet Jimmy at the courtroom door. They will discover that the judge has scheduled no appearance for Jimmy. But the judge will tell Jimmy to sit there with the other prisoners until the end of the day. At the end of the long day more than a hundred prisoners will be taken back down to the basement and returned to Lurigancho. The attorney will go with his client to the basement. The basement soldiers will know nothing about Jimmy's day, that he was never on the calendar. All they will know is that the lawyer is handing them documents—counterfeit documents—stating that the judge has ordered Jimmy's immediate release. So they will release Jimmy right then and there. And then Jimmy and his lawyer will skate.

I buy in. Richard and Arthur agree with me. If it works for Jimmy, I'll go next.

So the next time Diane visits, I introduce her to the little Colombian gangster. We make an agreement. If Jimmy gets out via the scam, he will get money from Diane to pay for the papers and for someone to pose as my lawyer. Not Ibarra. We all agree that Ibarra would rat us off.

By now Diane has lost the privilege of a military pass. The reason for this isn't clear. Instead she comes with the regular visit. On the regular visit the yard is packed with women visiting their husbands, boyfriends, and brothers. And it is packed with monstrous women from the village of San Juan de Lurigancho. The only habitation for many, many miles around, this village is the poorest of the poor. People live in the dirt. A house can be a few rusted-out car bodies fitted together to simulate rooms. The hideous women of this village come on visiting days into the cellblock. They offer to buy food and supplies for the inmates who can afford to give them money. This service is their entire livelihood. In the midst of such a society, I introduce Diane to a man I would not piss on if I found him on fire.

I want out.

Diane is falling apart. She's messing around, and she'll get herself busted. For that matter, the PIP and the DEA will just set her up and no one will question shit. As a matter of fact, they might be doing it right now.

Ibarra would probably love to have another American client.

The meeting takes place. If the scam works, Diane will hand Jimmy seven thousand dollars—everything I own.

I wait all day to see men returning from the bus that Jimmy would be on if he was returning. He does not return.

Neither does Diane.

Three weeks go by.

One of the guards tells me that he knows someone who saw Jimmy and Diane in town walking to a car and holding hands and kissing.

I go numb. The first feeling is sick to my stomach. I walk into our cell dazed. I am trying to side with the part of me that's fighting to say it isn't true, it can't be true—but it's a poor fight. The blow sickens me to the core.

"Hey!" Arthur slaps my face. "I said Hey! What the fuck is up with you? You look worse than you usually do! How come?"

When I tell Richard and Arthur what the guard said, they come back with other stuff like that, stuff they heard from some of the Peruvian inmates. Sometimes information gets to the prison even before it circulates on the street. "Why didn't you guys tell me something? What's up with that?"

Richard says, "We decided it's bullshit."

"What do you think?" says Arthur. "Is it bullshit? Would she do that? Turn on us?"

I've been set up.

It feels like I've been set up.

Nearly five years ago I walked into my house and announced to my wife Joleen, our little girl, and the baby boy that we were through. I moved out to be with Diane.

Joleen and I dated in high school, and we married when we were nineteen. She was a loyal, faithful, loving wife and a super mom. Now years later in Lurigancho Prison, thousands of miles from home and friends and family, I keep running Arthur's words over in my head. Would Diane betray us? I think I can hear Joleen's voice, talking about me back then when I walked out so cold and selfish.

Would he do that? Turn on me?

Would he do that to Eric, his little son who is Ed's little best buddy, the best buddy a daddy ever had? Or to Janell, his daughter? Ed loves her more than his own life, he said. Would Ed turn on them and leave them just like that?

Yeah. I did that.

Is the pain that I'm feeling anything like the pain that Joleen felt? Or am I just beginning to take the punishment of betrayal and desertion?

My own mind's voice assures me that the fun has just begun.

Ibarra comes. We go out and meet with him in the yard. The usual handshakes from Arthur and from me. Richard says hi but does not shake his hand. Ibarra's fat face is flushed and red today. His double chin is wobbling. "Boys, I must let tell to Eduardo. Diana and Jimmy, they living together at the house of Jimmy's sister. I believe they are doing the cocaine business. I know that man with Diana. He no good. I remember him from when I was a judge. They make to me give to them all joor monies."

"What the fuck have you been doing? Goddamnit, you are supposed to be looking out for her. And for us. How could you let that son-of-a-bitch get to her? I can't believe this shit. And you gave Diane my money!"

From behind me Arthur says, "You mean our money."

Richard is disgusted. "I've heard enough. I'm going up. Later."

Ibarra is embarrassed. He says, "Jess jess, I understand to joo. But you say for me to give her money and Diana she say me the money is for joo. She says you know everything."

"Oh fuck. You really piss me off. I thought you were smart. You're as dumb as a stick. Goddamnit, you old fuck. You know she's using cocaine, you know about cocaine, you know goddamn well you can't trust people when they get on that shit. Fuck, Ibarra, what the fuck is wrong with you, shit."

"Oh, you seem very upset. I am bery sorry."

Ibarra excuses himself, saying he will call Mr. Chula and try to get money.

I am too pissed to put out even one word more and turn and head back into the cellblock.

Arthur stays behind. I hear him say to Ibarra, "Yeah, call George. Tell him we need money in here to eat and live. Let us know."

Ibarra gives Arthur one last, "I am sorry. But I will work bery bery hard for joo boys don't worry."

Other inmates have heard this conversation with Ibarra, and now the soap opera is playing all over the cellblock. Soon it will travel the grapevine all over the prison. *Jimmy burnt the gringo for his monies and his woman.*

I can't get a full breath. The usual knot in my stomach is now the size of my entire gut. I want to jump a wall and run all the way to Jimmy's broken neck. I once watched my uncle gut and skin a buck elk in the forest. I know he'll be alive when I do that to Jimmy. I just can't decide if he'll be hanging upside down or by the neck.

I've actually got the spins. I can't hear the yelling and laughing of the men in their cells or the infuriating drumming coming out of every hall. When I get to the cell there's no table-thumping and yelling eat the bitch from the heart's game. Every man in the cell is quiet. They all know that being caged like an animal really exaggerates the feeling of having a low-life scum use cocaine to bait and fuck your ol'lady and then laugh at your dumb ass.

Now that I'm back in my cell, the rage catches fire and suddenly I'm burning up. No one except Ivan wants to make eye contact. I feel like I'm going to break like a dried old dog bone in the jaw of a grizzly bear.

"Hey," I say to Ivan, "can we take a walk, man?"

Without hesitation Ivan is on his feet. "Let's go." He knows I'm about to bust open, and I will slit my own throat to keep from crying in Lurigancho. My rage pushes me the same pace as Ivan. In silence we speed-walk down the hall and out to the yard and out of earshot of anyone who speaks English.

We join the traffic traveling east to west and back again. Our conversation is cloaked by the Spanish conversations around us, men joined in their own problems. Leaning over as if to tell me a secret, Ivan says, "You should put a hit on that motherfucker. Pelone can get a pistolero for you. Little more expensive than if Jimmy was back in here. If we could get Jimmy back in here with us, you could hit him yourself."

"I'd rather off him on my way out of Peru! I'm going to find Pelone. Comin'?"

Thoughts of Diane are sending ripples of weakness through me. My backbone is jelly, my legs very tired. What keeps me moving toward Pelone's cell is the need to off Jimmy.

Pelone is the boss in his fifteen-by-thirty-foot cell.

Every cell in Lurigancho has its own culture. We gringos manage to maintain a certain amount of floor space. But Pelone's cell is just a maze of men who live on the floor. A clothesline spans the room, tied between the frames of two steel bunks. The laundry looks like carwash rags. Men in the cell are chattering. One guy's mending a shirt. This one's doing a tailor job on a worn-out pair of pants. Some men are inventing a crazy dance in order to move around the cell. In the middle of the maze two men are playing chess and ten others are staring thoughtfully at the board. They've got the board set up on old tin cans, one at each corner. Nearly everyone is Peruvian, a few Colombians. They all come to attention when they see Ivan and me standing inside the cell door. The chess players glance over. Someone says, "Que quieren, gringos?" Another says, "Are joo lost, gringos?"

"Amigos, I need to speak with Pelone. Is he here?"

The cell grows just a little quieter. I notice several of the inmates looking toward the back corner of the cell. On the bottom bunk an old gray army blanket begins to move. Pelone's head appears from behind the blanket, which was covering him from head to foot.

Pelone stands out from the other men in the cell. His color is very light, as is his shoulder-length hair. His green eyes make him look European or even American until he talks. Then you know he's not a civilized man. In fact, he is feared. I can feel it in the cell. They also seemed to fear the two dark characters who lurk in the bunks above Pelone.

"Bueno!" says Pelone in a sleepy, friendly voice. "Que hacen, gringos? What's going on, mans?" Everybody in the cell takes the cue and goes back to his business. The place starts to buzz again— men yacking as they sew their raggedy clothes, which are all they have left after years in Lurigancho with no one bringing them clothing or anything else.

I say, "Hey Pelone, can we talk outside, man?"

Pelone knows that Ivan has no problem with him. "You talkie too, hombre grande?" I can tell that Pelone admires Ivan's frame. But I'm curious that he's not intimidated by it. Most Peruvians cringe when Ivan comes near. They even cringe when I come near because I have twice their muscle. But Pelone operates by different rules. He would never bother fist-fighting a big man. Just slice his belly open.

Ivan puts his giant hand on Pelone's shoulder. "No not me, my friend. But Eddie has business. I can give you two some privacy. You understand, Pelone?"

Pelone and me sit down on the cement against the east wall of the courtyard. We talk quietly while Ivan keeps other ears at a distance. He's out of hearing range, but Burt Weaver, the Los Angeles Sheriff's Department narc, is the person we can see most clearly. As usual for this time of day, he is wearing his navy Speedo and he's working on his suntan. He's got one of the crude benches from our cell, and he's down in the yard lying on it, tanning his back. From our angle we're looking up his ass. He has his arms and legs turned outward, deliberately trying to tan the undersides of things. He tells us that he was a model before he ever became a cop. Then he came to Peru on vacation and got busted at the airport trying to smuggle a pound of coke hidden in a carton of cigarettes.

Pelone starts by looking into my eyes. Then he cocks his head toward Weaver and says, "Es un puto. Si?"

"Yeah. He's a real whore." In other words, yes, Pelone, you and I know which side of the fence we're on.

The traffic of daily life in Lurigancho Prison goes on as Pelone and me plan a murder.

Back upstairs I go looking for Richard. All has returned to normal. Carlton is slamming down a spade and Tony yells, "Stop the old man. He's trying to run 'em." But Richard isn't in his bunk, only his paperback face down. His is the bottom bunk. Arthur is middle, below Hunter.

Kit answers Tony in that shrill Texas drawl, "I got him." As Kit slams down the king of spades, Hermes screams, "And Kit eats that big bitch!" He sets the queen of hearts down on the trick like lips on a tasty morsel.

I find Richard at the end of the building, in the bare room where we've been holding our little boxing matches. He's standing at one of the barred windows leaning over, bent at the waist with elbows on the window ledge, wearing only his faded blue boxers. I'm shocked when I see Richard's back. I can see every bone. His legs don't look strong enough to hold his weight. When we left California, Richard weighed about two hundred pounds and he was trim

I walk over to the window. "Jesus, brother. You need to gain some weight."

"Fuck you, Eddie!" he says with a knowing grin. I can see what he's reflecting back at me. I don't look any better.

And he's reflecting more than that. I can tell he's thinking about the fact that I deserted my kids. Because now he has a kid—the little girl whose picture he's been holding in his hand.

"What were you talking to Pelone about?" he says. "More coke?"

"No. He's going to help me kill that fucking Jimmy!"

Richard looks back at the picture in his hands.

"You know I'm no killer, R.B. But if I don't put all this rage in my gut toward killing that fuck, I'm going to go fucking nuts, man. I want him dead."

"You should."

"That's what Ivan said. You know, R.B., I'm feeling a lot of things I never have before. I'm feeling pain I never felt. Hurts like hell. Man, have I been that fucking absent from my own life? From my own kids? How could I have been so cold? So fucking cold." Now I am leaning my elbows on the window ledge.

Richard stands straight and turns his back to the window. He holds the picture of Amber close to his face and looks at the picture and then looks back at me. "THIS hurts like hell, Eddie" he says. "This hurts like hell, man. Look at those eyes. Those are my mom's eyes. And the hair is just like mine, except it's curly like her mother's hair. Yeah. I feel a lot, too, man. But we WILL get home."

"We will?"

"Believe me, man."

After a minute I say, "Where's Arthur?"

"Down there."

Richard points to the barred window on the north side of the room. I walk over to it and look down into the yard on the other side of our cellblock, the yard we usually don't see. Suddenly I notice the hubbub. It's visiting day for women down there. The yard is packed. Little weathered women from the village of San Juan de Lurigancho are down there selling food. They have fresh fish and freshly butchered chickens. Few prisoners can afford such things. If they can, they have to cook the animal somehow and immediately. Then they have to eat it all within two days, or else it goes bad.

"I can't see Arthur in that crowd. Where is he?"

"He's down there selling leche asada."

"What the fuck's that?"

"Rice pudding."

Now I spot him. His dirty-blond hair and fair skin suddenly emerge from the throng. He has before him a wooden tray. A worn leather band straps his neck to the tray, which holds five or six small pudding jars. The visitors are buying from him. I hear him yell, "Get your leche asada!" He makes the Peruvians laugh, and he appears to be having a good time.

Richard joins me at the window. I say, "Trip, huh? Arthur has a fucking job."

Richard asks without taking his eyes off of Arthur, "What about Diane?"

"I just want her to run back to New Jersey where she came from."

Arthur inherited the job from a Peruvian who went home a couple weeks ago. The business consists of a wooden tray, a recipe for rice pudding, and a certain cooperation from the guards. The leche asada man can travel the Big Hall. From the Big Hall he can go anywhere, even to the outer courtyard, to sell his little glass cups to visitors. He goes escorted, of course. Arthur won't go into the Big Hall without the protection of the guards.

And yet I believe somehow that Arthur will never have a problem in the Big Hall. Two forces keep Arthur in a state of grace. One is that people here actually like him—he has made a real effort to learn Spanish, and he has gained people's respect. The other is that René has a crush on him.

René is an extremely violent man. At the same time, he is flamboyant and feminine in his mannerisms, with a sweet, high voice. René always wears a beret, a drab brown beret, which he keeps tipped to one side of his head. Someone told me that he is bald and that he's really on a trip about hiding his head. He's a sharp dresser by Lurigancho standards—always a collared shirt and polyester pants that coordinate in color with his beret. His Latin face with its oval dark eyes looks puffy and pockmarked, and though he's my size he has a soft-looking build. But René is king of his own cell, the one across the hall from us, just as Pelone is king of his. Both men rule by the blade. In fact, if the stories are true, René is more violent even than Pelone. One man tells me that he watched René attack an inmate in the Big Hall and take out his eyeball. Another tells me of seeing René bite a man's jugular vein. I never saw that, but I did see him stab a man who was beating him in chess.

It happened like this. I was in my bunk reading and I got up to stretch. Suddenly there was a burst of yelling across the hall. I stepped out into the hall and looked into their cell. Chess pieces were flying everywhere. "Stand back or you'll get stabbed too!" a man yelled in Spanish. I saw René pushing men out of his way and men were leaping to get out of his way as René stalked to one side of the cell, yelling that a man was cheating and now he had to die. I could see that René was holding a butter knife—I knew it was sharp as a razor.

Without hesitation René went after the man who had moments before been his chess partner. The partner stood his ground and put his hands in the air as if to challenge René to cut him.

Now a crowd was pressing into the doorway and packing the hall, but my view was still unobstructed. René accepted the challenge and flipped the knife from waist level straight up into the man's lower stomach. Instantly blood spread, soaking the man's tan-colored shirt, blood dyeing the shirt dark brown. The cut man was struck numb and could only stare down at his own bleeding stomach. René stepped back as quickly as he had moved forward. Apparently he was satisfied with the wound. The fight was over. A group of men gathered around the wounded prisoner. It was useless to ask for a doctor. This prison has a doctor only on Tuesday, sometimes. The man needed stitches, but his friends would have to do the job with their sewing kits.

René still claims that the man was cheating. Everyone else pretty much agrees that the man was merely winning.

When René totally cuts loose, he's scary. But I think his sweet, sweet voice is even scarier. Once he said to me. "Oh, I love joor Arthur. Oh, he is soooo fine. Joo know?"

"No, my friend, I don't know."

"Oh! Joo don't love Arthur?"

"Yeah, I love Arthur. But not like you mean, René. I love him like a brother. You want to fuck him."

"Oh. I fuck *my* brother."

"René! You make me laugh! Thanks."

"Jes? Joo sell me Arthur?"

As for the Big Hall, it's going to be dangerous for that populace if anyone causes harm to Arthur. René would be on the warpath.

Meanwhile Arthur has a career in Peruvian rice pudding.

Arthur and his pudding tray disappear into the crowd again, and suddenly I remember why I came out to find Richard.

"You think it's time to break out that bud Chula left?"

"Why not?"

We return to the cell, and Richard pulls out a couple of Chap Sticks. He opens one of the cylinders and pries out the wax and then extracts a thick chunk of marijuana bud. He's sitting on his bunk. I'm standing in front of him to block the view. But view-blocking has no value in this crowd. These guys could be blind and still know what we were up to. From twenty feet away Tony shouts, "Holy shit! Do I smell skunk or what?"

Every man in this cell loves pot—everyone, that is, except Kit, our Texas cop. When it comes to getting high, Kit considers himself to be a proper mainstream American. In other words, he's a 1950s-style junkie who pops pills and experiments with household cleaning products. But now even Kit, all the way over at the hearts table, declares, "Hot damn, that smells like my daddy's skunk farm on a hot afternoon."

Richard tells Kit, "You and your daddy should smoke this skunk instead of doing that brain-eating glue, dude."

Carlton is sitting at the table with a smile on his face. He butts in, "Oh shit this is good. I'm sitting here with a bunch of criminals listening to them discuss the morals and ethics of getting high. I am entertained, gentlemen."

"What'd ya'll say?" says Kit. "Morals and what?"

Hermes is being patient but has to cut in. "You assholes really make me laugh. You remind me of the Stooges. What were those guys' names? Moe, Kit, and Curly?"

Kit says, "I don't want any of that smelly shit Richard has. Give me a valium, Hermes."

"Give? What the fuck is this 'give' shit? They are five bucks each, asshole."

The once-big-tough Texas cop starts whining, "Ya'll know, Hermes? You are a little queer rip-off little prick."

"Whoa, baby, I'm no little prick I'm the big cock to you, mister."

Kit looks around the room for support and says seriously, "I'm sick of paying a little Puto-Rican queer so much for that there valium."

"Well, big guy, go out there in the Big Hall and get them yourself," says Hermes. "You might get lucky and come back alive with a sore asshole."

The cell is quiet and still. Everyone is hoping that Kit will bite the bait. The only one who might warn Kit or slap some sense into him is outside now in the yard, tanning.

So Kit swallows. "Oh, you think I'm afraid. Those guys out there are just prisoners like us. I'll just show your ass, Hermes."

As a Texas highway patrol officer, Kit tried to do one big-time coke scam. He got a plane, and he bought a bunch of coke from the PIP. Now, oh shit!, here he is in Lurigancho—with "real criminals!"

Kit is one of the sentenced—one of the fortunate inmates who actually have a fairly good idea what year they will be released. He's been in Luri for three years and has only five more to go. He likes

Weaver, of course. But he doesn't like the rest of us much. He's as tall as Richard, with high cheekbones, and even though he's young, he's balding already. His bony face makes him look hard and tough and fearless. His icy eyes have a piercing look to them, set deep in his ghostly white face.

Kit dresses up for his new business venture. He puts on a nice new pair of Nike tennis shoes that his girlfriend brought him from Texas, plus a gold chain and gold cross, also from his girlfriend, and a Casio wristwatch. He's wearing a t-shirt with a picture of a Mac-10 automatic machine gun. The slogan says, "Kill them all. God will sort them out!" And he's wearing the biggest prize of all, a pair of real 501 American Levi's.

Kit strolls out of the cell headed for the steel door. He might as well be heading out for a couple of Lone Star beers down at the Billy-Boy Bar.

Most of the guys just shake their heads.

Hermes shouts from his seat at the eternal hearts game: "Hey, who wants to bet that Kit will score his little fucking pills?" He gets no takers. "Oh, come on. Bet!"

But Stan takes Kit's place at the hearts table and the game rolls on. Richard puts the bud away until Kit returns. For all we know something could happen with Kit and we might have guards back here. Then we hear someone pounding on the metal door at the far end of the hall. We hear a muffled screaming of words too hard to understand through the thick steel. This goes on for twenty minutes. When a guard finally opens the door, it creaks like the opening of "Inner Sanctum."

Meanwhile Arthur has come back to the cell to count his earnings from his leche asada sales. I am in awe. He's telling everyone how beautiful the visiting women are. Suddenly from the hall we hear wolf-whistles and smooching kisses. Stan jumps up from the card game and looks down the hall. "Wait till you guys see this," he says. "Oh man, it's too good." We are all staring at the cell door when Kit walks in.

He's wearing nothing but his jockeys.

With a red face and a very pale body Kit screams at us all: "It's NOT FUCKING FUNNY." He got his toys taken away in the school-yard and now all the kids are laughing. We have tears in our eyes. My stomach hurts.

When the laughter finally slows down, Arthur says, "Look at his neck!"

Kit lifts his chin. We can see the marks on each side of his Adams-apple and a trickle of blood from each knife-point wound.

"Ivan, you couldn'a driven a pin up my asshole with a sledge hammer."

Later, we offer, but Kit won't have anything to do with our Humboldt bud. So we divide it into enough for me, Richard, and Arthur, and then Rick, Stan, Ivan, and Carlton. Carlton brings out his Ovaltine can that he made into a one-hit pipe.

Pelone has a visit with his wife. It's one of those special visits, the ones given by the military, the kind that Diane had at first. When Pelone wants privacy, he gets it. Even the guards fear what Pelone is capable of doing to them from inside Lurigancho, the House of the Damned.

From my bunk looking down on the yard I can see Pelone and her sitting on a wood bench up against the opposite cellblock. Traf-fic in the yard is minimal. The sun shines down on them. They sit at the east end, as far from the latrine as possible. Pelone's wife has brought him a meal in a straw basket. Like Pelone, the wife is light-complexioned. Actually she looks as though she could be his sister. She wears a summer dress and sandals. Pelone has put on a long-sleeved yellow dress shirt with a button-down collar. He has slicked his long hair back, giving himself a Sunday-school look. They both appear so calm. After all, this is not Pelone's first time in Lurigancho for murder. Two or three years for murder, that's just part of his business. Outside, he and his wife and kids live like first-class citizens.

When I see Pelone's wife exit by the east-end door and hear the guard's brainless whistle that signals the visit is over, I go out of the cell to meet with Pelone to hear any news of a pistolero.

The hall is clogged with twenty or so men who have just come up from the visit. They are chattering and showing what their loved ones have brought them. Some have letters. On the other side of this throng I spot Pelone's yellow shirt, which stands out like bird shit on a black car. I see him go into his cell to deposit the brown shopping bags that his wife brought.

I work my way through the bodies. Then as Pelone comes back out of his cell, we are in step. As we walk toward the stairs, I say, "Pelone, how do you get a pass from the military when you're a cocaine dealer? My lawyer says that the military and the traffickers are enemies."

"Oh, my friend," he says smiling. "You are no stupid gringo. Do you not know? The military get millions of American dollars for to stop the coca. But to stop the coca is to stop Peru. All Peruvians know this. So the militario de Peru take the millions dollars. Then they kill some natives in las Amazonas. They show the dead people to the gringo government and they show the old coca lab in the jungle. But only nearby, the new lab, they don't show. Hey, Eduardo, if there no coca how the dentist he drill your teeth huh?"

"What does cocaine have to do with my dentist?"

"Joo know Alimans?"

"You mean Germans?"

"Si. How joo say? Germans, okay jes, Germans. Peru sell to German peoples the coca. Mucha coca to los Alimans. Those German give to Peru tanks and guns and monies. Mi tio es el general de militario. Entiendes?"

"Every Peruvian in here says he has an uncle who's a general. It's a bunch of crap. I happen to know... yo se... that tu estas aqui en Lurigancho for killing somebody. Por matar an hombre. But...."

"Pero," Pelone corrected me.

"Pero, pero, su tiempo is less—menos—than the sentence of los gringos por coca."

"Hey mans joo talk better the English. Everybody have tio en militario de Peru but not joo, huh gringo? Joo still a gringo, no? Maybe joo should ask joor American government, my friend. Ask them why the gringos do more time in Lurigancho for the coca than me and my friends do for murder. My people, all Peruvians, hate the PIP. So ask why the DEA works with the PIP and give the PIP weapons and big American dollars."

"Pelone, American people know nothing, nothing about this. Newspapers do not come here. But right now I don't give a shit. I hate Jimmy, and I want to know he's dead. Do you have anything to tell me?"

Pelone puts his index finger to his lips. By now we have walked to the east wall of the yard. He leans his head close to mine and whispers, "shhhhh." We stop and turn around and stand there watching a man squat over the latrine hole at the other end of the yard. "Joo will get a visit from my cousin. Joo will know him by his black fingernail, it is the mark of his business. He will come next visit for los hombres, for the mens. Joo understand me, gringo?"

Even though I have materialized my rage as a murder conspiracy, the pain I feel comes on hard at evening—the time when lovers hold hands and walk without talking, just feeling bliss. At night the torture nearly kills me. I'm locked in a cage while Diane is fucking Jimmy. A vice-grip is twisting my guts. The sensation starts as soon as I wake up. It goes on longer every day, pulling me inside out.

Could Joleen possibly have felt this degree of pain when I left her and ran off with Diane? My fucking God, Joleen. I'm so sorry. I had no idea.

The pills I take to make me sleep aren't working. I lie in my bunk still wired from the coke I got from Pelone. If we weren't locked in this cell, I'd go right now and get more coke from Pelone. My credit with Pelone is good. Too good. And that means my credit is good with the Lifers down in Pabellon Doce—Cellblock Twelve.

Every man in Pabellon Doce is here till death. Even the ridiculous justice system of Peru refuses to let these monsters prowl the streets with human beings. They control the coke industry inside Lurigancho. They order the guards to bring it in, and no guard would ever disobey. If he did, he would go home one night and find his entire family in the morgue.

These Lifers are Pelone's friends. And his bosses.

It is late. I have been awake in my bunk for hours, my mind taunting and torturing me. I am going mad.

"Damn it!"

Tony, above me, whispers, "Hey! What's up?"

"I can't—" I lower my voice. I started to say that I can't sleep, but now I am distracted by a sound out in the hall. "Do you hear that?"

From below Ivan reveals he is also awake. "What?"

"Sounds like a bunch of people walking on tip-toes and talking really quiet. Listen!"

Tony says, "You're on that fucking coke, man! I'm telling you—"

"It must be around two a.m."

Carlton's snoring dominates the darkness. Normally we can't hear Carlton because the rest of the snoring is so loud. Now Arthur is awake. He says, "Hey, you guys, it sure is quiet out there."

Stan raises his head, half asleep. His bunk looks directly at the cell door. He says loud enough to make everyone wake: "There's two armed soldiers at our door, fellas."

Then two more step into view on the other side of our door. Then I realize that the hall outside our door is filled with the real guards of Lurigancho—the military, soldiers in full uniform with rifles cocked and pistols drawn. Now the cold-blooded-killer lieutenant is unlocking our cell door. He has his nine-millimeter automatic chrome-plated gun drawn. At the instant the door unlocks, twenty soldiers start yelling in Spanish. I can't exactly translate their hellish howls, but I think the basic message is: "Die! Die! No one will help you! No one can! No one at home is going to recognize your body!"

The soldiers storm the cell. They pull us out of our bunks by the hair. Three of them jump Ivan as he puts his feet on the floor. One grabs Ivan's hair, another his right arm, the other his left. He stands and says, "What the fuck are you bastards doing?" Soldiers butt him with their rifles. The lieutenant yells orders as the soldiers flood the cell—far more of them than there are of us. "Hands on your heads! Fingers locked!" They order us out of the cell.

As we exit the cell, Carlton is shuffling and expressing in perfect Spanish his anger at being woken in the middle of the night. Now soldiers are tearing into his belongings. In Spanish Carlton is saying, "You inferior little bastards, you should be serving me dinner and shining my shoes. Your mothers should have drowned you all at birth." The soldiers seem to admire the speaking ability of this white-haired crazy gringo. They herd all of us down to the room at the end of the cellblock, and the soldiers force us to lie on the floor face down. The soldier at my side yells: "Hijo de las putas gringas."

Arthur is next to me, also face down. He whispers, "Hey, did he call us gringas?" The soldier kicks Arthur in the ribs. "Oh God, that hurts," he cries. Then the soldier kicks him again. This time his body rocks with the kick but he does not cry out.

Across the hall René and the men in that cell are crammed together to watch the entertainment. We can hear the guards tearing our cell apart and helping themselves to our meager stuff.

Then the lieutenant yells a command. As quickly as they have come, the soldiers retreat.

None of us wants to be the first one up. For a long while we don't know for sure that the goons are gone.

For some reason, Kit is the closest to the door, so he's the first back in the cell. I hear him saying, "Fuck, y'all. Look at this god-damn mess. You know why those bastards did this. They did this because y'all smokin' that shit. And then one of these little Peruvian egg-suckin', butt kissin' idiots told the guards y'all smokin that shit, that skunk shit that y'all call pot. Y'all's goddamn pot-heads."

I say, "You're a fucking glue-head, Kit. Did you sniff that brain-eating shit when you drove your patrol car, you idiot?"

Kit's voice rises to a higher and louder register: "Y'all wouldn't be talkin' to me thataway if we was out."

Richard says, "Kit, don't worry. If we were out, none of us would ever talk to you—period."

From the other side of the cell Carlton announces: "Gentlemen, good news. We still have my Ovaltine can."

"Some things are sacred," says Arthur.

Hunter says, "Kit is right. We're lucky. The guards never smelled skunk bud before."

Now Stan shouts, "One of those perverted pieces of shit took my ol'lady's picture."

Hunter says, "We're not supposed to have anything but a blanket and a bunk. You can probably buy your girlfriend's picture back, Stan."

Weaver has found his comb. He says, "If you ever want to buy it back in small pieces, one piece at a time, I can help you do that."

Ivan is picking up his stuff off the floor. He says, "Everything they touched, they threw it onto the fucking floor."

But we still have nearly all our little meaningless items that reflect memories of home. And nobody went to the hole.

The man with the black fingernail arrives. Everyone in the prison seems to know that a pistolero has come to see the gringo.

It is men's visit day, and the yard is filled with fathers visiting sons or the other way around or friends visiting friends. As with all visits, three or four armed soldiers walk among the visitors watching for contraband and giving protection to visitors. To have a visitor killed or missing or complaining would be bad news. The last thing the Peruvian military wants are outside investigations from any source. What goes on in Lurigancho stays in Lurigancho. I stand by the door, as Pelone instructed. Looking over the shoulders of the rifle-bearing guards, I spot the man.

Unlike Pelone, the pistolero has dark skin, short dark hair combed straight back, and a pencil-line moustache. He wears a short-sleeve white shirt and black slacks with matching shoes. A slender and serious man, he has the professional appearance of a department store manager. He keeps his hands in the pockets of his slacks and moves with a cocky walk that sets him apart from the rest of the visitors, not afraid, no hint of cowering. He's a pro. All he needs is a name tag.

As he approaches the iron door, one of the soldiers slings his rifle over his shoulder, and then the pistolero and the soldier give each another a brotherly hug. They exchange words I cannot hear well enough to understand, but clearly the message is friendly. Then the pistolero sees me and moves into the yard. The soldier stops the next visitor and asks a question, deliberately not noticing us. The pistolero slides through the jam-up at the door and walks directly over to me, his hand extended for a brotherly handshake. "Eduardo?" he says. "I am the cousin to Pelone. I am Fredrico, but you call me Frank."

"Yeah sure, Frank. You speak good English. Come, we can walk into the middle of the yard. The noise of all these men will be our privacy."

I glance up over Frank's shoulder. I can see Ivan, Arthur, and Carlton watching from our cell window above.

Prisoners have placed wooden benches along both cellblock walls and scattered about the yard. More than a hundred men are yakking loudly about news of home and family. Others are talking about their court process. Their own time is so precious. Besides, most of the men around us can't speak English.

"How do you know that soldier?" I ask. "Were you an inmate here before? Pelone did not say."

"Yes, I was in here, too. But the guard he is my cousin."

"How many cousins do you have in here?"

"Only two."

"Why were you in here?"

"Murder. But after a few years here, at my tribunal I was acquitted."

Frank says this as though he's talking about a traffic ticket. But I think he's telling me that he got away with murder.

We stand close, studying each other's faces for signs of fear or deceit. I say, "We have business?"

"Yes. My cousin says you have money with your Peruvian lawyer?"

I look deep into Frank's eyes and lie well.

I know from boxing and from street fighting that this is the moment of truth. As a kid I learned to attack any opponent upon the slightest show of cowering in the eyes. If Frank can see a bit of that in my eyes, he'll cancel everything. I'll do the same if I can see fear in him. But there is no fear in Frank's eyes, and my rage over Diane and Jimmy has smothered any other feelings.

"Not a problem, Frank. And Frank, my lawyer can tell you where the body is. It is at his sister's house with a woman named Diane." I get a chill up my spine calling Jimmy 'the body.' "I don't want Diane hurt. But I do want her run out of Peru and back home to New Jersey. And I want proof Jimmy is dead!"

Feeling a flash of paranoia, I suddenly look around at the men nearby, everyone yelling in Spanish. I can see in a glance that no one gives a shit.

"You will have proof, my brother. You know, in my country and in Colombia or Brazil we kill the woman. But my cousin tells me this Jimmy guy he tell to you he gets you out, huh? And then takes your woman while you are in Lurigancho?" Frank suddenly gets a smile on his otherwise serious facial expression. "Hey, listen. I can cut off his head for you, and you can use it for a soccer ball." Then just as swiftly his smile vanishes. "But it would be difficult to bring it to you in here."

I keep staring at the trademark of his profession, on his left hand the one long black fingernail. Remembering the time we spent at the PIP house, right after the arrest, I recall seeing that mark on the left-hand pinkies of a couple of the PIP.

"Say, Frank, what's the black fingernail about? Is that so you can see the coke in a dark room or what?"

Frank laughs. "Oh no. I let you crazy gringos take care of the coca, you and my crazy cousin. My business is safer. Your government doesn't give one shit who I take out. My nail is no for the coca. It is a mark of my trade. It is a mark people respect. Remember, I only do people who have been very bad, like your Jimmy boy. As long as I do no work with the coca, I have—how you say in your country? Oh yes. I have job security."

Frank's humor does not tickle my funny bone. I just tell him, "When the work is completed, my lawyer will give you the money you ask." I am lying, of course. But Frank has heard from Pelone that I have the money. And he appears to believe me—otherwise why would he get all loose and light with me, making a joke about his weird morality? But I don't have any money left. Diane and Jimmy have it, the last dollars I had left to use for my survival in Lurigancho. All I have now to pay with is my life.

I'll be happy to get rid of it.

A shrill whistle cuts through the ardent hollering of the men around us. The visit is over. Frank and me do a manly chest-to-chest hug, a little awkward because he is taller. Then we part with another hearty handshake. I say, "Good luck with business, Frank." My words are masked by all the talking and yelling. No one hears but Frank.

"I will return, my friend. Stay alive, Eduardo. Adios."

I turn and head back to the cellblock.

I've been through several ounces of coke during the past three weeks. I am much more frightened than I have admitted to anyone. I am going to die violently here in this cesspool. When I think of that, my mind explodes with rage over Diane. When the rage finally begins to settle, my helplessness overwhelms me and I fall into the deep freeze of despair. I have never experienced such brutality delivered through my own mind. I want to talk but I don't know what to say until Jim Hunter says, "Hey, you look like hell. Come on with me outside."

Walking out of the cell with Hunter and out to the yard, I can hardly hold my head up. We must be a strange looking pair of pals, the all-American lad with the Ivy-League haircut and me—I don't know what I look like, but it can't be pretty. I can't pretend that I'm not worried about paying for Jimmy's death. How ironic. I don't have time to feel guilt about causing a murder—I'm too locked in panic over the fact that I can't pay for the job. Fuck, I don't have a fucking war budget.

Out in the yard Hunter turns to me as we start toward the east wall. "You know how cold your buddy R.B. can be, Eddie?"

"Yeah, so?"

"Well, I hope I seem cold right now. You've got to come out of this disgusting frame of mind."

I wait. Then I say, "Is that it?"

"That's it. Cold."

"Brr," I say.

He blinks.

I say, "Hunter, I have completely lost it, man. I put everything into that bitch. I'm telling you, man, I actually have physical pain right here." I clutch at my stomach. "In the center of my gut. And I feel like I'm not even worthy of being called a man, Hunter. And I know it, too, and I know what you're saying. But I fucking can't come out of it, man. I feel like I've had my ass kicked. I've been taken down by a chick, dude."

"You'd better come out of it. Or you're going to die, Eddie, and I don't know if all of us together can keep that from happening. Read my lips. You are going down. I'm no saint, either, but I know better than to use the shit that got me in here. After I get out of here, I never want to see cocaine or anyone who has anything to do with it. And those pills…. Did I hear right—you're in here because of a woman? And now you're eating shit because of a woman? How much more do you want to suffer?"

Not everyone sees things the way Hunter sees them. Rock-band Rick, for example, has been more than willing to help me stay out of my mind. Besides, Rick can play guitar pretty damn good and for hours. The ends of his fingers are like old leather.

I tell him, "That guitar looks a lot like the one Willie Nelson plays."

He says, "Funny you should say that because you happen to be looking a lot like Willie."

"Really?"

"Yeah. Like Willie Nelson on a really bad day. Like, on the day he croaks."

The men's visit is at a roar down in the yard. I could give a shit until a runner is announcing my name: "Gringo Eduardo!"

Outside standing in the middle of the yard in front of God and everyone, there is my friend with the ridiculous but serious black pinky. He is surrounded by a fan club of Lurigancho inmates, or maybe they're his relatives I don't know.

Only in Peru. I imagine him at a cocktail party, delicately holding a glass of chablis. "Oh look, there's Charlie, he's a banker, and there's Marty, the lawyer, and oh there's Frank. He's a hit man. You can tell by that lovely black pinky."

Frank sees me and excuses himself from the love circle. "Hey Eduardo, que pasa, hermano?"

"You have news for me, Frank? I ain't feeling real well. Can we make it short?"

Frank shakes his head from side to side. "You look bad, man. You gonna let this place kill you? Listen, I have good news and bad news. What you want first, huh? I tell you the bad news. They get away. The clients they run away to his country, to Colombia. That is the bad news, okay? Now I tell you the good news, is we have Jimmy's sister. She married a Peruvian man. That is why Jimmy is here in Peru, he works with his brother-in-law. You understand? We have his sister. I want you to tell me and I will make her call to Jimmy to come back. Or else we will kill his sister. Oh and she is very pretty, huh? Too bad, huh? Well, that is business. So what you say, my friend? We do this business, yes?"

"No! We don't do this business. That's not business! Fuck. His sister didn't do shit to me. What the fuck would I want to hurt his sister for? No, that's not business. That's hurting an innocent person. That scumbucket probably burned his own sister in some way, too. No, I don't want you to do anything to her but let her go. Did you say you fucking have her? Well let her go. Shit, she probably has kids. Does she have kids? Never mind. Just stop the whole fucking thing, goddamnit."

"Hey. Take it easy, my gringo friend."

"Oh now I'm your *gringo friend*? What happened to 'my brother'? Just tell me, Frank—what do I owe you for kidnapping a little, innocent, little mother, Frank?"

"We are finished," he says, turning his shoulder toward me. "We have no business. You owe me nothing. But when the day comes that I get Jimmy, you will pay me. But keep your mouth shut. You understand, Eduardo?"

"Okay, Frank. I understand, man. It's over. Unless Jimmy comes back and you can catch him without hurting anyone else. I'm not into hurting women or children, Frank. Call me a gringo, but that's how I feel, Frank. Shake my hand. I got to go up to my cell. You understand, huh Frank?"

What I think he understands is that I'm through giving a shit about living—much less about whether he's upset that I called off our deal. But I don't think he understands the other thing. That even though I'm through giving a shit about living, I'm not interested in taking someone down who has never done a thing to me. I don't care who they're related to. I want the motherfucker who burned me, not his goddamn sister.

The cocaine runs out so now I'm doing pills only, as many as I can. I sleep all day and most of the night. Between the pills and the depression exacerbated by the pills I have become a master of dream control. I can be back in Tahiti on the white sands of Hua-hine, where I was before Peru. Or I can be back on Maui at Mala Wharf, surfing in front of the Buddha. At Mala is the largest statue of Buddha outside of Japan. The huge figure faces out to sea right in line with the perfect Mala wave. No matter what disturbs my dreamscape, I quickly return to the intense sunlight of Hawaii. In my real world, cold winter is settling into the cement and steel of Lurigancho and into the sterile desert around us. We are so far from home and family. So fucking far from love and kindness.

I sleep with my clothes on, the same clothes. I don't allow myself to wake up. Sometimes for water or a little food, but I don't care for drinking or eating. Anything I put in my mouth gives me the runs within seconds.

I give up the daily fight with dysentery.

2

CHIVO

Tony wakes me with a loud "I'm hittin' the beach for a walk!" He jerks the bunk when he jumps down. Then he jerks it again. "Man, you fucking stink!"

From below me Ivan says, "Eddie, we love you. You are our brother. But you fucking stink."

I open one eye. There's Tony, looking right at my face. He looks kind of mad.

When I first came to Lurigancho, Tony and I bonded right away. Our definitions of freedom run parallel. He's only thirty, but you can see by his freckled and prematurely creased face that he has spent most of his life in the sun, surfing and sailing. For him and for me, freedom means the ocean, a sailboat with wind-filled sails, a surfboard and a glassy wave at sunrise, a sunset on a Maui beach. I guess it's been about four months now that he's been trying to ignore the intensifying stench of my rotting ego and my deteriorating soul.

I pull the blanket up and say, "This whole place stinks."

"No. You stink. You. Stench rises, okay? Get out of that bunk, man. Bathe."

Now Ivan stands next to Tony. He puts his double-sized hands on his hips and says mournfully, "Do you want me to give you a bath? I'll do it, you know." He seems to be sorry as hell that he has to.

I hide a little farther into the blanket. If they keep shaking the bed, I might start waking up. Don't spoil this nonstop sleep I've got going.

Then the worst possible noise—the howling whine of Kit Karson's Texas drawl. "Y'all 'scuse me, but back home my daddy would hose down they farm animals that couldn't clean theirselves. Daddy always said we got to hose 'em down else they get infections and disease. Sure wouldn't want our boy to get no infections or disease."

The days and the darkness have been running together for so long now that every jerk in the cell thinks he has a right to make me wake up.

Makes me mad.

"You're big, Ivan. But you're not that fucking big, man. And Tony—don't do anything you can't take back, I'm telling you. And you know what, Kit Fucking Karson? Fuck your daddy."

Tony laughs. "Man, back when you had some muscles I might have worried about getting a threat from you. But that was before you turned into a fucking jellyfish. Right now any one of us could walk you outside and wash you down. Wash you in those stinking clothes and all."

Getting angry wakes me up even more. "You know what, you motherfuckers? None of you is going to do a fucking thing to give me a fucking bath."

Suddenly I'm fighting myself to make sure that anger is the only emotion I show.

Arthur says, "Hey man, we care about Eddie, that's all."

I yell back now with my eyes tearing up, "Goddamnit, Arthur. If you all care so fucking much, why don't you all help me pay Pelone and the scary hit man?"

Stan has been quiet. But now he says, "Hey dude, don't expect anything from us. We all have to learn our own personal lessons."

"You've learned a few of your own, I guess."

"Damn straight."

From across the cell Carlton calmly says, "I thought you were a tough group of survivors. But a little white powder seems to have taken you down like little girls. My suggestion to you, Eddie, is to start putting some spine back in yourself and regain some dignity. For God's sake, man."

Now I'm pulling myself to a sitting position and I have to stop, clinging to the bunk. I'm weak and my head spins. Carlton's words hit me like a fist. Now I've got tears running down my face. Great. Something more to add to the already shattered image of the man I thought I was when I came to Lurigancho.

Because of their conspiracy, I get up. As Ringo said, I clean up with a little help from my friends.

Weaver's bunk is next to mine. Weaver seems to be the only one in the cell who doesn't give a damn. He is making up his bunk and waiting for the guard to unlock the door. I spot a new bottle of Kaopectate on his windowsill.

"Hey, Burt," I say, "I think I'm going to die. I have the cramps and squirks so bad, man. How about a little swig of that Kaopectate you have there?"

"Sorry, Buddy," he says. He's slicking his hair back with an Ace comb. "What am I going to do if I get sick, too?"

Now the guard is at the gate. Suddenly the rush to survive daily life begins anew. Weaver flows out with the others, people spilling out of their cells, eyeing each other, filling the halls of every floor with wall-to-wall human traffic. Cold empty cement amplifies the sound amazingly. As Ivan helps me out of my bunk, he says, "That guy is your brother American?"

"He's a turncoat sissy."

I grab the Kaopectate. "Fuck him!" I down the bottle like in a cowboy bar.

"Ah, that's good!"

The only real reason I've stayed off the coke lately—and been doing pills only—is that Pelone wants to be paid for the ounces I've gone through. Not only me. Richard and Arthur and a couple others. But no doubt about it, I have been the little cocaine pig. Now I owe Pelone ten dollars a gram for two ounces. Twenty-eight grams in an ounce. You can't compare this to street value. Here the price you finally pay is death.

I do not have the money that Pelone owes to the Lifers. I do not have the money for the scary hit man. I never did.

I die.

At the time it all began, my rage and pain was such that I just wanted to know that Jimmy was dead before they came for me.

Down at the end of the cellblock there's the shower room. It's a joke, of course, a cruel joke. Just like the toilets, the showers don't work. But the tiled room is a good place to do a marine bath and to wash your sour clothes. I bend over a pail wringing out my pants while Hunter faces the barred window at my back. I look up at Hunter. He's looking curiously over my shoulder at the building next door, the same building where the stabbing took place, the murder that would have given Danny Dildo lots to talk about if he ever finally got back to Huntington Beach. Suddenly Hunter shouts, "Look! Quick, look at the shower room on the bottom floor!"

I turn to see. In the window of the next cellblock I can make out the back of a guard. His blue shirt is shredded. His bare back shows large bleeding cuts, four or five deep lacerations. Blood is turning his uniform black.

Hunter yells down the hall: "Blood across the yard!"

Men pour into my washroom, pushing me weak and almost naked against the window. Very clearly I see the guard begging for his life, begging that crazy bastard Juan. Juan and two of his gang are flashing sizeable blades, toying. Hunter is standing up close to me now as the shower room fills with inmates.

I say, "Looks like the same three that offed that Peruvian."

"Back when Dildo Danny was here."

I say nothing.

Over the uproar of voices Hunter shouts: "Did you ever hear the story, why Crazy Juan killed that guy?"

"No!"

"Story is, the bastard came from another gang, another cellblock. He came to Juan and amigos for a business meeting. Who sells what dope. Who has what turf. Juan agreed to meet but to come alone with no weapons. So the stupid son of a bitch did, and they killed him. Took his American watch and his Levi's, then they gave his body to their cellmates. Eventually they threw his naked corpse into the Big Hall like road kill."

"Who told you this?"

"Chivo. Know what the official prison report said?"

"No."

"Body found in the heron."

I feel weak. Why the hell does everybody have to shout all the time? I yell, "Looks like that guard is about to get the same treatment."

"I don't get it."

"I know. What can these idiots possibly want from that lowly guard? His whistle?"

"They sure don't want his uniform. They're cutting it to shreds."

" Maybe they just feel like cutting."

I can see to my right the roof of the Big Hall, which runs along connecting all our cellblocks. Because I'm on the second floor and the Big Hall is just a one-story building, I can watch what's happening on the roof. It's filling with soldiers. The soldiers are lining up along the edge of the roof, pointing their rifles and pistols at the windows of the crazy cellblock. Now the lieutenant steps forth, a bullhorn in his hand. The bleeding guard is still visible, his back blocking the soldiers' chance for a clear shot at Juan and the boys. The prisoners around me are shouting opinions about who is going to get blown away. The lieutenant barks into the bullhorn. Hunter says in my ear, "That's that cold-blooded fucker we saw shoot those poor bastards. He'll blow Juan and the others away and take the guard with them."

But Hunter is wrong.

The lieutenant speaks in Spanish. Hunter gives a line-by-line translation: "Let him go. Let the guard go. Let him walk out of the cellblock. We will listen to what you say."

Juan shows his face just over the shoulder of the wounded guard. More shouting. Hunter explains: "They want to see the warden."

"Who the fuck's the warden?"

"Didn't know we had a warden."

Within ten minutes the warden appears. "Look at that dude! He looks like a golfer from Orange County."

"Check out those slacks. Wing-tip shoes."

"American!"

"Got to be."

The shit is heavy down in the cutting room. The three crazies claim they represent the rest of the unit. They shout their demands. Comida, mas comida! More food. Better food. And they shout something that sounds like "Olympia."

"What is that—they asking for beer, too?"

"No, no," says Hunter. "Clean the place up. Shit everywhere, dirt and shit."

"I can understand that."

"But nobody ever comes into their cellblock. The door stays always locked."

"I can understand that, too."

In fact, if that cellblock ever received regular food at all, it would be a tremendous upgrade. I know that the guards would like to treat us gringos this way, too. They would like to torture us to death. Unfortunately we are American, Canadian, French, Australian, and so on, and our embassies are putting some kind of pressure, however limp, on the Peruvian government.

The soldiers surround the warden, rifles and pistols ready to fire. The warden promises that conditions will greatly improve. He actually gives a little talk. He expresses his gratitude to these three brave inmates for bringing his attention to the inhumane conditions in the cellblock. He will correct everything, he says.

The inmates shove the guard out into the Big Hall.

Everyone breaks up and goes back to his cell. It's the end of a football game. The fans disperse. Get to the car and get home.

Of course my pail and laundry are sprawled on the filthy floor. Arthur remains at the door as prisoners empty out of the washroom. "I have another bucket of water you can use," he says.

"Thanks, Arthur."

"Did you have a nice vacation?"

"I guess you could look at it that way."

"Yeah. Except when people get back from vacation they're supposed to look a lot better than you do. Anyway, I think you'd better talk to Pelone. He's looking for you. He's got some heavy shit going on in his head."

"I better go talk to him."

Arthur takes another look toward where the bloody guard was and he says, "Jeesh! No one back home would believe this shit."

"Just life, Arthur."

"No," he says. "Life has tits."

Arthur is gone. I'm using the water he loaned me. And now Pelone appears at the entrance to the washroom. His long brown hair is slicked back from his ghost white face.

I am taken by our difference in weight. I have become small and weak, and this savage motherfucker is projecting some violent vibes at me. Even more unnerving is the fact that I see his whole entourage behind him.

I hate this shit. When I didn't give a damn about living or dying, back when I was unconscious, I wasn't afraid of a thing. But now that my peers have so considerately brought me back to life, I am fucking terrified.

Pelone steps closer. I know him. He's a vampire. When he senses that a person is afraid, he gets stronger. He gets filled with the desire to kill. Certainly he doesn't have to worry about pulling a murder charge, not here in Luri. Here in Lurigancho he is free. He seems to be smelling my fear.

I start memorizing each face in back of Pelone. I want to know who exactly is willing to hurt me. Standing just inches from Pelone's back is his main man, Manuel. Manuel's size is worrisome. And I know he would like to hurt me because we once boxed together. Back in happier days, he wanted to put on the gloves. I peppered his face and body with stinging blows that he could not deflect because he had no skills. Now his dark eyes want revenge. At Pelone's other shoulder is Pepe. I am concerned about Pepe's reach as he has long arms and seems to be holding something behind his back. The other two gangsters are leaning in the doorway, one on each side of the doorjambs to my left and right. All five of these motherfuckers are the best dressed on our floor—but only on our floor. Below, on the first floor where Clower and the real Mafioso-types live, people are always dressed as though they are going to the office downtown. In the evening they are in their pajamas and robes. By contrast, these animals in front of me are wanna-bes. They have a passion burning in their eyes to fuck me up and kill me.

"How are you, man?" Pelone asks.

My body is suddenly trembling with adrenaline. "Bueno. Mas o menos."

"My friend, you no looking too good." He is sizing me up.

"What's up, Pelone? You worried about your money, hermano?" I am making great effort not to show my fear but I cannot control the shaking coming on and in my voice.

"Si, my friend. I looking at you and I worried."

"When we hear from your friend about Jimmy, I pay you all the money. Pay for the coky, too. No worry, Pelone. You have more coke for me now?"

"NO! Pelone no likey you no pay. My boss no likey you no pay. Big problem you no pay! I thinking you fucking liar!"

Fucking liar. That's what he says. All my life these words have caused people to try to kill with fist or gun. But all I can do now is let out: "Ooh man. That's bad, Pelone. You talk bad, my brother."

I'm a little braver now that I can see Arthur, Ivan, and Richard coming down the hall. Only one reason Richard would have a sweatshirt draped over his arm. I see Chivo and know that Chivo has passed a blade. Also, I have my eye on a weapon just out of sight of Pelone and his gang—a metal dustpan with a long, hard wooden handle.

"No, you fucking gringo. I no you brother. You womans run with that fucking cocksucker to his country, to Cali, Colombia. Now you need pay my friend go to there! You pay me now. I no likey. You pay!"

Now Pelone is talking very loud and his boys are moving in closer.

"You know what, Pelone?"

Pelone lifts his chin to look slightly down at me. He has a dare in his expression. "Yes! What you say, gringo?"

As I reach for the handle of the dustpan, my left hand over my right like a golf-club grip, real clear and real loud I yell: "Fuck you, asshole!"

Fast as I get hold of my weapon, Pepe hands Pelone a thick round club. At the same moment, Ivan and Richard make their moves. Arthur screams, "Watch out!" Just as Pelone seizes the club, I slam the dustpan hard into his anklebone. He's wearing only rubber flip-flops. Pelone lands hard on his ass and immediately grabs at his ankle cursing me. He looks like a rabid dog. His eyes are dilated. His brown hair now hangs in his flushed red face. If he had a gun, he would be killing me.

Then his look changes. He realizes that I am positioned for another blow, this one to his head. Suddenly I see the fear of death in Pelone's eyes. I experience great satisfaction. Someone yells, "Do it, kill that fuck!" Sounds like Tony.

Then things move real fast.

Ivan has already knocked three of the five cohorts to the floor. Richard is holding a steel shank to a fourth one's throat. Chivo has taken his position with his back to the scene, facing all the men coming to help either Pelone or me. Truth is, not many are coming to help me—just a few gringos who are busy getting stuck at the back of the crowd. Brawlers are yelling encouragement, a mix of Spanish and English. But every man in the hallway stops at Chivo's authority. Chivo crouches with his hands extended, shifting the razor-sharp shank from his right hand to his left. Everyone knows that he will use that shank with the ferocity of a wild animal and the expertise of a highly trained soldier.

So the battle ends—with Pelone being helped up, his bleeding ankle in need of a few stitches. He growls at me, "Look what you do me, gringo!"

"Pelone, we can't live like this, my friend. You know?"

"I no dead for you, gringo. You pay!"

Two of his cronies grab him before he can come back over to me and start up again. I stand my ground. The crowd backs away to let them pass. I wait.

My endurance has diminished to none.

Chivo disappears with the shanks.

As everyone breaks away, a guard comes up the stairs a few feet from the washroom door. He looks at me and says, "Que pasa, gringo? You have problem?"

I answer, "Quien, yo? No señor. There is no problem in Lurigancho nunca."

"How much you owe that maniac?" says Stan, back in the cell.

"He says I went through a couple oh-zees."

Ivan says, "Jesus! That's a lot of money. I thought you said you guys ran out of money. How you going to pay him?"

Richard says sarcastically, "You can help Arthur sell leche asada." Everyone gets a laugh out of that.

I am about to go back to sleep when a runner comes up the hall like an old English town cryer, yelling, "Eduardo Path-ee-ya, y Arturo Tomaa-so-oon, y Ricardo Brooo-ayrr." We are being called to the lower court.

"Anybody ever get out at lower court?"

Carlton answers, "Not as far as any one of us gringos goes!"

"Well that's bitchin' news, Carlton!" says Richard. "That's just what Arthur wanted to hear."

"You won't even get sentenced. It's just a bullshit formality."

Arthur says, "You don't know everything, old man!"

Carlton turns to Arthur and says, "Everybody in this cell had to wait until he got to higher court just to get sentenced."

"Except for Rick," shouts Stan from his bunk.

"That's right," says Carlton. "Rick managed to get himself sentenced in lower court, and he managed to get less than twenty years. That was awfully speedy." He looks at Arthur again. "You don't imagine you'll get *released* tomorrow at lower court, do you?"

The three of us have never openly discussed our court business, nor have we talked about it much in private. Mostly we want to believe what Chula said many, many months ago. So the less we talk about our situation, the less we know and the easier it is to cling to some hope.

Arthur crosses the cell to where Rick is in his bunk reading one of Richard's paperbacks. "Say Rick," he says, "what exactly happened in your lower court scene?"

Lucky for us, Rick is somewhat articulate today. He has been cleaning up a little—easing back on the drugs—because he is supposed to be released in not too far off.

"Well, it was real short. Like not even a half hour."

Ivan, from his bunk below me, asks, "Did you see a judge? Tell us what the fuck happened. Don't make us drag it out of you."

"Okay," says Rick. "Shit, give me a chance. I may have lost my memory since I've been locked up in here, with all the drugs and all. And I don't know about you, Ivan, but I don't think the food has made me any smarter. Yeah, okay, to start with I hired a lawyer the embassy suggested. It was a Japanese-American dude named Tano or Tanto, something like that. Anyway I heard all this same shit that you guys—" he points at me, Richard, and Arthur—"are being fed, but I listened to it and got to lower court in a couple months. At my lower court my lawyer just told the judge to refer the case to the high tribunal, and then I went to tribunal about six months later."

From over in his bunk Richard asks, "What did you say—I'm a cocaine smuggler, please lock me up?" A laugh goes off all around the cell.

"No," says Rick. "I told them I have a daughter and she's blind, she was born blind, you see. And with the money from selling the cocaine I could pay for an operation. And her sight would be restored. My lawyer about crapped."

"Why?" says Arthur.

"He thought I was going to tell them the truth."

Carlton is sitting at the hearts table holding a hand mirror, trimming his handlebar moustache to perfection. "Did you think they would actually believe that fairy tale?" he asks.

"Hey, old man, I brought on real fucking tears. In fact, I'm thinking about going into acting."

"No shit." Carlton stops what he is doing and looks at Rick instead of his little mirror.

"No shit, Santa Claus. I could make more money doing that than fucking with these fucking drugs. And no jail time."

Kit Karson, over in his little corner, gives a loud "Whahoo, ya'll! Rick's gonna be in the movies!"

"Kit! Shut the fuck up," says Arthur. "Don't make fun of Rick. He's got the same problem you do. He lost his mind. So, come on Rick what happened?"

"Basically the president of my tribunal ignored the prosecutor and the DEA. He told me he was sorry about my little girl, but many people try to get out of their problems by selling illegal drugs. He said he didn't want me to spend my little girl's life in prison so he was only giving me five years rather than fifteen. The lawyer from the embassy told me before we went to court that I'd be lucky to get less than eight. Anyway, you asked, and that's about it. I stayed loaded for this whole time. But now I gotta start getting right because I'm getting close to leaving."

Stan, as usual, has waited for the conversation to give him a chance to slide in and ask a question. He says, "Hey, Rick, I've been here with you for years. Do you really have a daughter?"

"Fuck no!"

When they brought us out here two years ago from the Brigada, they drove us in what looked like a Nazi armored car— a steel box on wheels, no windows, only small perforations in the corners of the roof for air. Now on this chilly Lurigancho morning, the morning after the Pelone-versus-The Gringo bout, we're getting ready for our next little ride.

Obviously this trip will involve more than just us. Judging by the shouting and tramping in the cellblock, this is more like a military muster.

Armed guards call me, Richard, and Arthur out of the cell. Once we're in the hall we see guards pulling several prisoners out of the other cells on our floor. In one cell the men are too slow, so the guards slam the door shut and lock them in. They bang on the door and shout, but they're out of luck. No chance in court today. They plead, and the guards seem to enjoy the sound.

Arthur says, "They are some cold motherfuckers. Aren't these guys their own kind?"

Richard, right behind us, answers. "They are their own kind, man. They are fucking sociopath animals. I bet that lieutenant hand-picked every one of these bastards. Look at 'em. They'd shoot us in a heartbeat."

We are in the hall, shuffling with the crowd of prisoners, and then the guards herd us out into the Big Hall, where hundreds of prisoners from nearly all the cellblocks are shuffling together. *Nothing happens for them. They just rot in Lurigancho, never getting to any court at all. They never get a ride through downtown Lima. They never get to see women, people, stuff!* Lurigancho is always noisy, the psychotic drumming and banging and shouting and slamming, but out here the babbling roar of voices makes my head swim. It's a bad situation out here if you're a snitch and somebody hates you. The guards gather up more men and then they herd us all through the Big Hall.

The smell in the Big Hall is "pasta"—not Italian food but the crudest form of cocaine, paste—being smoked by inmates who already have holes in their lungs, holes that are filling with tuberculosis. The pain of inhaling is numbed by what they're smoking. Of course, underneath the *pasta* smell there is, as always, the odor of sewer.

In the courtyard three buses are waiting for us. They're the size of the big yellow school buses that we all rode when we were kids. But these buses look more like the L.A. County Sheriff transport with barred windows. They were built to seat a maximum of seventy passengers, but we have about twice the number of prisoners out here as the buses were made to hold.

The system is to handcuff us in pairs. The guards put Arthur to my right, and they cuff our outside hands together—my left to his right. This creates an awkwardness of movement. Now I can see the guards stuffing pairs of men into the buses, hitting them, and I can hear their demonic shouts. Silhouetted in the bus windows, guards are striking downward blows at seated prisoners.

"Arthur, slow down," I say. "If we get on last, we'll get off first."

As we get closer, I catch on to the sadistic system of bus loading. Four pairs make one row across the bus. Instead of two men on each side of the center aisle, the way the bus was designed, the guards put three men. The fourth one on each side sits on the floor even though he's still cuffed to his partner on the seat. That's what all the beating has been about.

We manage to be in the last group of eight to board the bus. And there are no seats left. And the guards are ready to kill.

I'm pushing from outside the bus, pushing on Arthur's butt to get him inside, pushing hard. Arthur is yelling at me: "You fucking asshole, there's no more room in here! Quit pushing, you're crushing me!"

"Get me in there! I'm gonna die!"

Arthur finally turns around to see the soldier behind me who is having a hell of a good time beating on me with his billy club. Arthur gives out a cry of pity and rage, and then he turns back and shoves as hard as his small frame is capable. He shouts, "MOVE!" We surge forward. Then Arthur grabs one of my hands and a Peruvian inmate grabs the other, and they pull me inside as the soldier lays one last hard smack to the middle of my back and then another one across the backs of my legs. I cram myself into the steep well of the bus. The soldiers force the door shut behind me and there I am wedged in, crushed under bodies, buried alive. Maybe I'll be lucky and the door will bust open and I'll die quickly on the open highway.

"Su cabesa abajo!" Heads down!

First-timers like us don't realize yet how far down they mean—down between our knees is what they are yelling and screaming. Through the space between the other men's arms and shoulders I can see a soldier. He has an automatic weapon strapped to his shoulder, and he's swinging, swinging, swinging his billy club, beating the backs of heads. Another soldier moves down the aisle, kicking with his steel-toed boots to make room so that he can stand and swing his military baton.

Arthur whispers, "Glad I did a little yoga back when we were hippies."

We are forced to ride this way for the entire journey to Lima, about sixty miles. When the bus door opens, the only thing that keeps me from falling out on my back is the fact that I'm still hand-cuffed to Arthur. After the first few batches of men come out, the guards begin delivering random blows. Three soldiers grab a pair of handcuffed men, grab them by the hair, the arm, the shirt, and throw them to the ground. Then for no apparent reason they com-mence to beating the men with their clubs. No doubt this is a method of crowd control handed down over the centuries from one military genius to the next.

We are in downtown Lima standing in a paved courtyard behind a huge stone building, something built by the conquistadors along the general design of Dracula's castle. No doubt this is the Justice Palace, and we're at a rear entry. But there's little to see. Armed guards are thick around us. No sense trying to make a break when you're getting off this bus. Unless you've got an army of your own, it's suicide.

We are hustled down stone stairs and then released like cattle into a vast and cold-ass basement. The men find their kind. Some have no kind. Four or five hundred men gradually fill most of the frigid cavern. The guards take off our bracelets. That goes smoothly because everyone wants that done as swiftly as possible. Then the crowd relaxes and the background noises begin, the hacking and coughing and spitting of blood right onto the floor. I can smell *pasta* again, and it's a welcome relief. Here, just as in the Big Hall, the floor is slippery with shit. That's why we are careful not to lift our feet when we walk. Instead we do a sort of shuffle to keep from falling onto the filth. After some exploring I learn why the floor is so polluted. The latrine down here is constantly flowing, but its drains are clogged. So the material that the men deposit in the latrine eventually makes its way out into the main room.

This dungeon is a social place. This is a rare time to be together. People are hustling, trading cigarettes for candy or one drug for another. We are directly underneath the rooms where power is manifest in the form of the judge. That powerful little dude can cut us loose. But the DEA and other interests keep us gringos locked down.

"Are you guys Americans?"

The big dark guy talking is about as tall as Richard but nearly twice as wide. He has the classic face of a Greek warrior, a full brush on his lip that could probably out-handlebar Carlton if he put some wax to it, and a physique that could get him a spot on the Chicago Bears offensive line.

"I am," says Richard, and he points to me and Arthur. "These two are Peruvians."

Arthur says, "He's a moron. Hi. Yeah, we're Americanos. I'm Arthur. This is Eddie, and the moron is R.B., otherwise known as Richard."

I say, "Dude, you're Oso!"

"Uh, no," he says. "My name's Richard also."

"No. You look like a Chicago Bear. Bear in Spanish is Oso. You're Oso!"

"Where'd you come from?" Arthur asks him. "The PIP or the Brigade?"

"The PIP brought me here—Rubio and an Interpol cop and..." all three of us say it with him: "Del Gado."

Richard asks, "Where you from, dude?"

"Marin County. A little town called Fairfax. North of Frisco."

"We're from California, too."

I say, "Are you going back to Luri with us?"

"What's Luri?"

Then we know in our guts, we know without being told, that this brother from California has been deceived just the way we were deceived.

Richard says, "Luri. That's where we live. Lurigancho Prison."

"I don't think so. We paid a lot of money to Del Gado and Rubio and a lawyer who did the paperwork. They said I'd be going to court here and then released from the court. That way, it would all look legal."

"Oh yeah," I say. "Yeah, we know all about the released-from-court scam."

Arthur interrupts. "Hey, don't start whining and telling us all that heart shit. We'll all be crying and scared."

Oso looks worried. "Come on you guys! This ain't funny. My family took out a loan on their house. I gave up twenty grand and all I had. Those guys got like forty grand to let us go."

"Who's us?" I ask.

"Us is my partner, Pablo."

"Where is Pablo?"

"Is Pablo Peruvian?" Arthur asks.

"Yeah. Rubio said he got a judge's order on the fax to let Pablo go at the PIP. But I have to go to court because it will look bad to the American embassy and the DEA if I get out at the police level. Pablo left with his parents. Don't you guys think I'm getting out here? Today?"

Me and Arthur shake our heads, but Richard says it bluntly: "No!"

"Hey, lunch is being served, you guys."

There is a mad rush to get in line and get served. To keep us from fighting for the food, the soldiers are supervising. They are even giving us metal plates and spoons to eat with. But we already know what can happen when you eat what they give you. Us gringos anyway.

Oso says, "I'm not that hungry. You guys made me lose my appetite."

I get in the line and come back to the position we've taken in the basement.

"Hey big guy, take a look at this incredible lunch. I mean, what could be more like home than good old pork-and-beans?"

Oso sees that the pork still has a scalp of bristling, wiry hair on it, and he pukes right on the spot.

"I guess you're really serious about not wanting that lunch."

Richard says, "Sorry, Oso. Eddie's a son-of-a-bitch. He did that to me out at the prison. And he knows I have a weak stomach."

Arthur looks at me like he doesn't know me. "Why'd you do that? What the fuck is wrong with you?"

"Why should I apologize? He needed to puke. Puke up all that shit the PIP fed him. Let's get real, goddamnit."

No one says anything, so I keep going.

"I don't want to see this guy get taken down the way I went down. A lot of people tried to tell me that I was in for the fucking shock of my life, but I stayed arrogant until it nearly killed me."

Oso takes a couple of minutes to pull himself together. He starts wiping his mouth with his shirtsleeve, and then after a bit he pauses. Then he takes a deep breath and lets it out real slow. He looks at his shirtsleeve and says, "They have a dry cleaners out there?"

Oso not only does not go free, he doesn't even get out of the basement. Neither do we. But, unlike Oso, we were forewarned. Lots of people told us that these bastards will rush you out here—let you imagine that you are making a move toward freedom—make you wait all day in a state of burning anxiety without a word from your lawyer. And then the bastards will force you back onto the bus. That's court.

Today proves to be a textbook case.

Throughout the day we say things like, "Just in case you go home with us!" Of course he wants to know what our life is like. We talk about it as light-heartedly as possible. But we certainly undo the lies of Rubio.

Then, at the end of the day when they shove Oso onto the bus along with the rest of us, I'm hoping that something we said helped to prepare him for the shock. He's got his head between his knees, and he's discovering what kind of treatment forty thousand dollars will buy once you're caught in the web of Lurigancho.

Reality is becoming very clear. The only way out of Lurigancho alive is to go through this court process.

This is what I am telling myself riding back to the prison, my head down, my body and arms twisted to accommodate the awkward way we are handcuffed together and packed.

At the receiving yard in front of the prison, where the buses pull up, the guards take Oso away for the new-prisoner ordeal. The rest of us get a little time to loiter out here, which I enjoy just because I don't usually get to see this part of the prison. This is the area that public officials see—our ambassador, for example, or human-rights folks or reporters. They hear about our chow hall and our gymnasium with its sports equipment, and then they leave as fast as they can, their mouths tight. No one wants to go deeper into the Beast.

But who cares. I've learned not to wonder who visits Lurigancho. Either they want to make sure that we're still in here—and this category includes anyone from the U.S. embassy—or they are plain sadistic. For the most part, our families can't come, or they won't. That's just as well. None of us really wants to be seen here.

A couple hours later Oso gets to the cell. The fellas give him all the routine initiation lectures. Get a lawyer to sentence you right away. Don't even try to pay out. Eventually they get around to "everybody's woman abandons him in here." That's when Oso starts telling us what a great ol'lady he has back in Marin County.

"She is a really loyal woman, man. I'm lucky to have her. She won't let me down." Blah blah blah blah.

That's when I go outside to walk off the wave of pain.

Most of us have said the same words or thought those same words. No one disagrees, only listens. None of us wants to think it can't happen—even Carlton, who was married and divorced a couple hundred times before this test.

On the way to the yard I have to pass Pelone's cell. Pelone is lying there asleep, and his buddies are close around him, protecting him. From what, I wonder. Probably from the Lifers in Pabellon Doce.

As I pass, his buddies stare at me and smile like crocodiles.

The world of a cellblock is very, very small.

When I was in the fourth grade, I made up my mind not to live in fear. We lived in South Central Los Angeles, which had been at one time a decent part of the city. My grandfather built the house on West 99th Street where my dad was born and then where I was born. But I grew up in the years after the Zoot Suit Riots, the son of a dark-skinned father and a white-skinned mother. The white kids beat me up for not being white. The black kids beat me up because I wasn't black. And the Mexican kids beat me up because I wouldn't say I was Mexican. I could have learned to hide and cower. I could have developed imaginary sicknesses to stay home from school most of the time. I could have kissed ass with the teachers to build a false sense of security and protection, and then just stayed in the house after school. But I chose to fight back and get up and fight more. And if I got beat down, I didn't let that keep me from trying again. I chose to live my own little life even if I was scared.

Funny thing was, the stronger I got, the more the aggression stepped up. I started getting jumped by two or three at a time, then by more. Just before I got into guns, my parents changed family history and moved to Anaheim, where Disneyland had recently opened.

On the first day of school in Anaheim I did what any kid from South Central would do in a similar situation—I picked out the biggest kid in the schoolyard and tried to knock him down. In fact, I did knock him down with surprising ease. He didn't even resist. He just looked horrified.

In Orange County I began to realize what "white" means, and it

didn't usually include me. At the end of my first year at Anaheim
High School, my friends and I all applied to work for the summer
at Disneyland. They all got hired but not me. So I started using my
middle name instead of my last one. So instead of Ed Padilla I was
"Ed James."

Then my life was changed by the cultural events of the late
nineteen-sixties. The same is true for all my comrades here in this
putrid living quarters. We are all of the same generation. Not
Carlton, of course. Carlton's an old beatnik. He never got it, never
could have, and we all know it. But if you're from anywhere in
America or Europe and you came of age in the late sixties, you fun-
damentally share the same theme in your life—freedom! For you,
skin-color has nothing to do with anything important. But loyalty
to your fellow traveler is a high priority.

Out in the yard I'm walking laps. When I make my west-end
turnabout, I see a tall figure of a man in black.

*Is that the priest I talked to way back about getting married? I wonder
if he can get me out of here to get re-baptized or some shit.*

As I get closer, I can see this is not the same priest. Of course he
has the same uniform, with the black vest and coat and pants, the
white collar showing in the little square at the front of the neck. But
he's a big man with white skin and rosy cheeks, maybe fifty years
old, about six foot three, his hair a sandy color maybe from the sun.

"Say! Are you a priest?"

"Hello, mate. You sound as if you are American or Canadian."

"I'm American, Father."

"Actually in my church they use the term 'Reverend.' My name
is Reverend Robinson."

"Okay, Reverend. You have an accent like you're English or
British."

"I am British, and my family has been assigned to Lima for a few years. We live in Mira Flores. Do you know that part of town?"

"They call it the Beverly Hills of Lima."

"Yes. Well, it is pleasant."

"You want to come up?"

"Yes!"

"You seem pretty comfortable, Rev. You're not afraid?"

"Actually this is bad. But not a lot worse than many other countries I have been assigned to. I'm sorry to say that I visited a jail in the jungle that was nothing more than a large sewer pipe with a steel-barred door."

As we walk into the cell, Oso is still talking about his girlfriend and how she will take care of business. I interrupt him. "Hey you guys, meet Reverend Robinson. He came to visit us."

We head off Carlton before he can bogart the Reverend's attention, and we take turns describing our basic situation. The Rev wants to know how he can help. We tell him that most of us have been here for years without a hearing, a trial, or even a conference with a lawyer or a judge. Even so, the U.S. embassy treats us as proven criminals who deserve inhumane treatment. The embassy confiscates our mail and keeps the money that our families send. When the Rev leaves, he promises to come back every two weeks. He suggests that we have our families write to him, that he will smuggle their letters and packages to us. Smuggling for the smugglers.

Several of us walk the Reverend down the hall even though by now Carlton has taken over and the rest of us don't stand a chance. I say good-by at the stairs. When I turn to go back, Pelone is standing at the door of his cell. His ankle is bandaged. The look in his eye says he's not going to attack. He motions with his right hand that he wants to talk. I look down the hall and see Ivan standing at our cell door and he is looking directly at me.

"What's up, Pelone? How's your ankle, man?"

"Oh, it's okay, mans. Es un Padre come for to speak with joo?"

"Si, y los otros gringos."

"Maybe that Padre he give joo monies to pay to me, huh?"

What a surprise. Pelone has calmed down. I suppose he satisfied the Lifers somewhat by attacking me. I'm sure he told them a good story, bought some time. Maybe the pressure's off. Temporarily, of course. Maybe.

I answer, "Por favor, Pelone, escuchame. I will give you your money when I get it. I want no more trouble with you, Pelone. Entiendes? Okay?" I extend my hand. We shake.

Pelone's hand twists like a fish. I get the feeling that he has no idea why I shake it.

Now death by shank seems less likely, for the next few days anyway. And the pain of Diane seems to have stepped away from me about a hundred feet. In other words, I'm just plain tired of that constant feeling of twisting pliers. I want to think about something else. I want to think about the court system—about getting out through the court system. I want to write letters for the Rev to take. We're all writing letters. Carlton is creating a book addressed to Congress. I ask a few people for some money. I say that this is an urgent request, but I am too ashamed to say why. Things sure change when you get off drugs and want to live.

The work I have to do involves Richard and Arthur as much as me. We have to remember exactly what we told the PIP because that is the story we will testify to when we get to court.

Me, Richard, and Arthur go out walking in the yard for privacy. Richard says, "You know, as long as I've known you, Arthur, I have never seen you draw a fly."

"Oh fly up your ass," he says. "I can draw!"

I say, "R.B.'s right. Arthur, you told the PIP that you're an artist who came here to draw Machu Picchu."

Richard: "Yeah. Machu Picchu, my ass. What if the judge wants you to draw something?"

Arthur gets real defensive. "Nothing is going to keep me from going home at lower court," he says. "I'm sorry I have to leave you guys. But this is your trip. The way things look, I'm innocent and you guys are fucked."

That same night a runner lets Richard, me, and Arthur know that we are going to lower court in the morning.

Down the stone steps Richard, disgusted, returns to the basement of the Justice Palace. He has been gone only the amount of time it takes a somewhat civilized person to use the latrine in this place. But now his entire lower court experience is over.

He says, "I went into a small office with a soldier and one fat guy behind a desk. Papers and files were stacked higher than the fat guy's head all around him and on top of file cabinets. The fat guy looked me over. Then he started reading from a file with my picture in it. All the words were Spanish. He read for, like, five minutes. Then Fat Ass motioned to the soldier with a fat index finger across his fat throat, as if to say I'm dead. The soldier grabbed the chain between my handcuffs behind my back and lifted me. Fucker nearly broke my shoulder."

I go next.

Same story.

When Arthur comes back, he has nothing to say. He faces the wall, pressing his face against his hands. Then after a couple minutes he looks at Richard. "How the fuck did you know the fat fuck would ask me to draw?"

"Did you?"

"Yeah. Did you guys see the calendar on the wall in back of fatso?"

"What? You drew the flower on the calendar?"

"Yeah."

"What did the judge say when you showed him?"

"He did that finger-across-the-throat thing. Shit!"

"Say, I thought our lawyer would be in that room," says Richard. "What exactly does a lawyer do besides take your money?"

"If that Reverend dude comes back, we need to give him letters to my brother and your mothers."

Arthur says, "Don't talk about our mothers!"

"No joke, guys. We may be going to that higher court thing fast, now that this part is over."

We stand there in the foul pit doing nothing, and then Arthur says, "Are you guys sure you told that fat dude that you didn't know me? And that it was all you two's coke? And that you just met me in Tahiti? Did you?"

"Yeah! Sure, Arthur."

"Uh huh."

We look at each other. We look at him. He looks at us suspiciously. We smile at him.

I hope he realizes that we're just fucking with him. Truth is, both me and Richard feel responsible for him. We did invite him to come along from Tahiti, and we both told the judge so. Arthur would have been just fine if he'd stayed home.

Back at camp I ask Richard if he thinks that lower court trip was as bogus as I do. He answers, "Yeah. Bogus. But at the same time did you feel the looseness of this system with its paperwork?"

For a minute I think about what he might be implying by that comment about the paperwork. Then I say: "What do you mean? Are you saying that you think Jimmy and Diane were really trying to get me out?"

"Hey man! Get off that bummer right now! You nearly died over that whole bum trip. Let it go, or it's going to take us down. We need all our energies to get the fuck out of here!" Then he changes his tone. "What I meant was that the looseness gave me a real good feeling that these people will take a pay-off as long as it looks legit."

"We need to write a letter to get Chula down here."

Richard asks, "And what about that fat chump, Ibarra?"

"Looks like we're the chumps."

"Hey, knock that shit off, man. I'm telling you!"

"You know, it's pretty funny—you telling me about keeping it together. Yeah, you did quit smoking that shit. But all you do now is lie in your bunk and read."

"You should try it!" he says. Then he narrows his eyes and looks at me. "You know how to read?"

"Shit yes!" I say. "In fact, I used to be pretty good at it. At least I think I did. I'm rusty."

"How long has it been?"

"Well, let me think. I quit school as soon as I could legally drive. And then I went to work at partying. Got money doing construction work for my dad. Since about then I guess."

"You haven't read a book since you were sixteen?"

I look at him.

"It doesn't matter," he says. "If you can read your own arrest warrant, I guess you can read a fucking novel."

"But I could read very well. I thought I could, anyway."

Later, Richard hands me a paperback titled Captains And Kings. It's a brick—twice the size I had in mind and thicker than four years' worth of Marvel comics.

"Jeesh! That's a lot of reading!"

"Yeah, that's right, I forgot. You're real pressed for time, huh?"

"Give me the book. What's so great about this book? Sounds like a chick's book."

"Go read it. You'll be surprised when you open it."

He's right. That night, most of the guys are either writing or talking. Oso is full of current information about what's going on with the Dead and Jerry, and all the sports stuff. I crack open the brick. To my surprise the paperback turns out to be a story about escaping from prison—a French prison called Devil's Island and a prisoner they call Papillon who's stuck for life on an island surrounded by sharks and treacherous currents that sweep everything onto killer rocks. Hours pass, and now I'm in the spell of another world far from Lurigancho. When I go to sleep, I put the book next to my head so I can begin reading again as soon as I wake.

The next morning, I'm back inside the book. It's a new, peaceful place. About mid-morning Richard stops by my bunk to explain what happened with the cover. I'm not reading Captains and Kings. The book I'm reading has a false cover because the warden has banned it from the prison. Richard says, "The warden thinks it promotes the desire to escape. So you have to keep it covered just in case one of these guards figures out what it is, or one of these animals snitches just to fuck the gringos."

As he faces my bunk saying this, Richard looks out the window on the other side of the mattress, letting his vision wander over the bleak hillside just outside the prison wall. Suddenly he catches his breath and stiffens. "Oh, wow!" he says. Then, louder: "Hey, you guys! Remember all the shit those guys demanded a couple of days ago?"

Stan says, "What guys?"

"Our neighbors. The guard-slashers. Crazy Juan and the boys."

"Right," says Carlton. "What about them?"

"Well, I think those promises are about to be delivered."

Now the guards are blowing whistles. Arthur shouts, "What're you talking about?" We can hear cell doors slamming. They're chasing us back into the cells and locking us in.

Rick only has to turn his head to look out the window. Then he, too, sees the soldiers on the hill. "Ho, no shit," he says. "Look out there. Over the wall. On the hill." Ivan stands up out of his bunk below me and leans on my back to get a better look. "Uh oh," he says. "Somebody's going to die tonight."

Weaver jumps nervously out of his bunk. "Maybe they're just after Crazy Juan."

Kit is suddenly out of his bunk, too, his attention riveted to the window at the other end of the cell.

From above me I hear Tony say, "I hope so. Crazy Juan needs to get his dose of the hole. I hope they kill his ass."

Carlton stands a couple feet away from the rest of us. He's not watching; he's listening and twisting his moustache. "Looks like the warden lied," he says. "Can you imagine that?"

Hunter is quiet. Oso stands next to Kit Karson, silently observing out the window.

The men locked on the opposite side of the hall are yelling, "Que pasa? What the fuck is going on?" René is at his iron gate. "Oh, Arthur," he calls. "Oh, Arthur!"

Arthur walks over and takes a position by our door. He tells René what we are seeing. Soldiers with weapons on the hillside, he says. They get ready to shoot into this yard here.

René repeats the information loudly to his cellmates, and the word hits the cellblock like a match on gasoline.

Now everyone in the cellblock is yelling. Arthur adds more information, and we hear it back in the yelling. How many soldiers? "About twenty-five," he says. Then in the roar we hear "Veinte-cinco. Veinte-cinco." We also hear the Spanish words for semi-automatic rifles and forty-five caliber pistols.

One soldier laboring up the hill has on his shoulder a fifty-caliber machine gun. His tripod-hauling companion is close behind. I stare with an awe inspired by my complete impotence. My only function is to watch. The killers take their positions—guns and rifles, the machine gun locked in place on its tripod—and they aim at the cellblock across the yard.

Suddenly we all experience a moment of silence in the desert. For an instant we are equally alive. Then we hear the command:

"FUEGO !"

The hillside explodes with gunfire. At the same instant, the freakish screaming starts, the shrieks of trapped men dying and about to die. Bullets pour into the walls of the clay building across the yard. In its windows we watch men getting slaughtered, running and screaming and falling. The fifty-caliber is tearing huge chunks of brick as the gunner sprays every opening of the building, hitting men on the run or men standing in shock struck with the same bullets that are tearing apart the brick and cement. We see blood splash and splatter. Men in our cellblock are screaming, screaming out to the men being slaughtered even though their cries are drowned by gunfire.

Then an explosion rocks the prison from within. We pin our fingers to our ears. Soldiers must have entered the Big Hall and for whatever reason blasted their way into the doomed cellblock. The shooting from the hill stops. Now we get to watch heavily outfitted stormtroopers, all wearing gas masks, shooting as they enter. Shooting anything that moves. They shoot men who had nothing to do with the three crazies who cut the guard, men who are simply standing with their hands over their heads. We watch people choke on tear gas, waiting to be murdered. The soldiers shoot into every cell. Then the cloud of gas fills the building and obscures all the brutal details.

A breeze tears at that cloud and puffs a light, thin stream of teargas in our direction. Wisps of the gas begin rolling through our cellblock. Next breath, I get no air. Every next breath I keep inhaling more gas. I start to panic—I'm suffocating. I grab the old army blanket on my bunk and bring it to my face, but it makes no difference. Men are shouting to get their doors unlocked. Ivan yells to me, pointing to the floor. "Hurry!" The guards are surprisingly quick to open our gates.

Now the floor of the cellblock is carpeted with men, all of us scuttling cockroach-like to get lower than the floating gas that has set off a symphony of choking and gasping.

All night long hundreds of bodies, dead and wounded, are carted away. The people doing this gruesome work are the twenty or so cellblock residents who managed somehow to survive the massacre.

Around sunrise we begin to hear the whistles blow above the chatter developing in the halls of each floor of our cellblock. We are herded into our cages as the night passes into morning. The last remains are still being removed from the neighboring cellblock. The wounded, fifty or so, have been laid out in the Big Hall. Most of them will die right there, lying mercilessly unattended. Only ones gathering around the helpless are the animals that populate the Big Hall. Like vultures, they are stripping these dying men of whatever can be worn, sold, traded, or eaten.

A fire breaks out where hot lead has started a blaze in some mattresses, and flames and smoke spread through most of the shattered cellblock. What little our neighbors had in the way of food or any kind of comfort is now smoldering.

The horrible stench of burning bodies combines with the magnified stink of smoking gutter rot. When we look into the windows of that cellblock now, we see a uniform décor of soot and bloodstains.

By mid-day, life is back to normal—back to Lurigancho normal.

Gustavo is a Peruvian named in our court case. He is in his early twenties, taller than the average Peruvian and light in color—an upper middle class Peruvian. He speaks good English, which he learned by memorizing Beatles songs. He has been to Hawaii on a surf trip.

After we were picked up, we saw Gustavo once, briefly, at the PIP mansion headquarters. The PIP were keeping us in a downstairs closet. We lived in that closet for several weeks. On this particular occasion the guards left Arthur in the closet and brought Richard and me handcuffed to an upstairs office. The little nameplate on the desk said "Del Gado." The guards ordered us to sit in chairs facing the desk.

Then Del Gado came in. He was still dressed in his black Navy peacoat over a black sweatshirt, plus camo pants and combat boots, probably steel-toed. He sat at the desk, and the vicious look on his face made my heart sink.

Not long ago Arthur made the comment that Del Gado is the scariest man he's ever seen. Richard and I both agreed. For me, the threat is concentrated in his eyes—wild, black, shining pools that radiate power over life and death. And yet his entire presence feels dense and dark, with his brick-like torso and his ebony skin, heavy eyebrows, and black walrus moustache. His men all fear him. He's nothing but a sergeant with a platoon of non-uniformed cops—a little street army that finds its authority primarily in its guns, a gang of thugs who like calling themselves "Gestapo." But in the realm of the PIP, Del Gado is supreme commander; he can kill without consequence. He has the complete power to ruin your life, and he enjoys using it.

Del Gado glared at us. I moved my wrists helplessly in the bracelets. Then he whipped open a desk drawer and pulled out a zap. A zap is made out of long strips of hard, thick leather stitched together with a bunch of ball bearings in one end. With this you can beat people as close to death as you want them to get. Del Gado cracked the zap down hard onto the top of his desk, wham. Then he gave us a look that said, *I'll be back to use that on you two.*

He walked out of the room.

From another room down the hall about twenty feet we could hear Del Gado screaming: "HABLA, CUNCHA TU MADRE. HABLA, ORITA!"

We heard punching sounds, as though somebody was slamming beef carcasses with a baseball bat. Then someone fell hard to the floor. Then, muffled sounds of a man being beaten and screaming for mercy. Del Gado yelled again: "ERES UN TRAFFICANTE COMO LA PUTA MADRE, SI? HABLA!"

And so another confession was heard at the PIP palace.

That was the beginning of it, I suppose—the beginning of Lurigancho—me sitting in that chair, hands cuffed behind me, thousands of miles from any claim to human rights or any chance of rescue from these killers. What would keep them from murdering us and taking our money and selling our passports? No one would ever know.

The crying and screaming stopped sharply. We heard Del Gado give orders. Suddenly he appeared at the open door, holding a man who was bleeding from his mouth and nose. Both of the man's eyes had puffed shut, and his lips were so swollen that he could barely answer Del Gado's question. Del Gado was asking the beaten man if he recognized Richard and me. The beaten man gave a nod of his battered head, yes, he knew us. I seriously doubt he could see us through those swollen eyes.

That man was Gustavo.

Del Gado is the shorter of the two men, but he grabbed Gustavo by the back of the neck and pulled him upright. Then he shoved him back down the hall. On the floor where Gustavo had stood I could see a circle of blood about three feet across. I remembered noticing that one of his legs was soaked red from the knee down.

Then Del Gado came back into the office and took the zap from the desktop. He brought the zap down onto the desktop hard, hard enough to crack the wood. We flinched.

He pinned us with a stare of his cold, black glassy eyes. He put his hands on top of his desk, the zap still in his right, and said: "Dime, hijo de la puta!" His voice was low, slow, and violently threatening. "Habla! Joo two understand? Joo tell me Gustavo make to sale la coca to Dawson."

That was a long time ago. By now we have nearly forgotten all about Gustavo. But one cool autumn evening in Lurigancho, we see him again.

We're walking laps, Richard and me. About three hundred men are out here. Everyone's moving at the same tempo around and around the long oval route defined by the walls of the yard. It's dusk. We're all trying to get more time out in the night air before being caged.

Where we make our turn at the west end, there are twenty or so Peruvian men standing near or leaning against the wall. One of them gets our attention by lifting his head and nodding and softly saying, "Good evening, Ricardo." That stops us both, and we step out of the moving circle.

Richard answers the Peruvian, "Yeah, good evening to you, man. What's up?"

I won't say that I recognize him. But I do know his name when he says it—Gustavo. Ibarra has spoken of him because, strangely enough, Ibarra is Gustavo's attorney, too.

"Oh, right," says Richard. "The last time we saw you, you were working with Del Gado."

Gustavo looks confused. "Working with him? I'm sorry?"

"Yeah, dude, weren't you two working together to rearrange your face?"

Gustavo doesn't laugh, but he puts his hand to his face and says, "He work very hard."

I say, "Yeah, he seemed to enjoy his work. How's your foot or leg? There was a lot of blood."

"Oh, I can walk okay. But slow. I don't think I will ever run too much. But he did not kill me. I was thinking he will kill me. But may I tell to you something?"

"Of course. What's up?"

"I must tell to you instructions from Señor Ibarra and me mama. That is why I wait here in this dark place to not be seen by your gringo friends. One of your gringo friends, he is American police, si?"

Richard takes it personal. "Hey! It's okay this time, but don't ever call that cop my friend again. He's Eddie's friend."

"Don't listen to him. Tell us."

"We must not be together," he says. "We must not talk again like this. Lurigancho has many eyes that see from la courte suprema y los judges. They must not think we know each other before now. Ibarra will tell the court I am a sick man. Sick in mi cabesa and that is why I sell the coca to Dawson. Okay?"

Gustavo tells us that he will be going to court with the three of us, and that he will testify that he never met us or ever saw us, only Tom Dawson. Gustavo recites our story exactly the way the three of us have come to know it. We need to be in sync. He assures us that he has gone over and over the testimony until he can tell it like the truth, the whole truth, and nothing but the truth.

"You understand me? I am sorry for my English."

Richard says, "Yeah. We don't know you and never did. No connection."

I nod my head in agreement. Gustavo reaches out and hugs us both. Richard and me turn and continue our laps, silently considering this new information. We are slightly lifted to know there is some kind of plan. We have a chance to keep our time short if we can prove the coke wasn't ours.

But court can be a long way off. Can be years. A lot happens to people in Lurigancho before they make it to their court dates. A lot of men die.

We don't like seeing our Peruvian in this place. For a long time Gustavo was outside—free, for all we knew. Same is the case with Oso. His Peruvian, named Pablo, was outside. Now Pablo, too, has shown up in Lurigancho. Pressure applied from the DEA has finally put both of them in the belly of the Beast.

Gustavo and Pablo are from wealthy families. Both have attended schools in North America. Both have traveled to California and Hawaii to make friends and to surf. Now they are living in Pelone's cell. They are the new guys; we are seasoned prisoners. They still have shiny Nikes and the newest surf shirts. Nice pants. They are clean and well-fed. They don't have runny bowel movements yet.

In our minds we take Gustavo down from our shelf of hope. Too bad, because it is a very small shelf.

Damned if two weeks don't go by and Reverend Robinson walks into our cell. He has money in his shoes and under his belt. He has mail in his coat pockets and in his shirt. Not much chance the guards would search him. He wears all the same stuff, the collar and all, as a Catholic priest.

"Here are letters from home, men!" He has some phone messages, too. Some of our friends and family have called the Rev at his home or at his church.

The Rev says, "Well, I am certainly happy to see you all well and alive. Were any persons in this building hurt in the escape attempt?"

At first I don't know what he means. But I hear Carlton chuckling. He looks up from his regular seat at the hearts table and says in good humor, "There was no escape attempt, Reverend. It was a slaughter of hundreds of men over something pulled by a few. We saw the whole thing from these windows." Carlton looks past the Reverend, and the Reverend turns to see the building where this event took place. "The newspaper reported it as a mass escape attempt. The article said that more than two hundred inmates burned to death or died from smoke inhalation in fires that were started by the inmates."

Carlton describes what really happened, and none of us butts in. He finishes by saying, "The number of dead is actually more like six hundred."

The Rev says, "May God have mercy on their souls."

"Yeah." Richard can't help himself and comments: "They sure didn't get any here."

The Reverend is visibly shaken by the bloody truth of our world. Suddenly Kit Karson surprises us all with a humane remark. "Ya'll's rightfully nervous," he says, "but I want you to know these here letters mean a whole bunch to me, Reverend, and I want to say thank you much, sir." Then Kit walks the six feet over to hand the Reverend a letter to take out. "Another thing, don't y'all overburden yourself with that dang huge pile of paper of Carlton's there he has for you. It is so bulky that y'all ought to leave it."

We all laugh just to rile Carlton.

"And Reverend there's something else that you bring to us," says Stan. "You believe that none of us has ever done anything worth being treated this a way."

Rick's over in his bunk writing a letter for the first time in years. He says, "Whatever he thinks, he keeps his word. To me that's a big big deal. Thank you, Reverend Robinson."

Hunter says, "You changed our lives. We can write something and know that our letter will eventually get to that person—because the Rev keeps his word."

"Without that, we have no motivation to write," Weaver says. He looks up from where he's sitting at the hearts table, next to Carlton, writing an address on an envelope, and adds, "Unless one of us happens to be Carlton writing a manuscript for the U.S. Supreme Court."

Carlton reaches over and pats Weaver on the head. "You will understand one day, my boy."

The Rev unbuttons another button of his shirt and reaches in and produces more letters. Out of them he picks through and hands me several and says, "These are for you, Ed. You have quite a few people who care about you and love you."

"Thanks, Reverend. I think these guys are trying to say you have restored our faith."

The Reverend's face is flush red, but he smiles and looks at a small paper from a tablet, a list. "This is my list of who called me on the telephone over the last two weeks. Some very important people calling me about you there, Mr. Carlton."

Carlton says, "Thanks to you. Those godda... Oh, sorry, Reverend. I mean to say those people from the embassy refused to take my letters…."

"And you, Mr. Hunter, have the most delightful parents," says the Rev, snatching the focus back. "We spoke about you, and I assured them you would be back in Hawaii soon. Did you attend Episcopal church with your parents, Jim?"

"I'm sure they told you, Reverend. I attended with them until I was about fourteen, and then all I wanted to do on Sunday was surf or dive or just go to the beach."

"I suppose those other activities are valid in the eyes of God."

"To me, Reverend, those things are done in God's real house. Churches and temples sit on God's ground under God's sky. Waves from God's ocean have taken churches and temples out to sea in one big splash."

The Rev says, "I will not disagree with you, Jim. I truly pray you will enjoy those wonderful days in nature again very soon."

"Thank you, Reverend. If my folks call you again, please tell them I'm fine, I look fine, look fine. Someday I'll tell you what the acronym F-I-N-E stands for, but for now just say he's fine."

Arthur asks, "Is that what kind of priest you are? Episcopalian?"

"Yes, Episcopalian. May I sit down?"

Ivan moves over on his bunk for the Rev to sit next to him. "I must empty my shoes. And under my belt as well."

The Rev has money for us, sent from home. Carlton gets a stack handed to him. The Rev hands me five twenties. He tells me that my ex-wife wired the money. "Her message says that the money is for the three of you. She hopes you enjoy the card."

I pick out an envelope from Joleen. As I open it, Carlton sees the cartoon and says, "Oh, yeah, that's from your ex all right!"

The cartoon shows a bone-thin man with a beard to his waist, his arms stretched above his head chained to the wall of a cell, and on the inside of the card it reads, "HANG IN THERE!"

The Reverend says, "Oh, there is this small package that goes with that card. Here it is." He hands it to me. Inside the box is a family-size jar of Vaseline petroleum jelly. When I take it out of the box, we all have a good laugh. With his Hollywood grin Weaver says, "Hey—Hermes will pay you plenty for that."

Hunter says, "You guys, knock it off while the Reverend is here. Have some respect."

As we sit with the Rev, a small crowd gathers outside of the cell. Pelone is not exactly standing in the crowd, but for sure his little spies are working. They certainly spot the cash. This is our food money—a hundred bucks to be split between me and Richard and Arthur. There's scarcely enough here to put a dent in what I owe Pelone. I sure hope the little spies are good at math.

The Rev leaves, walking down the hall with Carlton at his ear. Arthur crosses over to ask Hunter, "So what's F-I-N-E stand for?"

I go between Arthur's bunk next to the wall and another bunk to my right. I'm facing the wall inside one of those narrow alleys between bunks, counting the money.

"When you say 'I'm fine,' most of the time you're saying 'I'm fucked-up, insecure, neurotic, and emotional.'"

"Right. The good old days."

Peruvian inmates have started to penetrate the cell. They're holding treasures such as bars of soap and rolls of real toilet paper. Tony hates to have intruders in the cell. "Out!" he shouts. "Get out. Do your thing out in the hall or in your cell. Stay the fuck out of my house." Richard stands up from his bunk and starts herding people back toward the door. He says, "I think it's obvious these animals saw the Reverend passin' money to us."

At my back I hear a quiet, violent voice say in a low tone: "Dame me plata!"

I twist the upper part of my body around in the cramped space where I'm trying for privacy. It is Pelone, wearing a leather jacket zipped to the top of the neck.

How did he…? Slipped in. Where's R.B.? Usually R.B. is right here in his bunk.

I can hear Ivan laughing from way down the hall. I hear Carlton talking Spanish close by but out in the hall. Stan is coming in the cell. *If I yell, Pelone might go off.*

He has a crazy, goodbye look in his eyes, one that many other men must have seen as he killed them. I turn to face him, putting my hand on his shoulder. *Tell him about the money, the small amount.* Very quickly Pelone pulls from behind his back the longest blade I have ever seen in Lurigancho.

He's been hiding the shank under the back of his leather coat. The blade is twelve inches long and razor-sharp on both edges. A leather strap tightly binds the end of the steel shank, making a handle. The same leather also wraps around Pelone's wrist, binding the warrior and the weapon.

Oh man, if he was holding a gun, I'd make a play for it. But this fucking blade. I'll lose my fingers.

He pulls the blade up shoulder high and swings it right at my face.

There is suddenly a silence—nothing but me and Pelone, him trying for a quick silent kill with no escape for his victim, me. *Don't turn away man remember don't turn away. Remember what Dad said. "You can't defend what you can't see." Face this crazy motherfucker.*

A defense technique I learned from boxing takes over as an automatic reflex. I use my shoulder to ward off the blow. The blade slaps flat on my shoulder.

This bastard is really going for it. You'd better do something. Don't stand here like a little girl letting him smack you with that fucking blade, goddamnit!

Pelone swings the blade again, faster. This time he turns it as he draws it back, aiming the deadly point at my neck. He lunges.

It's just like an overhand right cross coming at my jaw for the knockout punch. Being left-handed gives me a big advantage in this situation. Having my left out front, with him in a right-handed stance, gives me more control over the moves. With all the speed and strength I have, I smack Pelone's right hand just before the point of his shank stabs my left cheek.

This asshole can use that blade like a pro, man. You have to take him down now!

My block sends Pelone's arm and hand straight up in the air. But the blade is securely attached to his wrist. Now Pelone skillfully alters the momentum of my blow to bring the blade around and down to aim the point of his sharpened steel at waist height. He is aiming at my groin.

I have no Bruce Lee moves. I can only bring my hands together in front of my crotch.

He is going to kill me.

Holy fucking shit! This is it? Here in this stinking hole? This is what I woke up for—to die in Lurigancho, my buddies laughing out in the hall?

Once I came up too high in the lip of a pitching wave at Honolua Bay, and the wipeout was brutal. I got held down on the reef for too long. Then when the wave let me up I was in two feet of sea foam. I gulped a breath of foam and then got sucked back down. I thought it was over then. And right now it looks just as bad, without the glory.

Suddenly over Pelone's shoulder I spot Carlton's face looming forward, with its white handlebar and Carlton's open mouth shouting at urgent volume, "Hey what the hell's going on here, stop!" And he grabs hold of Pelone's elbow. He shouts, "HELP! GET OVER HERE!"

Pelone snaps his head to look at his elbow, then instantly up at Carlton's face, and then back at me. He has changed. Now he's a trapped beast, like a tomcat trapped in the corner of an alley that knows it's about to die. *He's fucking scared! Get him!*

Pelone reaches up with his free hand and grabs my collar and starts pulling me toward him, but Carlton demonstrates that he knows a few moves. He deftly twists the blade-arm behind Pelone's back, and he twists until Pelone starts to crumple. He says directly into Pelone's ear: "LET GO, MAN. LET IT GO!"

Ivan is at Carlton's shoulder yelling, "What the hell's going on here, stop!" Carlton has both of his mitts wrapped around the wrist with the blade, and Ivan reaches to untie it from Pelone's wrist.

Now my death-fear turns to physical rage. My heart is pounding. My spinal cord is shaking. "You fucking son of a bitch, you tried to...."

I look right in his eyes. He's bending forward because Carlton's twisting his arm, and he's staring at me. My hands are still at my crotch. I throw a punch with my left fist that lands square on the bridge of Pelone's nose. I can hear the nose cartilage crack.

"...KILL ME!"

I shove my right hand, open, into Pelone's face. My palm splatters the blood gushing out of his nose up into his eyes and all over his face. He's still holding onto my shirt. Carlton knows that the next move is to take Pelone down, so he unbends Pelone's arm as I plant my left hand on the man's chest. I throw my whole weight into slamming Pelone to the floor.

Ivan yells at Carlton as they go to the ground: "Watch that fucking blade!"

As Pelone goes down, Ivan shoves himself between us, breaking Pelone's hold. Ivan plants his two hundred and fifty pounds on top of Pelone, with hands and knees pinning him to the floor. Now Richard gets a good hold of Pelone's free wrist, and his other hand grabs the shank-wielding right arm that Carlton is still gripping firmly in his two strong fists.

I pull back out of the grapple. Stan's coming in now. A wave of alarm hits me and I shout, "Don't hurt him!"

Stan reaches for Pelone's wrist. Pelone is cursing in Spanish, spitting like a rabid psychotic. The rest of us are yelling at Pelone, yelling at each other to get him down, yelling to get that blade. Carlton looks up and says in a controlled voice: "Stan, take the strap off his wrist."

Stan unties the knot, frees the leather strap, and pulls the shank out of Pelone's hand. Pelone cusses in Spanish like a snake. I can hardly breathe. I feel like I'm going to puke. How-ever, years of living in Lurigancho have taught me to not puke where I live.

Man, I am in bad shape. This nut almost killed me.

Arthur and Hunter are yelling at Pelone to stop. I'm leaning against the bunk to catch my breath. Ivan takes the shank quickly from Stan, then he stands up and walks away with it.

I finally notice that Richard is by my side. "Tight place to make romance," he says. "You guys didn't fuck up my bunk? No! I'm impressed."

Pelone starts kicking wildly. Richard drops down on Pelone's lower legs with a grip on his ankles, using his weight to hold Pelone's feet still. Now Richard, Carlton, and Stan all hold Pelone so he cannot move. Pelone looks at me with wild animal eyes, black, glassy, dilated with rage. At the cell door Kit, Rick, and Tony are blocking Pelone's gang of four. I hear all sorts of loud yelling between them.

Then Carlton stands up. He's out of breath as though he's been running. Panting, he barks at Pelone, "Cuantos soles te debe Eduardo?"

Pelone just stares at Carlton.

Carlton turns to me: "How much do you owe him?"

I am breathing hard as well. "I think it's around four hundred dollars."

Carlton says, "Okay, listen! I'm going to give you the money to pay him. This has got to stop. One of you is going to die. Or else you'll get a real bad infection from getting cut, and you'll die from that. So give Pelone this."

Outside and inside the cell everyone is quiet. Some of us are breathing hard. The rest are holding their breath. Carlton pulls bills from his pocket—the money he just received from the Rev. Then he tears open the lining of the old coat he always wears. He takes money from the lining of the coat and puts it together with the money from his pocket, making four hundred dollars.

I take the money and show it to Pelone. Pelone's nostrils are stopped up with blood that has begun to coagulate down his lip and chin. He promises to be cool. Pelone and Carlton talk in Spanish.

Business finished. Pelone has been paid off.

Now he is standing in our cell, and peace has returned to the unit. Those in the hall are satisfied that Pelone is cool. Pelone brushes himself off and straightens his clothes and touches his lip looking at the blood now on his fingertips. His face is still very flushed, and there is sweat on his forehead. He looks for a moment at each of the men who interfered with his business. Then he shakes his head. The gesture seems to say, "Okay, you took my little toy away, but you didn't hurt me. Revenge is not my business.

Pelone turns to me and says, "I telled you, my friend. I no die for you. No more problem, my friend?"

"Yeah, Pelone, I want no more problem."

Me and Carlton walk out to the yard where as we walk I profusely thank him but that is not enough.

Carlton says, "You owe me. And this is what I want in payment. I want you, no, I expect you to pay me back by completely stopping all and every drug use. Take a hit of pot when you can. I'll share my Ovaltine can with you. But that's it. Okay? Is that a deal? Don't lie to me."

"It's a deal." I say it, and a sense of relief comes over me.

Carlton and me are now at the west-end turnaround. Men playing chess and checkers are sitting on the ground, or a few have a box or even a bench up against the side of our cellblock where the sun hits first and it's warm all day. A small-built man walks toward us fast and out of time with the rest of the crowded yard. He's a dark-haired, dark-skinned Peruvian, and he steps into our path and stops us. "Are you Eddie?" he blurts.

"Who the fuck are you? Slow down."

Carlton says, "Calmate, hombre! Habla despacio por favor!"

"Please, are you Eddie?"

"Si! I am Eddie. What's up?"

Carlton says, "Que cosas, amigo?" I put my hand on the man's twitching shoulder.

"You're friend Murphy, no?"

The man's statement is so strange to me that I stand still just puzzling it. He says it again:

"You're friend Murphy?"

Murphy? I barely know one guy named Murphy. That friend of my brother. The guy's a social misfit who went to Alaska and made a lot of money in real estate and construction. I did borrow some money from the guy one time. Then I ended up here. Does he want to be paid now? Get real.

"What about Murphy? Who are you, little guy? How did you hear that name?"

My brother wouldn't have let Murphy come down here without informing me through the Rev. Or would he? Maybe Murphy came to give Ibarra more money. But what would any of that have to do with this little Peruvian guy? Shit, look at him. He's so scared he's going to cry. Now he's got four of his brothers around him. They're all hopping from foot to foot, wringing their hands.

I start to laugh. Then I don't.

Carlton's not amused. "Better listen," he says.

I have that tightening in my gut, a sure symptom something real bad is about to go down. "So, amigo." I look over his shoulder at the others. "Or amigos, I guess. What is your message for Señor Murphy?"

"You must stop him from coming to get the coca! Tell him stay away. No come."

"Why would I do any such fucking thing?"

"They are your friends. You are El Jefe!"

"El Jefe!" The leader! The boss! Now I am yelling. "Hey, you fucks! What the fuck are you guys talking about?"

The little guy and his companions are so worried that my angry outburst doesn't faze them. Now I'm yelling at them. "Who else thinks I'm the JEFE in your fucking scam? Were you guys at the PIP? Who arrested you five geniuses?"

"Muy negro hombre. Muy peligroso!"

The conversation has intensified to such a tight focus that I don't notice Richard until he says, "Was the scary man's name Del Gado?"

We aren't clear as to what has happened until that night when the guard shows up at the door with another inmate.

As I lie in my bunk, the new guy enters the cell. The guard re-locks our cell door. The new guy asks, "Who is Eddie?"

"I'm Eddie. Eddie Spageddy if you're from Hawaii. Who are you? Why are you looking for me?"

No one is asleep. Everyone wants to hear this.

"I am Javier. You know Murphy, yes?"

"Murphy who? Why do you think I know Murphy?"

Javier remains standing where the guard left him, only a few feet inside the cell door. He says that he has been arrested for a small amount of cocaine. He is going to be in Luri just a short while, he says, and then he will be deported back to Uruguay because his parents brought thousands of dollars to Rubio and Del Gado.

"The PIP mens, they bringed Murphy in the PIP house. Yes? You understand my English?"

"Don't worry, we'll help you if you get stuck."

The Uruguayan describes how the PIP and the DEA used him as interpreter at the PIP mansion in Lima. The PIP have arrested a man named Murphy for trafficking cocaine. The Uruguayan was present for the entire interrogation, and he translated Murphy's confession. At one point the DEA came in and told Murphy that they already knew all about Colombia. Whatever the DEA meant by that, no one asked because at that point Murphy started begging the DEA boys to let him go home in exchange for snitching off everyone involved.

The DEA promised Murphy a flight back to Alaska in exchange for a full confession. And this is the story that Murphy told them:

Murphy was contacted by Diane. She invited him to come to Colombia to meet Jimmy and to make some easy money. When Murphy asked if Eddie Spageddy was in on this plan, Diane told him yes. She told him that a lot of the money from the coke scam would be used to get me out of prison.

So Murphy flew down to Colombia to form a plan with the two conspirators. He brought along twenty thousand dollars to leave as a down-payment for the coke.

When he arrived in Cali, Diane and Jimmy told him that he had to take the money down to Peru. They warned him not to visit me, not to try to make contact with me in any way. That would draw the heat.

So Murphy flew to Peru and gave the twenty thousand to Jimmy's sister. Using that money, Jimmy's sister paid for the manu-facture of the cocaine. Murphy went back to Alaska.

Jimmy's sister hired a bunch of cooks—who were the little Peruvian men who accosted me earlier today. In order to process the coca leaves, the cooks needed to gather huge amounts of strange ingredients—literally a swimming-pool full of battery acid, horse piss, and a whole gamut of poisonous chemicals. In the course of gathering the materials, the cooks drew the attention of the PIP. So Jimmy's sister and the cooks snitched off Murphy.

At that point, all the PIP had to do was wait for Murphy to show. They notified their counterparts in Colombia, the DAS, to watch for him. The DAS intercepted him in Bogota. They took five thousand of the twenty thousand he was carrying, then they let him go.

When Murphy connected with Diane and Jimmy, he told them that the DAS had nabbed him at the airport and taken five grand. Diane and Jimmy shrugged it off. They said that the seizure was a kind of south-of-the-border fine for not having declared the money. They sent him on to Peru, where the PIP were waiting.

Now Murphy is in the hands of the PIP. The DEA has promised to send him home on the next plane because, according to the Uruguayan, Murphy signed a confession stating that I, Eddie, set up the entire scam from Lurigancho Prison!

The Uruguayan tells this story without a stop. The rest of us haven't spoken a word. We all know that the man's story is true.

I break the ensuing silence by asking Richard if he has any valium.

"Oh yeah," says Richard. "Want a handful? How about some coke from Pelone?"

Then Richard yells with his hand to his mouth to amplify the call: "Hey, Pelone! Ed needs some coke, dude. Hurry."

"I get the point, Dick!"

Richard hates to be called Dick. Not because of the penis thing. He says it's because they called Nixon "Dick." For him there is no greater insult that to be compared in even the slightest way with Nixon.

Ibarra comes out to the prison the next day. We haven't seen Ibarra often enough to know yet if he owns more than one suit. Today he's wearing the same one, dull brown with scuffed old brown wingtips. His tie is crooked, as before. His puffy brown bald head waggles. But he doesn't act like a drunk. The eye is clear. He carries himself as though everyone knows him.

Richard watches Ibarra walking toward us and says, "Alfred Hitchcock."

Arthur and me give a little laugh, and Arthur says, "Yeah. Hitchcock with a tan. He's coming out with a new movie—Psycho in Lurigancho."

"Hello, boys. How are joo?"

"Hey, you old fart!" says Richard. "We know you don't give a rat's ass about us. Why did you come?"

Ibarra laughs a phony laugh.

Arthur says, "I want to know why you weren't at the lower

court. You said you'd be there."

Ibarra turns to me and asks, "Do joo have a friend called Murphy Burns? He is an American boy also?"

"Who?"

"Murphy Burns. He tells the PIP that he is your friend and he works for joo with your cocaine business. Is this true?"

Arthur shouts, "Hey! Answer me, goddamn it!"

Ibarra says, "Jes jes, Arthur, I will tell joo. Please you must understand. The only time I may defend joo is at joor tribunal. Don't worry, boys."

Richard cuts in. "Yeah, so what about this guy Murphy?"

Ibarra tells us what we already know. What we didn't know till now, though, is that I have been charged with another trafficking beef. This new thing, Ibarra says, has a bigger punch.

"Y Eduardo, you must be firm at lower court with Señor Murphy!"

"What the fuck are you saying?"

Richard blurts, "We heard Murphy confessed and is going home."

"Oh no. No no. He will come here to Lurigancho."

"Why am I going to court with that fuck?"

"Court is the place where you may claim your innocence."

"Oh fuck!" That's all I can say. The real knife in the gut is that Diane and Jimmy got me again.

Richard asks, "What does this do to our case now?"

"Oh, this is very very bad. For if joor present case is put together in the same court or heard by the same judges, it will be bery bery bad for joo boys. Not only for Eduardo, but also for joo, Ricardo. Both of joo could get twice as much sentence here in Lurigancho."

Richard is silent.

"But do not worry, boys. I will make them to be in separate courtrooms. I am a bery good lawyer, boys."

Arthur actually turns pale. "What about me? I don't know that Murphy dude at all, man. Huh, what about me?"

"No, Arthur, joo do not have to be worried. Murphy he says

nothing about joo."

Now Richard explodes. He shouts loud enough to attract the attention of everyone in the yard. Prisoners and visitors all stop what they are doing to listen. "You know what!" he hollers. "That motherfucking punk put me in another case! I'll kill him if they send him out here! He'll be dead before any court scene!"

"R.B., shut the fuck up. Man, sometimes!" I feel like slugging him. "We don't even know the son of a bitch, remember? Stop advertising to all these people that you're going to kill someone, man. Are you losing it or what?"

Richard is hard at me now, right up touching his chest to my body, losing his temper and spitting when he yells slightly down at me, yelling in my face: "You got me into this. Don't tell me to stop anything. I ought to kill *you* for this."

"Yeah, right. You know what I have to say about *that*, killer."

Arthur jumps in between us. "Hey, both of you knock it off."

Ibarra says, "Oh please, boys, do not fight with each other. Joo must help one another in this terrible time."

Richard says to Ibarra, "Okay, yeah. Never mind what I just said to Eddie. I'm just thinking about my new baby girl, and my lawyer—you—are telling me I could be here the rest of my life. This just keeps getting worse and worse, darker and darker. Pretty soon we won't be able to see any light at all. And what have you done as our lawyer? Not a thing—except you keep telling us what a great lawyer you are."

"Oh, Ricardo, I am working bery bery hard for joo boys' freedom. But we have very little monies now."

I say, "Monies for what? Richard is right, you know. You have not done a thing that we know of. You didn't show up at lower court. You know how fucking disgusting it is down in that basement. You didn't even try to send us a cup of coffee or a sandwich. You knew we'd be there all day, and you did nothing. Monies? Do something about getting us the fuck out of here, goddamnit. Have you even called our families to tell them anything? No!"

"Oh, but I am working hard for joo. I will try for to call joor families, boys, but it is very expensive the telefono internacional. You will see, boys. Everything will be okay, boys. You must be patient, boys. I must go now to see about this Murphy."

Ibarra starts to go, then he turns back toward us. "Goodbye now. I will see joo again soon, boys. Not to worry."

We stand where we are, watching him leave.

Arthur says, "Does he have a little waddle?"

Richard says, "I think Chula fucked up when he hired Tubby."

We just stand there for a while, feeling real heavy. The three of us make a very small circle in the yard full of inmates and visitors. "R.B., don't let this place go to your head, dude. We are still Americans. We are not Pelone. We're not Chivo. Don't be talking in public about killing another American. We're not criminals, man. We will get back to America and to our kids. If that guy Murphy comes out here and ends up shanked or has a bad accident and you've been talking about killing him, guess who the FBI and DEA are going to crucify?"

Richard says, "And now this guy Gustavo, too."

"We'll get through it. Let it go for now, man."

Arthur says without thinking, "Man, I sure am glad Murphy don't know me."

"Isn't that thirty to forty years? Don't tell me I won't kill him. I'll kill him and stuff him down the hole in the yard with the rest of the crap."

"You know, maybe they tortured him, R.B."

Richard points across the yard. "Out here in the yard right now is a man in a fucking body-cast. The PIP broke his back. They broke his ribs and his arm. He still didn't give anyone up."

"Listen, whatever he told the DEA and the PIP, he had to make up. He lied. So at court we can show he's lying."

"Man, what has happened to your head? He is a fucking snitch. He has no honor. No one stuck a hot electric wire to his balls. No one broke his arm or finger or anything. He snitched because he is a snitch. I never really put it together before, but remember all those war movies we were raised on? Remember how the Americans always felt when they found out that somebody was a traitor? Well, flash news here—traitor, snitch, traitor, snitch, same-same."

"I don't know, man. I'm not into that gangster crap anymore. This is no John Wayne flick telling me I should hate Japanese and kill snitches. Man, I'm going for the God thing."

"What the hell are you talking about now?"

"I'm not sure yet. But if there is a God, then maybe I can get closer to whatever that is and be guided or some shit. I can't really say it yet because this is new for me. I don't even know, but something is changing in me. Pelone almost killed me. Then something bigger than us walked Carlton back into the cell just in time."

Richard scoffs.

"No, really. Remember how it went down? Carlton walked out of the cell with the Rev. He practically had his mouth glued to the Rev's ear. You know how Carlton is when he gets onto one of his rolls. He never stops. Am I right?"

"Right."

"So what happened? Why the heck was he the first person back in the cell? I think—no, I feel—that something bigger will get us out of here. But thinking like Pelone is the wrong direction."

"Pelone would kill Murphy."

"That's what I mean. Lurigancho is Pelone's life. He chooses it. I'm choosing something different, something that I see is guiding the Reverend. I'm not turning religious. No way. But something is happening, and I want to learn what it is."

Richard keeps looking at me as though he's trying to say something but can't figure out what that is. Finally he drawls, "You sure are taking some big leaps."

"We need to take big leaps, R.B. We're in a deep fucking hole."

I go to find Chivo for the first time ever. I don't know where to begin. Usually Chivo finds me. He will simply appear. Like when Pelone tried to nail me in the shower room—there was Chivo passing out blades and ready to defend me to the death.

Chivo has been watching me from a distance from the very first day I got here. Even when I just arrived and I was still up front at administration, I saw him over in the corner. It was as though I knew him and he knew me. He just had a look, that's all, a look I recognized from my travels in Mexico or perhaps somewhere in Central America. Later he said to me, "You will find out who you are in Lurigancho."

Those words repulsed me at first, but still I was curious. Now they seem to haunt me, now that I have woken again. Or maybe I'm just now waking. Certainly my opinion of Chivo has changed. At first he was an animal among animals. Now I realize that he is a respected citizen of Lurigancho, a leader, a man of honor, a man of his word.

"You will find out who you are." I sense in my gut that his words are the clue to my escape from this place. Above all, I do not want to become what Chivo is—a first-class citizen of Lurigancho.

At the bottom of the stairs I stop in front of the thick rusted iron door to the Big Hall. When I look at the door and imagine going out there alone, I feel fear seizing my gut. Suddenly I realize why I am looking for Chivo.

Yes, I could kill Murphy. And I would do it right. Not like Richard. Not out of anger or the desire for payback. I would do it out of responsibility for the tribe. I would do it simply to adhere to the morals that govern life in Lurigancho. That sense of responsibility, that's what Chivo thinks he sees in me. A true brother. Murphy is a gross example of the most powerful threat to the Chivo tribe, disloyalty, dishonor—snitching.

The sense of responsibility, this is what distinguishes Chivo from Pelone. Pelone doesn't give a shit about who snitched, as long as it wasn't him. Pelone murders for business. But Chivo's true business is honor.

Suddenly I realize what it is that frightens me most about the Big Hall. It's not that the Big Hall is full of people like Pelone. The Big Hall is filled with the tribe of Chivo. The Big Hall is a moral place, a place of honor. But the code of honor in the Big Hall is so harsh that few men have the courage to survive it. To walk in the Big Hall, one must live beyond fear.

"Eduardo, que piensas?"

Chivo is standing behind me. He looks serious, like a business partner who has just looked at our profit-and-loss report and realized that we have to boost production. He reaches out with both arms as if to hug me. I step toward him, and when we hug he whispers in my ear, "I kill the new gringo."

I'm sure he feels the shock that goes through me. Gently I push him back. "Chivo, listen. Por favor eschuchame bien, Chivo."

"It's okay, my friend. No worry, my friend. No one know. Nobody. We hide the bad gringo his body. Only pay un cartone de cigaros. Yes?"

"No, Chivo, no! You must not kill the gringo. He is American. The DEA knows Murphy. They know he knows me. Tu entiendes?"

"Si si. Okay, mi hermano. Por usted, es un packete de cigaros."

"No, Chivo. He must not die. The DEA will make for me a murder charge in the United States."

"Okay, I kill him for you because I like you. You are American brother."

I don't know why Chivo says this. He has never suggested that we have sex—even though he sometimes mentions his "bitch" back in his unit. Maybe he sees something special in me. A lot of Peruvians look at me with curiosity, even admiration, because I speak English without a Latin accent and I live with the other gringos as one of them even though I have skin like Chivo. I think I give them encouragement. To me, that's weird. I can hope that someday I'll be back in the U.S.A. These inmates and guards have no hope of that.

I'd like to explain many things to Chivo. For example, I don't want rage to burn up the good energy that I'll need someday to get out of Luri. Besides that, why should I do anything? Murphy is on his way to hell, so why should I try to deprive him of the experience? I can actually sympathize with the fact that the poor bastard was lured and lied to by Diane. Maybe Jimmy rolled over on Murphy.

Regardless of all that, Chivo wants to bring me into the tribe. He wants me to accept the code by murdering Murphy—whether by doing it myself or by letting him take the lead. Such a choice would give me a tribal membership and a pass to the Big Hall. It would make me a resident of Lurigancho.

And yet Chivo sees that I am serious. He is very disappointed. Even so he grabs my shoulders and embraces me again. "You say Murphy live, he live. You say Murphy die, he dead."

After all this time I still have trouble believing this existence.

Chivo waves his hand at the guard inside the office, which is right next to where we are standing. He points to the door and tells the guard in Spanish to hurry up. The guard practically jumps out of his old wooden chair.

As the howling hinges release the rusty door, I say, "Chivo. Adios." Go with God.

Chivo turns to me. With his right hand on the half-opened iron door and with his left fist striking his own chest near his heart, he says, "Dios es aqui no mas." Then he walks out into the deadliest hallway in the world, where he is respected, feared, and beloved.

Night has begun. Men are cooking. This is a good day. Everyone has something to eat, the toilet is working out in the yard, and almost for sure the water will be turned on in the morning. As I lie reading a paperback, Weaver walks into the cell. I look up. "Say, Weaver. I know we hardly talk. But I want to know something. It might be kind of personal, I don't know."

Weaver says with a laugh that shows the gold in all his molars. "Hey, just ask. Nothing much around here is personal, but go ahead."

"Okay. What do you, as a cop, think about snitches?"

"Wow, that seems like a loaded question."

"Yeah, I guess."

Stan is lying in his bunk and he says, "Oh yeah, what do cops think about snitches?"

Weaver answers, "No cop could make a bust without a snitch. The prosecutor couldn't prosecute without the informant."

"Everybody knows that. They show that on television. I mean what do you think about them? About rats. About people without honor or loyalty. People who roll over their own kind so that those people will do their time for them."

"It depends."

Richard can't handle this procrastination. "Oh fuck, man, just answer him. What do you think of a snitch?"

"Well, I think they're pretty rotten." Weaver sits on his bunk. He looks up at me and says: "Why? Is that guy who dragged you in his case coming here?"

"Yes, he is. According to my lawyer he is."

"Mind if I give a word of advice?"

"No, go ahead."

"I wouldn't hurt him. He can...."

Richard cuts Weaver off. "You're lucky we don't bounce YOU around, you fucking cop. How many snitches have you made, Weaver? You're just a snitch with a badge. Now that you don't have a badge, you're in the same fucking hole as us. But this ain't television. In here you're the bad guy and we are the good guys."

Weaver takes his health in his own hands. "Get over it, Richard. We are all in the same boat, man."

Richard ignores Weaver and goes back into the pages of his paperback.

Kit Karson is over near the cell door, and he announces, "Hey y'all, there's a blue guard from downstairs a comin' this a way."

The guard in blue knows me. At the cell door he points at me and makes a hand motion. I follow. On the way down the hall the guard tells me, "You gringo friend, he say his name Mooffy. He es in mi oficina and he very scared. You gringo brother, Murphy—no?"

"No brother. Only gringo. What this gringo tell you?"

"He say you kill him."

"No. No. I no care this gringo. I want this gringo live, stay here with you. I go to America, yes?"

The guard laughs as we walk toward the stairs.

As I pass the other cells, the inmates are watching me. It's as though I am getting a package. Pelone gives me that cut across the throat with his finger, like the judge did in our lower court appearances. Some people are smiling, as if to say, "Hey all right, man! The goat is here to be slaughtered!"

Once downstairs I push through the crowd that has gathered at the door of the guard's office. Everyone is staring at the new dog. These are the lowliest prisoners. Life has never shown them anything better than Lurigancho. Most of their crimes were motivated by starvation. They know all about the new gringo of course. News travels fast from the PIP to the prison. They know that this gringo snitched another gringo and now he is here. They already regard him as a carcass.

Given the circumstances, it would be ridiculous to pretend that I don't know Murphy. Over the heads of the ones that I don't bother to push aside, I see Murphy sitting in a chair, his head down so as not to look at the demonic crowd.

"Hey, Murphy! Come up with the guard. No one is going to hurt you."

He looks at me, his pale pockmarked face out of balance with his eyes of bright blue, eyes so blue that you imagine they belong to somebody attractive. His hair is greasy blond, and I see that he still parts it on the side the way his mother combed it. He's wearing a red flannel shirt with a lumberjack's checkered pattern, blue jeans, and sturdy sandals with black socks—a shining contrast to the crowd's filth-stained t-shirts and crumpled shorts and thin legs and wafer-thin rubber slippers. He looks pathetic and scared literally for his life. He is shaking.

By the time Murphy walks into the cell, I have gone back to reading my book. No one but Weaver gives him a word or a welcome. Weaver is overly friendly, greeting Murphy as though he's been accepted into a college fraternity. But Murphy is deaf to Weaver, and he's numb to the silence being observed by everyone else. He looks around for me and walks to my bunk side, and looks down at me with big cow eyes full of fear.

"I'm sorry, Eddie."

Richard shouts, "Hey! Sorry's for chicks, dude."

I simply say, "Hope you like it here. You're going to be here a long time."

Weaver takes on the buddy role. He does Murphy's orientation. No one else talks to him except as necessary.

Carlton walks with me in the yard and asks for the story.

"Murphy went to high school with one of my brothers. I got to know him when I needed an investor to buy a container full of surfboard blanks from California to sell in Hawaii."

"Who'd you buy the blanks from?"

"Clark Foam."

"Oh, they're good."

"Carlton, I keep forgetting that you're a Newport Beach surf bum."

"Not a bum like you, but I surfed with Duke Kahanamoku."

"I know, you say that. But what does that mean? I never asked you this before. Same wave?"

"Not the same wave. But the same day."

"Same day. Same place? Same shoreline?"

"We're not talking about that. The point is, did you make any money selling the blanks?"

"We made a profit but not much. Other people copied the venture right away. And there was never any warmth between Murphy and me. But Diane figured out that he had money. Talk was he was a good businessman."

"Cold fish often are."

"But I never heard of him doing anything illegal."

"Do you think you're being too hard on him?" Carlton speaks as the elder. Which he is. "Didn't Diane tell him it was to get you out of prison? I mean, Ed, he may have done the only illegal act he's ever done in a sincere, courageous effort to help you out. The most gut-and-heart-felt endeavor of his life. For you. I mean, how do you really feel about that, Ed?"

I stop walking.

"I know you saved my life and everything. But I have to say that your theory is horseshit. Yeah, Diane probably tricked him. She sure as hell lied to him. But he did not come down to Peru with a rat's ass of sympathy for me. Hard on him? More like, I'm the only thing keeping his throat from getting cut."

Carlton walks silently for a while and then says, "What about Richard? He keeps staring at Murphy."

"Yeah, I know. But remember. R.B. is in my case just because he was in my bungalow when they arrested me. Now just because he knows me R.B. has another charge. Fifteen more years. No parole in Peru. And R.B. just had a baby girl. Imagine that. A complete stranger lies, and you lose your whole life. Murphy's lucky that R.B. hasn't hurt him."

When the runner comes down the hall, he announces that I'll be going to lower court with Murphy. This is good news and bad news. The bad news is that I am actually being charged in Murphy's case. The good news is that Ibarra finally has been right about something.

Going to court with Murphy, it feels wrong. Richard and Arthur remain behind. The grueling bus ride is the same except I'm not attached to Arthur. This time I am cuffed to a Peruvian from one of the other cellblocks.

At lower court the judge finds me involved enough to go to tribunal with Murphy and the Peruvians. Oh happy day. Ibarra is right again. I have a second case.

Shortly after the lower court decision Ibarra comes to the prison to talk about our upcoming military tribunal. He gives us copies of the prosecutor's opinion in our case. The prosecutor feels that Arthur should get three years on top of any time he's already served. Richard has an opinion of fifteen years. My opinion is twenty. And in Murphy's case my opinion is another twenty-two. In Peru sentences do not run concurrently.

Ibarra tells us that we will fight. He reminds us what a fantastic lawyer he is, and that he used to be a judge. But he stops any conversation about getting us released. He talks now only about getting us less time. And he needs more money.

We do get him to promise that he will keep the cases in two separate tribunals. Me, Richard, and Arthur in one courtroom. Me and Murphy in another. Hopefully, never on the same day.

The weather has changed. Summer is coming. While Rick plays some great blues on his guitar, some of us are kicking back. A warm, soft breeze is coming through the holes where the plastic windowpanes used to be.

Some of the guys are writing. Some are reading. Arthur is at another building selling leche asada. Ivan is sitting in his bunk below me, using the thread and needle he bartered for somewhere downstairs. He's sewing up the knees of his jeans. I am reading a paperback called The Jackal.

Murphy has been with us for a while now. By now I've heard a few of the guys admit that they might have done the same thing sooner or later. We all have to look at the reality of torture. But R.B. remains unforgiving. "No one laid a finger on him!" he says.

Still, on this perfectly peaceful afternoon I cannot resist a little humor in this living morgue. In the center of the cell and in the middle bunk of a three-man bunk Murphy is sawing logs. His bare toes are sticking out the end of his bunk.

I find a scrap of paper and write "Toe Tag" on it. Then I put a little string through the tag and tied the string around Murphy's big toe. Murphy wakes up because everyone is laughing at him.

More and more I find that I have less rage. More of my thinking is about the high court and that process. My priorities are changing.

As I become more and more conscious, I start thinking about my own bullshit attitudes about cocaine. I always say that I came to Peru to visit the amazing ruins of the Incas. But, like Arthur, I mainly wanted to taste Peruvian cocaine.

I've been studying the transcripts from lower court and from the PIP station. They are exact.

"Hey, R.B. I know you don't want to hear it, but have you read these papers?"

"Yeah right! Like that shit is going to matter."

"But we need to know…."

"That the papers don't matter. We need to know that our entire lives depend on one statement by one person."

I thought he wasn't paying attention. But suddenly I realize what he has known all along. Whether we're acquitted or sentenced to hang out in Lurigancho until our grandkids are old enough to visit, this decision hinges on the testimony of one person. Sergeant Dracula Bonebreaker Del Gado. He'll take the stand, and he'll answer the question about whether our story is true. If he says no, we are doomed.

I am waking up to how impossible it all appears. But I don't want to go back in that death sleep until I die or it all goes away.

3

ZOILA

I am awake now.

I check my watch, which hangs by a string from the rusty springs of the bed above. I turn my watch toward the fluorescent glare that streaks into the cell from the hall. Not yet four a.m. The usual. These days I pop up awake long before the barrel rolls across the yard. I wake for the silence.

I have found a new way to live. I have slipped into the present. The routine is stable now. Reverend Robinson shows up every two weeks with our mail and money. I have discovered the beach that Tony has known about for several summers. Beat-up paperbacks have become precious. Like Richard, I have gained an ability to escape into the writer's world, hear the voices of the characters, feel their emotions, laugh out loud as a witness inside someone else's story.

I start writing a letter using the light from the hall. But something funny comes to mind. I realize that if I keep thinking about what I'll write in the letter, I'll lose the silence.

Not so long ago the silence troubled me. But now I let go of any thoughts and let it be. Nearly all the snoring has stopped. I close my eyes and become still in myself. Wide awake.

Quietly I slip out of my bunk and sit at the hearts table, sit on one of the crude wooden boxes we use for chairs. With my eyes closed

I can float free. There is ease in my gut. My breath comes with the same ease.

This is what I do now. I do it for twenty or thirty minutes every day between three forty-five and four thirty a.m. I connect with something greater in the silence. I don't know any religious practices. But I've heard of people sitting with their eyes closed. Could this be what they all do?

This morning the silence is like a breath of air.

The condition of my mind is what brought me to Lurigancho. Sitting with the silence will clear my mind and show the way to move on and out.

Then the fifty-five-gallon drum rolls across the yard and everything starts, and I roll into my daily routine.

The guard opens the gate. We all line up and count off, then we go back in the cell. Once we are counted, Ivan and me grab eight buckets each and jam down the hall, down the stairs, and we push and shove and punch if need be. Ivan keeps a shank tied around his calf under his pants, but by now we know that no one is going to challenge us. He stands at my back while I fill the buckets. This is our job. We supply our cellmates Carlton, Oso, Kit, Tony, and Hunter with daily water. And they provide our daily bread.

These guys could get their own water, but they still have family sending money. Me and Ivan could beg for more money from home, but this servitude is what we have chosen. We need it for our own self-worth.

No drugs. A clear mind. A job. And the feeling of being within myself. This has become my new life in this same old disease-infested, stinking prison.

And while we're at it, we always get water for Richard and Arthur.

Ivan and me fill our buckets at the six-faucet trough. As always, René is standing at the next faucet over. His beret tilts to one side. His shirt has the top three buttons undone, showing a gold cross he won in a chess game. The cross and gold chain are the only thing on his hairless chest. René always wears slacks, and his shirt is always clean and ironed by one of his homosexual slaves. He stands there while his guys fill water buckets, and they keep filling buckets until the water is turned off. That's his mania—he hoards water. And yet he is always pleasant to me and Ivan. He respects our work ethic. "Oh good morning, Eduardo," he says. "Good morning, Mr. Ivan."

Later, I clean the cell and write a couple letters. Writing home to my mother really gets my gut in a knot. I refuse to write anything except, "This prison isn't that bad, mom. The food is good and I am healthy. Love you always." Then, to bring myself back to the here and now, I leave the cell to walk a bit.

To get a view, I walk down to the end of the hall to the big empty room where we used to have our boxing tournaments. I go to the barred window at the north side. From here I can look into the other yard, the one that René looks into. That yard is exactly like ours, with a cellblock on either side. From two stories up I see that the yard is full of women.

I see Arthur walking among them yelling, "Leche asada aqui! Aqui su leche asada. Veinte soles." He carries his white skin and his blue eyes and his well-worn wooden tray with little glass jars. Everyone who buys his pudding has a smile. They laugh with him.

I notice one old man who has nine or ten women around him. The women have prepared a small picnic, and they are laughing and making the man feel good. He is their grandfather figure. Four of them hold babies in their arms. One sits close to the old man, and she is the same age and quite obviously his wife. They have brought the old man packages and a few shopping bags of food.

One of the ladies somehow rivets my attention. She seems young—eighteen or even younger. It's strange to me that I am attracted to her.

I can't quite get a full sight of her until she turns around to look at the prison, at the buildings and the windows. Her attention sweeps the sad architecture, and I see it coming and then, bam, she sees me. In the barred window. We make contact.

She is not attractive. Rather, she is beautiful. Her eyes have an exotic oval shape, almost Asian. Her face is as soft as the new baby lying next to her in the arms of an older woman. The moment of contact lasts a long time—a few seconds.

Then the young woman looks away, catching herself, embarrassed. *Is she having the same feeling?* My heart is beating faster.

Her hair is in a pile on top of her head. It's curly, like an expensive perm, with rings of dark hair dangling around her long neck and her ears. From two stories up I can see the fullness of her mouth and lips. Her skin is golden. She has turned her back toward me, and I see that her dress has tiny yellow and blue flowers on light pink lace around the neckline and the hem. Here in Lurigancho these slight impressions are explosive. The soft cotton clings gently to her small frame. I want to look into her eyes. I want to see her on level ground, no bars or walls between us. Somehow I have to reach her.

Carlton. Shit, he knows Spanish so well that he reads Don Quixote in the original.

Now, back in the cell, I interrupt the eternal hearts game, this round being Carlton, Kit, Weaver, and Hunter. "Hey, Carlton. I need you to help me write a note. Sorry, you guys."

Carlton brushes his perfect handlebar moustache with his tiny moustache comb. "A note for what?"

"For a girl."

I have butterflies in my gut.

"I love nothing better than writing notes to girls. And where did you find a girl to write to, if I might ask?"

"Down in the yard next door. A visitor."

Carlton already has a small tablet of paper for keeping score. He folds back the top sheet. "Okay, what do you want to say? I want to see her after we finish this bit of literature."

"There's not a whole lot of time. Write that I am Eduardo. You are a very attractive lady, and I want to meet you. Ask what is her name."

Carlton shouts, "Oh for god's sake, is she a young girl? And with her family? A Latin family?"

"Yeah, it looks that way. Why?"

"Because there is such a thing as being culturally correct, even in this dungeon. Who is she visiting?"

"Looks like her father or grandfather."

"You must pass the note to him, and he will decide to pass it to her."

"Yeah, sure, okay. But come on. Write."

Carlton tells us what he is writing as he writes.

"Señor, I respectfully request permission to compliment you on your loving and caring family. If you would permit me, I would like to know the name of the lady in the pink-flowered dress—unless of course she is engaged or married. My name is Eduardo. Thank you, Señor."

I say, "Tell him that I just want to get close enough to smell her. Come on. Arthur is down there now selling his pudding."

I take the note to the window. A troop of my cellies clusters behind me. At the window I am overwhelmed by the feeling that she might look at me again. And she does. She smiles and ever so slightly nods her head to me.

Carlton, next to me, says, "Unbelievable. No wonder you want to smell her. But I would not get too hyped up. Remember where we are, Ed."

In back of me Stan says, "Her? Yeah, she's okay. But she looks like any other Peruvian chick to me, man."

Kit says in that fucking high pitch, "Y'all may think she's a pretty one, but them eyes are a lookin' Japan or somethin' foreign to me."

Without taking my eyes off the lady in the pink and lace dress, I say shaking my head in disgust, "Kit, you are such an ignorant son of a bitch. But then, if you liked her I'd be worried about myself."

Hunter says, "Okay, we saw. Let's finish the game."

"Just a minute," says Carlton. "I want to watch this."

The girl in pink has now turned toward the man they are visiting.
"Well, that's a good sign," says Carlton. "She seems glad you re-
appeared at this window, barred as it may be. But she has respect
for that gentleman, enough respect to give him her full attention.
What are you waiting for? Throw the note before the damn visit is
over!"

I yell. "Arthur!"

Carlton says, "You'd better yell louder than that. Must be a hundred and fifty people talking at once down there."

After two good yells I get Arthur to look up just as he walks under
the window. I take aim, waving the note. The folded little square of
tablet paper floats down, a slight breeze gusting it toward the girl
who is seated with her family.

The girl in pink and most of the visitors watch Arthur as he chases
the floating paper. When he catches it, he is about twenty feet from
the intended.

I say to Carlton—who is the only one interested enough to hang
out—"She looked up here, and now she's looking at Arthur. I think
she knows that the note is for her. You think?"

"I think, Ed. I think."

Arthur is looking up at me.

"Not her!" I shout. "The guy, the man she's visiting!"

I don't think Arthur can hear me. But I put my hand out through
a missing windowpane and point Arthur to the gentleman in the
center. He hands the old man the note, and the old man accepts it.

"Mission accomplished, Romeo," says Carlton.

I am experiencing a feeling I have not had since I was thirteen.
Or maybe never. *Oh cool, he's handing the note to her. Oh wow how cool
this is.*

She reads the note that Carlton authored. Finished reading, she
looks up with the most wonderful smile I have ever seen.

Now her family visit is ending with hugs and tears, and the
small baby-carrying tribe embraces the beloved old man, and they
walk through the east-end door out of sight.

When Arthur returns, he assures me that Zoila is a cutie but not his type. "She's Peruvian. Give me an American woman." And yet he hands me a note.

Carlton says from the hearts table: "How did she respond, Ed?"

"She says thank you for asking about her and for complimenting her family. Her name is Zoila."

"Zoila? That's a name I've not heard before. I thought I'd heard them all."

Weaver is at the table writing in his journal and says, "I thought they were all named Maria something."

I have a warmth inside me all day.

A runner announces we are having a visit. "Todos los gringos vengan. Su embajada ha llegado."

Today is visiting day for people with passes from the military—people with connections, people with clout. Unlike other visiting days, these events are short, just an hour and a half. But they bring a better class of visitor. Arthur gets down in the yard with his leche asada tray right away. Pablo has set up a cluster of benches with his family members; Oso is with them. The rest of us start gathering in the middle of the yard, leaning against our cellblock wall and looking down to the east end of the yard, curious to see who might have come out to meet us from the American embassy.

Carlton is practically vibrating with excitement. He's saying, "... those sons of bitches just left us here to rot, they don't take my letters, they don't want to face the truth that the DEA is supporting a travesty of justice...."

"Hey, Carlton," says Richard. "Don't use up all the oxygen."

"Yeah man, make sure the rest of us get a chance to talk," says Stan.

Now a woman comes through the door. The blue-uniformed guard is holding the iron door open for her. He nods his head and

then turns toward us and points. He shouldn't have bothered. All it
takes is one glance at the crowded yard to see who the gringos are.
And vice-versa. One glimpse and you know that this woman is as
American as a can of Pepsi Cola.

She's dressed in a dark-blue business suit, her shiny white blouse
buttoned nearly to her chin. She wears her hair short, almost a boy's
regular cut, a Newport Beach look, a Coast Guard look—blonde
with the hair on top combed in a big wave that tapers down to
stubble around the ears and the back of the head. Her small silver-
ball earrings don't make her any more feminine than do her wedgy
black shoes and functional socks. She carries a black briefcase under
her right arm; her other arm swings in time with her march toward
where we are all standing.

Now she will see how desperate we are—unsentenced Americans
in hell.

Right behind the American woman is a bearded white man who is
talking with the guard. Carlton recognizes the man as the Canadian
rep. He warms up his voice by yelling toward our cell windows:
"Ivan! Your embassy is here!"

Richard, standing next to me, says, "They should send someone
just to represent Carlton."

As the stiff American woman approaches, Carlton bolts forward
and gets in her ear before the rest of us can even say hello. "My time
is almost up," he says. "Are you bastards going to make sure I get
out of here and back to the States?"

She blinks rapidly, her sand-colored hair bouncing as she turns
from Carlton's intensity to us and back to Carlton. "Give me a break,
guys. I just got here. Would you men mind identifying yourselves? I
have read everyone's file and have some idea. Just let me know who
you are, please."

"I am Henry Carlton. I haven't seen you before. And you are?"

Even though Carlton towers over the woman, she gathers her
focus and aims it at him: "Oh yes, you're the one who drove around
Latin America smuggling pot from country to country." Suddenly the

temperature seems to drop twenty degrees, and now she's looming over Carlton. "Why are you being so rude with our agency, Mr.
Carlton? Did you think we would be sympathetic—you, driving
around with a huge bag of marijuana?"

Carlton opens his mouth, and then he just shuts it again.

She turns back to the rest of us. "My name is Laura Schmidt. I am
your American counselor."

"No one here needs any counseling," says Stan. "But I have reason to believe you guys got money from home for me. Do you know
anything about it?"

She places her briefcase on the wooden bench that we brought
down from our cell, and she flicks open the two clasps of the briefcase. Richard says, "Hey, you want to stick around for dinner? We
have a can of Spam that we've been saving for a special occasion."

Laura Schmidt looks at Richard and then instantly looks past
him toward the west wall and says, "Oh my God! What are those
men doing?"

"They're shitting, lady."

"I'm so sorry," she says. "Could you gentlemen come to this side
of me, please?" She indicates the direction of the east wall. None of
us objects. We are satisfied to know that she is shocked by her one
glimpse of our living conditions. Of course, she will never see the
Big Hall. I will never be able to offer her pork and beans.

From her briefcase Laura Schmidt extracts the Los Angeles Herald
Examiner. Carlton has re-gathered a bit of his cool. When he spots
the newspaper, he says, "Can I see that?" She hands it to him and
proceeds to get more stuff from her briefcase. Carlton opens the
newspaper with his long arms.

"You people are sadists," he says. He spreads open the paper
and holds it up. It's full of square holes, as if a schizophrenic was
trying to cut paper dolls.

"We don't want to upset anyone with bad news from home. But
you will find the sports section intact."

Then she adds, "Stanley, we did receive one hundred dollars

from your family. Here is ten dollars of that money. I am authorized to give you ten dollars every time I come."

All of us laugh.

Kit, standing at the back of our little group, says, "Damn, I'd like to make her come."

If she hears, she gives no indication. She hands Stan the ten-dollar bill.

He says, "Thanks. But how long do you think ten bucks is going to last in here?"

"We know you are supplied with your meals and basic needs. So we estimate it should last between our visits."

Stan just turns away, shaking his head, too disgusted to continue the conversation. He heads back to the cellblock.

She is unaffected.

Weaver and Murphy are last to join the little conference. Now they are standing directly in front of her. Weaver has dressed in a cowboy shirt, red and white checked, and he's got the top buttons open. The shirt has been ironed. He must have paid Mariposa, the big homosexual two cells down, to do the job in a jiffy. He's wearing Levi's and reddish cowboy boots. He looks like a Hollywood version of René. "Any news for me?" he says with a wink. "I'm Burt Weaver."

"Yes," she says. "You are one of our policemen."

Kit offers, "Yep, and I am the other one."

"You two should be ashamed of yourselves," she says. "My God, what kind of role models are you? You are a disgrace to Americans."

Kit replies, "What a tight ass y'all are, lady." And he turns to join Stan.

Arthur has walked over with his wooden tray of little glass pudding jars. He says, "What else you bring? Any mail?"

Ignoring him, she reaches into her briefcase and pulls out a bulging, magazine-size envelope. She hands the envelope to Carlton, who has his arms crossed, one hand fingering his perfect moustache. "Here are some answers to the letters you have been writing to Congress, Mr. Carlton." Carlton takes the envelope and leaves the yard without a backward glance. Again Laura Schmidt appears not to notice.

Arthur says, "Well, that's two unanswered questions. How about, you want to buy a leche asada?"

"Do you have a serious question?" she hisses.

Arthur just looks at her for a moment and then shrugs. "Yeah. Why'd the first American woman I've talked to in years have to be you? And when are you going to do something about getting me out of here? I didn't have any drugs, and I do not deal in drugs. How is that for a serious question? Is that serious enough for you?"

"Yes, I can appreciate your situation. I have read your case, and I have seen your photo. I suggest that you learn to be more careful about the company you choose. I believe you know who I mean— these friends of yours that you say you don't know. Richard Brewer...." She looks at Richard, then she looks at me. "And Edward Padilla." She keeps looking at me. "You people come to these countries and just think you can do whatever you want. And then this happens. And it's our fault."

"That's your answer to my question?" You hardly ever see Arthur get mad like this. "Listen, lady. Your job is to help us. Not to torture us. Not to lecture us. Carlton is right. You're all a bunch of bastards. You know about us. You know that we're Americans and that we've been fucking stuck in this stinking prison for nearly three years now and we haven't even been sentenced. And you come in here to tell us that we think we can do anything we want? It's you and your kind, you're the Americans who are down here doing whatever you want in 'these countries.' Breaking the law. Shitting on the constitution. America stands for human rights—but you don't. Thanks for coming. Thanks for nothing." And he walks away.

Schmidt is unaffected.

Oso has walked across the yard from where he is visiting with Pablo's family. "Hi," he says. "I'm not supposed to be here. I think those PIP guys lied to me."

That gets a laugh from us all, including Laura Schmidt.

"Yes, I am aware of your case. But you have chosen your own attorney rather than one from our list of preferred lawyers. We really have our hands tied when you do not take our advice."

"Lady, do you think I look that stupid? I never got any advice from you or anyone. But one of you people called my mother and told her not to do anything—not to send money, not to help me hire a lawyer—because her son is guilty. Guilty until proven innocent. Because he's a smuggler, and good Americans turn their backs on those guys even if it's, like, your own son. But advice? No, no advice, lady. So don't start giving it now."

Oso looks her over from head to toe one time, gives a last "Hmmph," and goes back to Pablo and his mom.

Ms. Schmidt is unfazed. "Which one of you might be Mr. Murphy?" she says.

Murphy is still wearing the same checkered shirt and Levi's that he came in. Looks like he lives on the same ranch as Weaver. "Yeah, that'll be me," he says.

"Yes. Well, there seems to be some problem with your file not being ready for me this morning. So I am afraid I have nothing for you right now."

Murphy responds with a shrug. He seems relieved, as though he got away without getting spanked. "Oh, that's okay. I'll see ya next time." As he turns to go back to the cellblock, I can see Richard staring at him, giving him the stink-eye.

"Now which of you is James Hunter, and which is Anthony Phillips?"

Richard interrupts. "If there's no reason to be out here, I have a lot to do, lady. Excuse me." He goes.

I say, "So, no more mail or anything?"

"No. And I am surprised at the small amount of mail. But I did bring it all. We are not keeping any from you."

Obviously she knows nothing about the Reverend and his deliveries. That's good. And she doesn't seem aware of any connection between Murphy and me. She's just a machine, performing her tasks. I walk away while she discusses an exit plan with Tony and Hunter.

As I walk toward the west wall, I'm thinking it's strange that she knew the three of us better than she knew everybody else. And yet she had nothing to say to us. Maybe she's thinking, these guys are so fucked what's to say.

From across the yard Oso calls: "Eddie, hey Eddie! Come over here!"

Pablo is waving me over. "Eduardo!" he shouts. "Come meet my mother, come!" Richard has something in his hands that he is eating; he shakes it at me and motions with his head. I change directions and start weaving through the crowd. People are gathered in small clusters and pairs, standing and sitting, laughing and hugging. A young girl is crying on someone's shoulder. Each group is a world of its own.

"That embassy lady is co-old," says Oso. "Like ice."

"Well, it looks nice and warm over here," I say. "How's everybody?"

"Eduardo, meet my mom. Mother, this is Eduardo. He is Ricardo's friend."

Richard says, "Now wait a minute."

"Oh, stop clowning. You guys are tight. Say hello to my mother."

"I am very glad to meet you, Mrs. Herzog."

"Si, mucho gusto. I am happy to make your acquaintance, and I am so glad my son has friends."

Mrs. Herzog has a European look, her red lipstick outstanding against her white skin. I am surprised when she speaks Spanish. She wears a chiffon dress in the colors of autumn leaves and a bonnet of tight-woven white straw. Judging by her manner and dress, she is a woman of high society.

Next to Pablo, sitting with a can of Pepsi in his hand, is a strikingly handsome man about thirty years old with a God-given Hawaiian tan. His brown hair, short and combed back, is sun-streaked blond. He's clean-shaven. His light blue eyes shine, and so do his bright white teeth. Built like a baseball player, he's wearing a brown sport coat, tan slacks, and sandals with brown socks.

As I hold the gloved hand of Mrs. Herzog and very gently touch my cheek to hers, Pablo says, "And please, Eduardo, this is my older brother Lucho. Lucho Herzog. He is a celebrity on the television in Peru. Lucho, this is Eduardo."

"Really, you're on TV? A soap opera?"

Richard says, "Hey Lucho, you look more like a gringo than Eduardo. And you speak much better English."

Lucho laughs out loud, exposing what I see is the Herzog family trait—perfect teeth. Lucho's features are finer, but he and Pablo are definitely brothers, and clearly Mrs. Herzog is the mother of both men.

"No," he says. "I am only in a couple of commercials on a local channel. Actually I am a professional travel guide."

"So you show people the ruins and stuff?" says Richard.

Lucho laughs again. "No, and I am not laughing at your question. It's just that the wages for that kind of a guide would not buy my sandals. No, I have been much more fortunate. I am an international guide. Actually I take groups from South America to other countries. I speak several languages. And I made many connections when I attended school at your University at Berkeley in California. I like America very much."

"Yeah, Berkeley," says Oso. "Great place. Lots of diversity and freedom going on."

"Yes, of course. I am always treated so well there. Maybe we can meet in Berkeley one day." Lucho speaks English like a Californian, with less accent than most Spanish-speaking American citizens.

Mrs. Herzog insists that I eat some of her home-cooked food. "Actually, the maid did the cooking. But she is a very good cook."

Suddenly I am eating roast beef and potato salad. It is the best food
I have ever eaten.

"When you are free to leave this place, you must come to visit
Pablo at our ranch," says Mrs. Herzog. "You can relax and have a
good time with our family. You are welcome."

Lucho says, "Yes, please. If we can help you when you leave
here, we will be very happy to. You must come to our home. After
that, you will not leave Peru with a bad taste."

I see that Laura Schmidt is exiting the gate at the east wall. No
one escorts her. No one had any affect on anyone else and nothing
worthwhile happened. Mission accomplished.

Now the Herzog visit ends. We all walk to the gate. At the iron
door Mrs. Herzog sheds tears and gives Pablo a long embrace.
Lucho turns to Richard and me and says, "Please remember what
we have offered you from our hearts. We welcome all of you to our
home. I am sure I speak for the entire Herzog family."

We stand at the door and watch them go, Pablo throwing kisses
to his mama. Lucho is a hard reminder of all the good times we're
missing. We have only to look to the soldier's rifles or the prison
gun-towers to remember that we're trapped inside a desert world,
waving goodbye.

A soldier slams the iron door shut. A visit like this gives everybody an emotional hangover. We go off to deal with it each man in
his own way. I go up to my bunk to start one of the novels Richard
gave me.

Gustavo comes out of his cell—or should I say Pelone's
cell—just as I enter the hallway. We have to pass each other. There's
no way around it. He walks with a hobbling limp—his souvenir
from Del Gado.

Most of us are walking around with some kind of Del Gado souvenir, whether it's obvious or not.

"Hola, Gustavo."

He says hello back, and we go our separate ways.

The hallway is filled with men sharing news from home or news about court, sharing candy or new magazines. Men are hustling, already trying to sell or barter the gifts they've just received.

Carlton looks up from the hearts table and announces: "Laura is a dyke."

"Doggone it," I say. "I was hoping she'd fall in love with Weaver."

"Yeah," says Stan, who's sitting at the table, too. "Then the two of them would run off together and leave us the hell alone."

"She's another sadist, I'm telling you," says Carlton. "I know what I'm saying. No compassionate human being would leave me sitting in here. I know goddamn well that they can pull me out of here anytime they goddamn please. All they have to do is threaten to cut funding and these third-world governments do whatever they're told, right or wrong."

Richard has already cracked open a book. I climb in my bunk to do the same.

Ivan walks into the cell. "I'm sure glad that guy comes to see me," he says. "He is always positive, and he knows we are not having a party here. The guy knows I have no family to send me money. He just loaned me twenty bucks out of his pocket. Pretty good, huh?"

When nobody responds, he looks around and says, "How is it with that woman for you guys?"

I lean over the side. "Don't ask right now."

"Yeah," says Richard. "Or ever."

And yet for me the feeling of missing loved ones has changed. No more waves of sadness. I welcome the mail. I welcome the little that there is to welcome.

For example, I welcome the sight of bricks and gravel and cement when it is delivered to our yard three days after the visit from

Laura Schmidt. She may not be the answer to our dreams, sexual or otherwise, but the little bull-dyke ambassador has been moved to humane action by one aspect of her visit—the sight of men crapping in the middle of the open yard.

After the bricks are delivered, we are visited by three grubby workmen. Guarded by armed soldiers, the men labor silently and quickly, finishing the job in just a couple of days. Now, thanks to Uncle Sam, we have a brick wall four feet high that will block the American embassy's view of our toilet.

One good thing leads to another. I am reading a novel the Rev brought when suddenly I hear a runner calling my name. Runners are select inmates sent from administration. Running is their job; for pay, they get the freedom to explore the prison while they deliver their messages.

Today the runner has something far more marvelous than a message—a plain brown shopping bag and a note. I open the note. It reads:

> *I am so sorry I could not get past the soldiers for visit you this day, Eduardo. I must find my birth certificate because the soldiers think I am under the age to be without my parents at the visit.*
>
> *I will come back.*
> *Mucho amor.*
> *Su amiga, Zoila*

I open the brown bag. Inside is a cellophane package containing new jockey shorts, a new cotton t-shirt, and an orange.

An orange.

We are not allowed to have fruit. We are not allowed to have anything that will ferment and make booze.

"Oh my God! Hey! Look at this!"

We pass the orange around the cell. We watch it as it travels the room. It shines like a gigantic ruby in our little cement-and-excrement-colored world. Each man smells the skin. Each of us gazes as though it's a crystal ball.

Then comes the big moment when I break the orange open. Arthur quickly puts a cup under my hands so as not to lose any of the juice.

"Look at the color," he says.

Everybody gets a piece, peel and all.

I say, "Hey. Someone go get Oso. And get Pablo. Man, after the food we got from Pablo's mom, we gotta share this with them."

Pablo knows the ways and culture of Peruvians. He examines my jockeys and t-shirt. "She cares for you like you are family," he says.

"But we've never even talked."

"Yes, of course. But she still feels for you. I would say a very strong feeling for you. It must be very difficult for her to come here on the bus alone. As mi madre would say, she is guided."

When Pablo says "guided," I think about the four a.m. silence. Did the guide send Zoila?

When I felt Diane twisting with pliers, was I just torturing myself?

In the silence, my mind is the only sound I can hear. I want to go deeper into it.

"What is the guide, Pablo? You mean she's guided by her uncle?"

He just looks at me. "Eduardo, have you been getting a lot of fruit in here?"

Everyone in the cell laughs, or else starts bitching. I say, "Most of us haven't seen fruit in many, many moons."

"Zoila is telling you that she has power. Small power, but enough to get you an orange." Pablo gladly accepts his portion. "No, my friend. It is not her uncle or her mother or her father. It is a spirit guide that she has been taught to live by. Perhaps the closest thing I can give you for an example would be what Americans call a woman's intuition. If you like, I can tell you a little bit about the tribe she comes from."

"Please!"

Carlton adds: "For god's sake, don't stop now."

Hunter from atop his bunk says, "Got my attention."

Arthur gives an opinion. "She's starting to sound a little scary. Like she should be Chivo's ol'lady."

"No, not Chivo," says Pablo. "Chivo is a warrior, a protector of his tribe. Like the mayor of a city. No. Zoila is more of the highest level of rank in the Amazones. I know her uncle. He is the one she visits. They are from la selva de Amazones. His brother, Zoila's father, is an elder of that tribe. They have developed a custom or a tradition different from the other tribes that are becoming extinct for many reasons. Zoila is here in Lima to carry on that new tradition."

Pablo sits at the card table, now talking to nearly everyone in the cell. Richard appears uninterested. He has a paperback on his chest.

Ivan looks up from where he has been lying listening with interest to Pablo and asks: "You mean Zoila is a native? Like a native in the jungle?"

"Well, not like you see on your television travel programs. Not running around with their clothes off, getting high on some kind of root, no. These people work hard. They farm and make what they need, and they hunt. Most of her family lives in small villages in the Amazon. Excuse me. I must taste this."

Pablo bites into the fruit of the orange and then stares at the wall for a moment. Then he says, "Zoila came to Lima to attend school. That is the new tradition. To send a strong spirit to the city. The tribe sends her. They pay for her living expenses, her books. When Zoila is not in classes at the college, she works. I know these people. For this girl to come to Lurigancho to visit you is a great honor for you. Her family lives on a river's edge in the jungle. They cannot go in the water except by canoe because the river in the Amazon is very dangerous. Their language is Quechua. It is what the Incas spoke. The name "Machu Picchu" is Quechua. It means man and woman. These people are very rich in spirit. They survive thousands of years in the Amazon. They are honest, and they possess great honor."

"Pablo, why would such a spirit come here to give me this orange?"

Pablo looks at me like I was a kid asking why the sky is up. "You passed the note to her. She is only visiting her uncle. What are you afraid of?"

"Not much these days. It's already happened."

"Then why are you afraid of this girl?"

Silence rockets back and forth through the cell, more potent than the smell of an orange.

"I'm more like ashamed."

"Of what?"

"Who I was."

"Oh. So you're ashamed of who you are not?"

"Hey, Pablo. You can be pretty quick, brother. Yeah, you're right I guess."

"I am. Look. When Zoila visits, just be grateful. If it is just one visit, be grateful. Remember where you are. Remember what a gift this person is to your—"

He looks around.

"Your own miserable life."

Then Kit Karson offers his opinion: "Well, it would be an honor to have her suck my dick."

Murphy is the first to say, "Oh man, Kit, you son of a bitch. This is a real pretty story. Then you open your mouth. Why do you have to be such a jerk?"

Even Weaver backs that up with: "Hear hear. I agree."

Tony leans his head out over the rail of his bunk and says to Kit Karson, "Are you that stupid?"

Carlton has been listening intently, slowly twisting the ends of his perfect moustache. "Splendid description of a wonderful people. Ignore the ignorant over there, Pablo. Thank you."

Hermes hasn't said a word until now, as if coming out of a trance. The flamboyant Puerto Rican says, with one hand on his cheek and loudly in that sing-song voice: "Oh. My. God. Is that romantic or what—I ask you. Really sweet. Anyone want to play hearts?"

The honor actually comes.

Zoila enters through the steel gate. Until now I have only seen her from the second story. My stomach has elevator drop. My breath goes short. This is the sweetest little human being I have ever seen. This is the softest, gentlest creature that God ever created.

Zoila stands inside the door just a few feet into the yard. I see her looking for me. She locks eyes with me. Carefully I approach this delicate being. At ten feet away I am close enough to see how dark but bright her eyes are, so awake and full of life. She stands, and the moment is slowed by my awe-struck brain. I sense we are not stared at. No one is stopping to gawk. There are no gringos here in this moment. We are meeting and about to touch. The moment is like painless birth. We drift into a warm experience of one another's physical appearance. Now I am close enough to smell her. Her skin has a golden glow in the desert sun. Today her hair waves gently in the breeze. It flows down her shoulders, thick curls black with auburn streaks from the sun. Her earrings are handmade of glass beads, deep red and dark green, strung with white seeds. They hang from her ears covered by thick ringlets that frame her high cheekbones and oval eyes, her thick lashes and brows and eyelids all appearing to have heavy makeup, but looking closer I can see she wears only what she was born with—her lips parted, white perfect teeth exposed, mouth forming a slight smile, moist and ready. She wears a soft cotton dress. The hem-line touches the tops of her handmade sandals. Her sandals expose the color and smoothness of her small feet. Her dress presents lavender and pink lace around the neck-line. Her waist is wrapped with a fine cotton velvet of deep maroon. Her scent is gardenia or—now that I am a foot away from her—a pleasurable, indelible groove on my brain. The scent of the trail home.

Her dress touches her hipline enough to show that she is young but that she has become a woman.

Zoila.

"Hola, Eduardo."

I can't speak.

She looks at me and raises an eyebrow. She points toward a bench in the partial shade at the east wall. "Sit? May we sit there?"

I mechanically follow the beauty of her pointing arm.

With its first words, her voice enters my being. As she reaches her hand out for mine and we actually touch, I can't keep the tears from flooding my eyes. Zoila, with her hand in mine, never doubted that this moment would be ours.

Her hair and skin, her scent. Suddenly she pushes a piece of fried chicken at me, poking me in the chest with her wrist. With a giggle she says, "Cometelo. You eat!"

Now she is talking to me as though we have been madly in love from childhood. Establishing how much Spanish I speak and how much English Zoila speaks gives us both a few laughs. She is so light. We cannot possibly have sex. There are no conjugal visits at Luri. And yet we mate.

"You cooked this food."

"Jes. Excuse me—" She works hard to make the sound—"I mean yes. I prepare this meal for you. I know the food here. My uncle he tells to my auntie everything about Lurigancho. Lurigancho is called by my people 'Casa de Diablo.'"

"House of the devil? Who is el diablo?"

"The devil lives here in the dark, hiding and waiting for the ones he owns."

"Who are they?"

"The ones who hurt and make to suffer women and children." Then, as I obey her and bite the food, she says, "He waits for

Del Gado."

"You know Del Gado? Has he hurt you?"

"No. I pray I never know Del Gado."

The yard is buzzing with women. No one is listening to us. The instant feeling of knowing Zoila has flowed like a liquid to merge with the majority of men and women in the yard. Suddenly I have a sense of family, as when I was a little kid at Grandma Pearl and Grandpa McClesky's. Before I knew that I was both white and brown on the outside, I learned the strong spirit of both family names.

"My uncle was arrested for feeding his family," she says. "The only reason his family does not starving is because his brother, he owns a bakery in Lima that does very well. This brother supplies the hotels with their breads. He takes care of my family."

She hands me a piece of chicken. "My uncle who is in this prison has cut wood for the traders in the Amazon for many years. And his father for many years. And his father before him. It is the resource of our tribe. With his profit he has put the two oldest sons to college. His wife, my auntie, she has her own house and it is pay for. But now the government says he cannot chop the wood on his land in the Amazones. It is illegal to him now. My poor uncle will stay in Lurigancho I am afraid until he dies. But he does not care about that. He only cares that his family is not starving in the street."

For over an hour I sit on the bench with Zoila, our backs leaning against the east wall. Pure in heart, she tells me what I had never imagined. I realize that I was ignorant, thinking that her people belonged in Lurigancho. But the true story of Zoila's people sounds like today's version of the destruction of the American Indians— steady, slow genocide.

Now the guard, his blue hat pulled down tight to his ear, stands in the middle of the yard and blows his whistle, both his cheeks puffing out to maximize the irritating shrill.

Zoila quickly reaches into her basket and pulls out an apple. "Eat this before I leave. I promised to the guard at the entry that I would have you eat it before I leave. It is important that you eat fruit and remain strong while you are in this place."

"Will you return?"

"Do you want me to return?"

"It is hard to ask anyone to come to such a terrible place."

"I will come once a week. I have a pass now. I come to see you, Eduardo, not this place. Eat the apple."

The whistle is herding all the visitors toward the iron door at the end of the yard, which is where we are sitting. The crowd blocks us from being seen. We stand. Zoila takes my right hand and places it on her hip. She takes my left hand, raising it up to dance position. And she begins to sing in the sweetest voice a tune in her native language. She sings while she moves closer, touching her legs to mine, her five foot six inch height a perfect fit. She is looking into my eyes. There is nothing between us. The crowd slowly drifts out the iron door, not noticing us for their own chattering and saying goodbye.

Zoila holds my face with both her hands. Softly she touches my lips with hers. Our bodies are touching fully. She says, "I will come back. Please wait for me."

"Hey, when's the wedding?" says Arthur.

Richard is true to form: "There is something seriously wrong with that chick!"

With a smile from ear to ear I ask, "Why?"

"Oh! Give me a break! This fine little chick comes into this fucking hole just to see you? What—because she *likes* you? She doesn't even *know* you!"

"She knows a lot."

"Oh fuck! Right, dude. And then when this one gets you all fucked up and twisted like the last one, you're going to go into another fucking coma on us. And you can bet she'll run off right when we need your ass to be together for that fucking military shit court trip. Yeah she knows a lot, man. Like a lot of chicks, she knows how to fuck you up."

Carlton jumps in, laughing. "Come on, man. Ed just got a visit. A visit! Out here in the middle of a god-forsaken desert thousands of miles from home. As you said, I believe—a fine little chick came to visit Ed." Then he adds: "Say, Richard, are you talking about the women that *you've* known?

"Okay, old man. You tell me. What the fuck would someone looking like that be doing coming here to see one of us?"

Ivan booms out his opinion. "Hey, R.B. You are just mad because she did not come for you."

"Bullshit, Ivan!"

"No, I am sure of it."

Richard lies down on his bunk and grabs another paperback. "Yeah, right."

Hunter, three beds high, says, "You know she's related to one of the inmates on the other side?"

"Yeah. That's how I met her."

"Her family buys a lot of puddin'," says Arthur. "They're cool."

Once a month Richard receives a letter from Robin, and every letter includes a photo of their little girl Amber. He continues to write no one.

For Richard, fun is walking up to you when you're fifty pages from the end of a book and telling you what happens. That's why whenever somebody's cooking spaghetti I like to grab a noodle, walk past Richard, sneeze, and fling it on his bare skin. Oh, R.B. can hand it out but he can't take it.

Now tonight we happen to be exchanging stories from our bunks. It feels like summer camp. No one out there is screaming or getting stabbed. No one is desperately sick. The night is hot but not unbearable.

Richard tells how him and his buddies were practical jokers at a

Boy Scout camp-out. They filled a sleeping kid's hand with shaving cream, and then they tickled his nose. The kid spread soap all over his own face while they laughed.

Later, Richard dozes off.

I whisper to Ivan, "Got any shaving cream?"

Ivan gets his cup with the soap in it and starts whipping up foam with a little brush. Kit and Stan are both at the card table writing letters. Hunter and Tony are playing chess on a homemade set that uses bottle-caps and pieces of paper for knights and pawns. Carlton is standing with his back to us, reading a book that he has placed open on the middle bunk. I break a straw from our cell broom.

Richard lies sleeping with his paperback on his chest, his hand hanging over the edge of his bunk just the way he described it back in the Boy Scouts. Arthur is in his bunk right above Richard, watching, not saying a word. I scoop out cream from the chipped cup and carefully fill Richard's unmoving palm. Now I take the straw. Ivan goes back to his bunk and hops in. Carlton and the rest of the guys know what I am doing. At this point we become conspirators.

The instant I touch the straw to his moustache, Richard swings his cream-filled hand. I dive for my bunk. Ivan is already laughing. Richard yells, "Hey, who the fuck.... It was you, Eddie. I know it was you, man!"

Arthur, lying above Richard, lets out a howl of laughter. Most of the other guys are still waiting for Richard's full reaction. He jumps out of his bunk and comes over to where Ivan and me are laughing. He's standing right in front of Murphy's bunk, and he has shaving cream wiped all over his nose, moustache, and chin. The sight of him puts the whole place in an uproar.

"Eddie," he says almost mournfully, "I never thought you would do anything like this to me."

For some reason, that comment makes Murphy laugh twice as loud. Richard turns and looks at Murphy, who's lying in a middle bunk, right at about Richard's chest. Now the sight of Richard's slobbed-up face looking right at him pushes Murphy over the edge into hysteria, and he's laughing so hard that he shuts his eyes and clutches his stomach. Murphy's head looks as though it's been served to Richard on a platter. At the same time, Murphy's doing exactly the right thing to drive Richard crazy—laughing in his face.

Richard leans down and grabs a hunk of the hair above Murphy's forehead. With his right fist—not drawing his fist back fully but just to about a foot from Murphy's face—Richard punches him two hard, quick blows to the bridge of the nose. The second punch is delivered just an instant before Murphy gets his hand up to protect himself. After the second stiff, deliberate punch, Murphy smears his own blood all over his own face. Richard stands straight and tall and proud. He looks at me for a couple seconds, and then a big grin breaks through the shaving cream.

Weaver is at Murphy with first aid, pressing with a towel at the bloody mess. "Keep your head back," he's saying. "Breathe through your mouth." The rest of the guys go on with their business.

Weaver says, "Look what you did to him. Fuck. Why so violent? And you think it's funny? Fuck. I can tell it's broken. You broke his nose. You broke his nose, Richard!"

Every man in the cell takes a turn. "You broke his nose, Richard. You broke his nose, Richard." Each man uses a taunting voice that dates back to little-asshole days in the schoolyard. Then a team of silence forms as everyone waits for the old Great White Hippie to pass judgment. And now Carlton provides his comment:

"You broke his nose, Richard."

Richard patiently waits to respond. Then he says to Weaver up close, bending to adjust to Weaver's five-foot-nine. Looking deep into Weaver's face, he says, "No. This is not violent. Violent is when I take your gun and stick it up your ass and pull the trigger. This here is only somewhat violent, mister policeman-slash-coke-smuggler."

Arthur can't pass up this opportunity to support Richard. "And a dumb smuggler, too."

Weaver blames it all on the female he brought with him to Peru. He claims that he brought her along to take the spotlight off himself. She did attract attention all right as she partied hearty around Lima—too much attention and the wrong kind.

Weaver had come up with a smuggling scam that was as ingenious as it was stupid. He opened a carton of brand-name cigarettes and took out all the individual packs. Then he carefully opened the bottom of each pack. Inside each pack he hid an ounce of coke tied up in a condom. Then he re-sealed the whole carton as if it had never been opened.

This scam was so clever that it made a hero out of the airport cop who caught him. The cop was doing a routine check of carry-ons and noticed that this carton of cigs was extraordinarily heavy.

The PIP took Weaver to their headquarters at the Pink Panther, the mansion that they had confiscated by executing the owner and his family. Weaver tried to tell them that he was an L.A. sheriff on an undercover operation. Over the telephone, the L.A. Sheriff Department admitted that Weaver was one of theirs. But they told the PIP to do whatever they wanted to Weaver, then after they were done send him back for further punishment.

So the PIP did what they wanted. They took Weaver to the upstairs bathroom, where there was an old-fashioned claw-foot bathtub. It was winter, and the PIP filled the tub with cold water. Then they played a dipping game with Weaver. They made him strip and lie on the floor on his stomach. They cuffed his hands together behind his back, and they cuffed his ankles, and then the goons ran a pole under the cuffs, lifted Weaver into the air, and carried him over to the tub.

Weaver got the full treatment, including the legendary black hood tied over his head. The PIP had a great time bringing Weaver to the brink of death, laughing as he revived himself sucking air through the hood, then starting over.

They had long since found out everything they wanted to know. They were just taking advantage of this unusual opportunity to torture another cop.

When Pablo told us about his own experience at the PIP station, he took the darkness away from himself. What I mean is that we were suspicious of him at first because he had given Oso's name to the PIP. He even told them where they could find Oso. But the idea of him snitching got a little easier for us to understand after Pablo told us his own horror story.

The PIP arrested Pablo on the street, right out of his car. They'd already picked up the man who had supplied Pablo with Oso's cocaine, and after considerable torture that man had rolled on Pablo. Then the PIP went to work on Pablo. Pablo showed us his burn marks from both electric wires and cigarettes. The PIP hung him up to the ceiling and beat him unconscious, then burned him to bring him back around and then beat him some more. One of the times Pablo regained consciousness during this ordeal, a PIP was trying to stick a bottle up his ass. After this little treatment Pablo couldn't go to Lurigancho right away. To keep him alive, the PIP had to take him to the hospital. That explains why Pablo managed to stay out of Luri for a while even though Oso was in.

Ivan gave us his own testimony about the PIP ways of gathering information. He said that the Canadian embassy people saved his life. The little PIP rats had cuffed his hands behind his back and tied him to a chair. They tied his ankles to the chair legs and lashed a rope tight around his chest and stomach. Then they beat Ivan unconscious. When he came to, the Canadian embassy rep was arguing furiously with the PIP. So they quit beating Ivan for information they already had.

By now, routine has become my life. Trick is to have a life. Have neighbors and friends. People living next door. The guards become servants, opening and closing doors for us.

This morning as usual a few of us—me, Ivan, Tony, and Rick— are at the gate, ready to do the day as soon as our servant opens our protective steel door. Ivan and me are ready with the water containers. The cells are busy with men getting up, farting, coughing, and hacking.

A man in another cell yells for the guard. Ivan, standing behind me, says, "Something is up. It is past time!"

"It's going to get real noisy around here real quick."

It goes like dominos falling. Another man yells for our servants to come open the cell. Ivan says to me, "You remember the last time the water was turned off?"

"Barely. That's when Richard and Arthur got me a water bucket because I was too gone on coke and pills."

"It got bad."

Tony looks at Oso and says, "The shitter was unbearable. You had to beat the flies away with your rubber slippers and get your business done quick."

Oso says, "Why would they turn off our water?"

Four or five guys answer in unison, "Rats!"

"Man, I'm not staying at this resort next time I come to Peru."

Three days later, still waterless, we are feeling downright grateful to Laura Schmidt and her walls. We're down to drinking water only—no boiling water for pasta or for re-boiling the sickening rice that the prison provides. Now I dread going out in the yard.

As I walk down the stairs I can smell the latrine, and above the stench I hear laughing. Inmates have gathered to watch a man hard at work inside the shit pit—Ballhead. He's wearing only a pair of old ragged pants rolled up over his knees, also his helmet cut from an old soccer ball. At last the water is back on, and our self-appointed janitor, detached as the fucking Buddha himself, is stomping the three-foot-high pile of waste with a smile on his face.

Not so long ago I thought of this man as mentally deficient. Now all I see is his courage. What I can't see is his mystery. He must have the peace of the silence within him. I feel weirdly envious—here is a man who lives free and beyond fear even in Lurigancho. I want to let something go, but I'm not sure what it is.

My greatest relief comes with Zoila. I listen to her soft voice tell me about working at the bakery and attending classes at the university. We have our usual spot now. Before the visit begins, before visitors even start entering the yard, I place a bench at the east wall. Then I spread a clean cloth over the bench. I treat her like royalty. Any small way I can show her respect or provide her with comfort, I do.

Chivo gave me the cloth, a handwoven fabric with no stains, a cloth of a softness deserving of Zoila. He bargained for it in the Big Hall. "This is for your señorita de la selva," he said. "She knows who you are, my friend. She knows before you do." Then Chivo went off laughing to himself.

Each time Zoila visits we become easier with each other. We begin by hugging and pecking a kiss. Then we evolve to caressing and holding—though very briefly because soldiers sometimes patrol the yard during visits. After several months of visits the soldiers begin to turn their heads, and we hold each other longer and less nervously.

She wants to help me. "Help me?" I say.

"Jes! I am sorry, I will get better, I mean to say yes. Yes, I will help for you. My family know many peoples."

"Zoila? Please don't misunderstand when I ask you this question. If your family knows these people and can help me, why can they not help your uncle?"

"Oh no, Eduardo. My uncle's problemas son problemas de politicas."

At each visit Zoila learns a little more of how I came to be in

Lurigancho. I tell her that a jealous rage has caused me and my two friends to be imprisoned here, the rage of a man who thought that his wife and me were having an affair.

"I understand how the man became crazy with jealousy. Men will be jealous of you because of who you are, Eduardo."

I answer with a question that sounds perhaps a little suspicious. "Zoila, do you know a man called Chivo? He lives here in Lurigancho."

She is amused: "No, Eduardo, I only know you and my uncle. And now I only wish to make the visit with you. But why do you ask me if I know a man named after a goat? Is that your friend?"

"Yes, I think you would say he is my friend. But I ask you because he has said the words you use—when you say *because of who you are*. You and Chivo see something, and I have no idea what it is."

"Oh, Eduardo, it is your spirit. You belong to the Great Spirit. You walk with the Great Spirit leading your way. When I saw you at the window, I thought at first you are one of our warrior hunters from my tribe in la selva. And with your long black hair and your little bit of face hair and your high cheeks I thought you could be from the jungle. I could see your eyes have a deep understanding of humans. I could see that from two stories. Without your shirt, even though I could only see your shoulders, I can tell you have the muscular body and color of our great warrior chiefs—the ancestors of my people before the traders and governments began taking our land of food and our rivers of fish, causing my people to become weak and small."

"You like my hair?"

Our thighs and hips touching, she reaches up with her small, long fingers. "Oh yes. I would want all my children to have this hair."

"Zoila, I must tell you that my mother is white. Total gringo. I only have this color because of my father's skin."

"We do not see that you have dark color or white color or yellow

color. We can see your spirit, Eduardo. What is important is for you
to see what we see. Do you understand?"

"I will try."

"You must live this way. You must talk this way. You must know
what I am telling you. This is how you will leave Lurigancho. You
must know the Great Spirit is with you, waiting for you to know
who you are, Eduardo. When you leave here, do you think you
would visit me and go to see my family in the Amazonas? I would
like this. But I will understand that you have been in this prison for
so many years and you want to go back to your country and see
your family."

"Zoila, it means so much to me that you would invite me. Yes, I
would like that very much also." I pause, looking into her dark eyes,
gold flakes in the deep dark brown. "Do you know the quiet time of
the morning? Before the light begins the new day?"

"Oh yes. The hunters of my people wake to hunt at three-thirty
in the morning to be ready for the animals when they begin to look
for food. The warrior hunters sit in silence waiting for the wild boar
and other animals of la selva."

I want to ask more about the silence, but I do not have the words.
I can only ask, "And you? You hunt in the silence?"

Zoila gives a laugh and says, "No, I do not hunt. But I have been
taught to light a candle and sit in the silence of the night until morning and listen as the sounds of the creatures begin, first this one
and then that one, and then the wind and sometimes the rain and
the jungle is alive. The elders teach us this practice. They say only
humans can do this, and it gives us rule over the jungle creatures."

"Now that your people have sent you to school, to the University de Peru, do you still do this practice—still light a candle and sit
like that when it is so early?"

"Oh yes. At the university my first class is at seven a.m., and
I help with my uncle at the bakery before I must take the buses to
the university. So to carry on my people's simple custom is not difficult because I must be up and begin helping at four-thirty every

morning."

"Zoila do your people marry, like in Lima or the United States?"

"Oh yes, of course. But it is different. If you would come to the Amazon and suppose you would marry me, well, I would want you to marry also my sister. Because this is our custom. Because there is a need for men and more babies. My people have been robbed of our land. Perhaps we will die forever if we do not educate our people. Bring them into modern life and out of la selva that is no longer able to provide the food we need. To fight the traders and the governments will only lead faster to extinction. American drug war soldiers are killing our people. They burn our villages because we could be making the cocaine even though we are not. And the soldiers show the burned people and the burned village to the DEA and to the American officials and tell them, 'Look, we have burned out another cocaine-making village.' And so your American government gives millions to these men like Del Gado. I am sorry Eduardo, but I tell the truth."

Each time she leaves, the feeling of love is stronger and the feeling of loss is more intense. I have never experienced a relationship like this. When I think of her voice, her hair, her feet, I feel a comfort as though she were right with me. That cold lonely feeling has not overcome me, not since the day I first saw her visiting her uncle.

When I return to the cell, Gustavo has news from his mother. She says that we'll be going to tribunal very soon. "My mother is sure you will go home after tribunal."

"Why, Gus? What makes her sure?"

"She is sure because if you do not go free, it looks very bad for me."

"You think that? But why?"

"You must know about your DEA. If my government does not do what your DEA wants, your government will cut off the drug-war funding. You must know that is millions of American dollars for the rich people of Peru, for the politicos."

"Yeah and so?"

"If you are not put into prison with me, no one from your government will care if I am in Lurigancho or home eating fried chicken with my mother. You must go. You understand?"

"Perfectly. Believe me, I want your mother to be right."

Rick's release date is tomorrow. Eight years down the toilet and gone. For twenty thousand dollars he got to stay high the whole time.

It is real important to everyone in this cell that each man gets out when he is supposed to. We all take it real personal.

Rick is at his bunk. It is still morning. He has his head down, sorting through all the stuff and letters he has rat-packed over the years. His long curly rock-star hair is hanging around his head. Then he looks up to Tony above me and says, "You're the only one who wants to learn to play bad enough to practice. I am bequeathing you my guitar."

Tony steps down to my bunk frame and then to the floor where Rick is holding the guitar in his two hands. "Wow man," says Tony. "This is the first gift I ever got in here. Thanks, Rick. Maybe next time we meet we'll sit down and play some tunes together."

"Hey, if you get to San Francisco, look me up," says Rick. "My dad's in the book. And there's a club in the city called the Great American Music Hall. I'll be there a lot. Lots of pretty ladies."

Oso says, "Hey, watch out. That's where I met my ol' lady." Then he adds, "Maybe I'll see you there, too."

Tony reaches up and places the gift guitar on his bunk above me and then he turns and reaches his arms out toward Rick saying: "Rick, good luck, man. If it gets too heavy out there, remember— you can come back any time, buddy. But really, brother, it's been good to know you."

Ivan looks out of his bunk and says, "Be sure to say hello to that poor little blind daughter of yours."

Rick and the rest of us laugh with Ivan. Rick reaches into the pile of stuff on his bunk and pulls out a small mirror. "Ivan, I know how you like to keep a look-out for Carlton while he's smoking on his Ovaltine can. So here's my little mirror you can see down the hall with."

Carlton is the first to give something to Rick—an envelope. "Here, Rick. In here is my phone number and address. If you can't memorize it, then remember that my brother has the same last name and I don't think he'll be moving from Newport Beach in this life-time. So look me up in a few years. I'll be around." They give a hug.

Now that I have decided to live life awake, Kit is the number-one pill freak in the cell. Rick looks over his bunk down to where Kit is reading on his bottom bunk. "Kit, I know you want these. You must not be an addict because an addict would have stolen them by now. Here." Rick throws a folded-up piece of paper with pills inside. It lands on Kit's chest.

"Hey thanks, man."

Rick looks at my wall and sees that I have replaced Farrah and Jaclyn with photos of the Amazon jungle. "Wow, I didn't see that you changed your wall, Eddie. If you want, man, I have some great lady pics here."

I'm lying on my right side watching the sentimental proceedings. "No thanks, Rick. I got a different trip going, man, but thanks."

"That little Amazon chick has really got your head, huh?"

From across the cell Arthur says, "Hey, she got to his head not mine. I'll take the girly pictures."

"You got 'em, Arthur. Hey Murphy, look. Here's a flannel shirt I had under my mattress so long I forgot about it. You want a second flannel to wear?"

Murphy has been watching with a serious face. "Sure, Rick. That's real nice of you." Murphy gets up off his bunk to try on the shirt. It fits.

Rick says to Weaver, below Murphy, "Hey, Weaver, here's my stash of Kaopectate. Eddie says you need it more than the rest of us."

Without a word Weaver puts down his writing tablet, sits up, takes the plastic bottle, and places it on the shared windowsill.

Before Rick can give Stan something from the pile of souvenirs, Stan lazily says, "Don't bother. I know I'll see you later back home."

Rick looks over to where we keep our water buckets and do most of our cooking. Turning toward Carlton and trying to include everyone, he says,

"You can have my water buckets, too. That way, you guys will always have an emergency twenty gallons."

Arthur has been writing something. "I live down south, Rick, around Laguna Beach. So here's my mom's number." Rick steps over to Arthur, where he is in his bunk above Richard. Richard gently bumps Rick's knee. Looking up, he says, "You're a really good dude, man. You'll be all right out there. Take it easy. We'll run acrossed each other some day and laugh about this." Richard leans onto his left side and reaches out to shake Rick's hand.

Hunter, above Richard and Arthur, reaches down from his bunk and shakes Rick's hand. "You have been thoroughly entertaining, Rick. Great to know you, man. Maybe someday you'll make it to the Big Island."

"That would be cool. Hawaii must be the farthest from Lurigancho that it gets, huh?"

He waits in the cell joking with us. Around noon he takes a couple laps in the yard. Dinner goes by, and so does the day.

No one mentions the fact that the runner hasn't come—no one except Richard, who tells Rick, "Man, you ought to start a letter about that lawyer. Get your money back and send it to someone who gives a shit."

Now Rick gives up standing at the cell door. He borrows his guitar back from Tony and starts strumming a tune. And that's when, finally, the runner comes. The toothless Peruvian waits until he is right at our door before he yells as though he's shouting for someone a mile away: "REEECK LOOKLACE!"

Rick jumps out of his bunk. "Yeah, that's me. Come here, give me a little kiss."

The runner says as he turns away, "Goodbye, gringo. You come back to Lurigancho, I give you kisses, yes?"

Every man in the cell gives a cheer, and Kit Karson gives a cowboy-on-the-range "Yahooo!" Richard gets out of his bunk, and now he's hugging Rick and saying that he knew everything would work out, and they both laugh together.

Rick leaves the next morning. No one wants to walk Rick out and down the hall. We say our final goodbyes inside the cell.

As soon as he's gone, everyone returns to the routine. If you linger in the letting-go, your gut will put you in a tailspin.

Tony and Hunter are next in line to leave. But they don't say so. They don't even think so. Both are masters of "freedom in prison," too disciplined to comment on the future. But good old redneck Kit has no such reservations. "Man alive!" he shouts. "You two are next to leave this fucking shit-hole!"

Arthur corrects him. "Hey, watch your mouth! This is where I live."

Our cell now has an empty bunk. But we all know that another occupant will show. The PIP are out there right now, working with the DEA even as we speak, gathering people for the beast.

In fact, the PIP enjoy their sadism so much that they have created a big problem for everybody else—overcrowding. For the legitimate soldiers of Peru overcrowding means more of this rotten jail work. For the judges at the Justice Palace overcrowding means longer days in the courtroom. For the clerks at every level overcrowding means an impossible pile of paperwork. But for Tony, who regards himself as the elder of our cell, overcrowding is a personal violation.

Suddenly a guard appears at our cell door. He's unlocking it. Three Peruvians are standing behind him. They look like the same poor bastards that the PIP keep locked up at the Pink Panther—use them as slaves whenever they want some cleaning done or cars washed. Or stick them in the gringos' cell now and then, make the Americans squeal.

Prison slaves. Thieves and snitches. Their crimes are petty. The PIP scoop them up and pack the prison with them. That way, Peruvian officials have a reason to ask for more subsidy from the USA. And that way, Peruvian officials can pocket the money and share the benefits with the PIP. Now three of them are coming to live with us.

Tony leaps down from his bunk and blocks the cell door. "No mas! No mas!" he's shouting. "Afuera!" He crowds the door, towering over the guard and the new inmates. Trouble is, he's stark naked. His fury is so intense that he forgets the taboo against public wagging of one's member. (In Lurigancho murder is entertainment but nudity is unforgivable.) "Nosotros no hemos animales," he shouts. "Muy mucho hombres aqui ahora. No mas."

Ivan says, "Tony, give them a break. What can they hurt?"

"They steal our shit. They fucking stink, too. What do you mean give them a break?"

"Of course they stink. They were locked up at the PIP house. Fuck, let them in."

The guard, angry, shoves Tony back from the door and pushes the three Peruvians into the cell. Then he locks us down.

Disgusted, Tony climbs back into his bunk without another word.

Carlton is at the hearts table writing his congressman. Being the most fluent in Spanish, he gently explains to the new cellmates that if they want to stay, they must bathe right away in the morning. He offers them soap and points out the extra water they can use.

Next morning, four a.m., I sit next to the cell door to do my meditation. One of the Peruvians is lying on Rick's old bunk, on top of an old army blanket that he brought with him from the PIP. He has the eyes of a cornered cat, dilated, looking for a way out. I whisper to the man, "Es mi tiempo de la paz"—my time of peace. "No piensan tanto mis amigos." You shouldn't think so much. Thinking can make you "muy loco."

After the morning count, the three Peruvians go out into the hallway and start making friends with some of their countrymen. Later, walking past the shower room, I can see them having a good time splashing water and getting off the grime. One of them—the one I spoke to in the dark this morning—sees me in the hall and yells: "We no can take bath at PIP casa. The PIP they treat us very bad. They treat dogs more good. The PIP mans, they very bad mans."

I tell them, "Mucho gusto, mi amigos. Enjoy getting clean." Keep smiling. *Because the water may be shut off tomorrow.*

Then I'm out in the yard doing my one-hour morning walk when Chivo approaches. He's speaking softly and shifting his glance around the enclosure. "Oye, Eduardo. Todo los gringos van por Pabellon Once! Y tu tambien, 'mano!" All the gringos have gone to the Hole—aka Pabellon Once. Block Eleven. Now the guards are looking for me. "Eduardo Padilla! Eduardo Padilla!"

No questions asked, I follow Chivo into the cellblock, quickly moving past the guard's office undetected and down into the first floor hall, Chivo holding my elbow, pushing me along, both of us looking back over our shoulders. Chivo says, "You no go with los gringos. Many no come back from where they go, or become sick and die. Come, you hide with my friends."

Your friends? In the fucking Big Hall?

Chivo puts his index finger to his lips. No, he does not pound on the steel door to the Big Hall. Silent, he guides me into the depths of our own cellblock, down to the far end of the hall. This cell is so dif-

ferent from any in Lurigancho that the first glance makes me imagine we have somehow escaped. These guys have real chairs and a
real store-bought table. There are fucking curtains on the windows.
There's room to walk around and stretch. Toward the back I can see
a stockpile of food—a gunny sack of rice, another of beans, stacks of
canned goods, and a couple dead chickens plucked clean hanging
from the end of a bunk by their skinny necks ready to cook. Over in
the cook area, these guys have four stoves and they're hard at work
whipping up a savory lunch. One of them has a pasta sauce going
with fresh tomatoes and real onions and celery and garlic. The cell
is alive, like a house full of family—only in this case the family consists entirely of brothers.

Chivo enters the cell as though he lives here. I've heard about this
cell—long-term prisoners with political connections. Their guards
are paid many more times normal pay. At the special visits they
have their own section of the yard. They wear expensive jewelry.
Zoila tells me that she never has to stand in line for the special visits
because these women take kindly to her and walk her to the front of
the line. Now I'm starting to see the connections.

The cell residents surround us and joke in Spanish with Chivo.
They appear to be pre-warned that I was coming. This is not the
Chivo we see upstairs; this is not the man we treat like a goat. Upstairs, he bows to the gringos—what do you need, food? Coffee? A
razor blade? Once he even scored some reading glasses for Carlton. It's Chivo's little franchise, the gringo cell, and no one else goes
near it. To run his franchise, he plays a role—cringing, meek, crafty.
Suddenly I see what a scam it is. He must be laughing to himself
the whole time. Because as soon as he comes back down here, he is
himself, an equal—no, a man above men, a warrior.

Chivo directs his attention to a wrinkled old man who's lying in
a middle bunk. The old man nods to Chivo and pulls himself out of
the bunk. Once he's standing, he motions with his hand for me to
get in. Then he pats the mattress. I climb into the bunk, and the old
man reaches down and produces a newspaper from the empty bunk

below. "You read," he says. He holds the newspaper up so that it covers his face, and then he hands it to me.

Far out!

Chivo stands in back of the old man, observing, until I am in the bunk with the newspaper in hand. There's a card game at the far end of the cell. The card-players have real chips, plastic chips in red, white, and blue. Nearby, men are playing chess with genuine plastic chess pieces. A man leaves the card game and walks over to me. He's wearing flannel pajamas and a floor-length bathrobe. "I am Clower," he says. "I remember seeing you when they brought you to the PIP. Chivo he says you are his friend. You may relax here. The young girl who comes here to see you—?"

"Yes. Thank you for making it easy at the gate."

"If she would like, my wife can pick her up and bring her. You tell her we will be happy to help. She is from a very strong family."

"Thanks, Clower. Thank you very much. I will ask her. But, like you say, very strong and independent, I think."

"Well, I admire her tradition. Tribal tradition. Saving their kind by sending the smartest child to school, and all of them work to pay for the school. I only hope the young girl is as intelligent as she is beautiful."

"You guys have a lot of comfort down here."

"Yes. But the soldiers come every few months and take it all away, and then we buy it back from them. It is a small game we play in order to have some things during the time we must live here to show your American government that La Cosa Nostra de Peru is in prison. Excuse me. I must finish our card game. You stay. But remember—when it is time to count, you must be back in your cell or they will say you are *escapado*."

That fucking guard calls my name all day. Twice he comes into this cell and I cover my face with the newspaper. In fact, when the

guard comes in, he's not even looking for me. He's just stopping
by to say hello to these guys and to make sure they're okay. Then as
soon as he walks back out into the hall he starts yelling: "EDUARDO
PADILLA!" over and over. Finally in mid-afternoon he gives up.

At the end of the day I slip back to my own cell for the count and
lock-up. The place is empty except for Ivan, who's lying on a bunk.
But not his own bunk—Carlton's. He's using Carlton's nice mattress and Carlton's real pillow. He's reading Richard's new book,
the one that the Reverend bought brand-new for him. In fact, this
is the first un-read book that Richard has owned since we came
to Lurigancho, and now Ivan is enjoying it—along with one of the
many notebooks that Weaver normally hides under his mattress.
Weaver is always writing in those fucking notebooks—a cop in our cell,
writing secrets! Ivan looks at me as I walk in. He says, "I got that
fucking cop's books. I'm reading them. There is nothing about us.
It is all letters to people in government and to his sister. And some
stuff about a case in New York with the syndicate."

"What syndicate?"

"Must be the fucking Mafia. It's a letter to the attorney-general
of New York."

"Heavy shit. Where the fuck is everybody? You look pretty
comfy."

"That fucking Tony and his flapping dick. He got everybody
thrown in the hole for embarrassing that guard last night."

Now Ivan rummages through Kit's stuff. "Look at all the fucking pills this motherfucker has stashed! Look," he says, "I found his
glue tube."

The sound of men gathering and walking in the hall grows to
its fullest. Now the guard blows the nightly whistle—lock-down.
Arthur always says that he wants one of those whistles so he can
give it to his next ol' lady. The large keys on the big brass ring jingle
as the guard locks each door for the night. The jingling comes
toward us down the hall.

"How did you keep from going to the Hole?"

He says, "I was in the washroom washing all my clothes with my towel wrapped around me. One of the guards told me to stay and watch the cell. He told me that all the gringos were going to talk with the warden."

"Is that what they all thought? That they were going to see the warden?"

"I don't know what they thought. I was just a naked Canadian. All I knew when I got back to the cell is that the Americans were gone." He makes a gesture with his hands. "Gone."

"What did you think?"

"You mean when I saw that?" Ivan smiles, then he extends his open hands to encompass the entire cell. "Fucking A," he says.

Now the new resident Peruvians are standing at the door of the cell. One of them speaks a little English. "Excuse please. Por favor? May me, my cousins, we come in? Jes?"

"Yes, of course."

Ivan and me laugh. Tony's in the hole and these humbled guys are here.

Later the guard asks me where I have been all day. I tell him that I was visiting friends below and writing my mother a letter. The guard says, "Deja ver." Let me see. So I show him a letter I wrote to my mom a few days ago. He takes the letter and pretends to read it. Then he says, "Joo berry lucky, gringo."

Then he locks us in. We're safe from the Hole.

The next day everyone is brought back. Not talking, they enter the luxury of our pad. No one even looks at Tony.

Richard walks in behind everyone else and says, "I will never do *anything* to get put in the Hole!"

I say, "Yeah, right. You mean you're never going to get *caught* doing anything."

Ivan and me have already put everything in the cell back the way it was. Now Ivan is standing with his back against the steel frame of the bunk bed. "Well, come on," he says. "How bad was it?"

Arthur gets into his bunk and says, "It's dark in there. The only light is cloudy, dark gray. The stench is so bad we all tied our shirts or whatever around our mouth and nose to keep from puking."

Everyone is going right to the bunks. Suddenly I notice that they're all barefoot. "Hey, why you guys so tired? And where are your shoes?"

Carlton is supine already. "I haven't had to sleep standing up since I pulled midnight guard duty in the Marine Corps. None of us has laid down or sat down since they threw us in Once."

Oso says, "We've been standing in shit to our ankles this whole time. I think I can handle your pork and beans now, Eddie."

Weaver says, "I wore my dress boots. They're ruined."

Kit Karson stretches out in his bunk and says, "Hell, a good pair of boots ain't really broke in until they got shit on 'em."

"Not human shit, you idiot."

"Hey, I ain't the idiot what got us in the stinkin' Hole."

From above me Tony says, "Hey, how many times you guys want me to say I'm sorry? My shoes are ruined, too."

Over in the far corner Richard shouts, "Hey, which one of you two got into this book?"

"Eddie did."

"Ivan did."

Hunter reports: "The Hole looks older than the rest of the prison, as though it was here first and the rest of the prison was built around it."

Murphy says, "Man, it's like a movie in there, man. Folks back home think that things in Alaska grow big. But they would not believe the size of them rats we had to feed in there."

"Oh come on," says Ivan. "Bigger than the ones running around this cellblock?"

Oso says, "They was big, Ivan. And mangy-looking, like if one bit you you'd die from rabies or something terrible. So we took turns feeding the damn things to keep them from getting interested in how *we* taste."

"We heard men screaming all night, man," says Murphy. "Screaming like you never heard."

Tony can't stay out of the conversation. "At first I thought they were doing some welding," he says. "But every time we would hear the arcing sound of the electricity, it would be in sync with a man screaming and then crying. Then it would stop and start again. I think they were torturing more than one guy. And I think they killed whoever it was because the screaming and the crying stopped for good."

"And you guys all thought you were going to see the warden?"

"Oh yeah," Arthur says. "That was a set-up. They were ready, boy, you shoulda seen it! The blue guard comes to tell us we're going to see the warden. So we get all dressed up. Chivo is with the guard, and he tells us he'll go get you because you're out in the yard. The blue guard tells us all to follow him. That's when we see Ivan naked except a towel, and the guard tells him to stay here. We think we're going to go over to the east wall and out to administration. Instead the guard opens the door to the Big Hall and in we go. About ten armed soldiers are waiting for us in the Big Hall, and they fucking march us right to this fucking ancient dungeon. Thanks, Tony."

At the iron door of the east wall I wait for her. A blue guard gets his roster ready. Then the door swings open partway and a soldier appears, waving his baton and bawling in Spanish: "Away from the door! Move to the side!" I'm standing with about fifty other men. The soldier swings nearer now. As we all step backwards, I can see Zoila ahead of the other women. She is almost running—it looks as though she's skipping or springing ahead of the others. Her thick hair blows back out of her face, fully exposing her smile as she sees me. Today she is wearing a cotton dress the color of emeralds, its hemline touching the top of her thin leather sandals. She has tied her waist with an earth-colored sash. I can vaguely detect her small breasts as the breeze pushes the soft cloth against her body.

This incredible female.

The soldier knows my face and he knows that my only visitor is Zoila. Today he surprises me by motioning with his head a couple of times. Go on out, he's saying. I step outside the door to greet Zoila with a total embrace. We wrap our arms tightly but gently around one another as the other visitors rush past us. We stand touching from our knees up to our lips. I have an erection. Zoila tips her head back, looking into my eyes, and relaxes her pelvis. "You are very happy to see me, I think." We laugh about the obvious. We turn toward the iron door and plunge slowly into the rush of people waving their identification, chattering, women yelling to their men, conversations bottlenecking at the door, runners inside the yard yelling names of visitor and visited, and away in the background Arthur calling, "Get your leche asada. Leche asada. Muy sabrosa y muy fresca."

I stand with Zoila as she produces her documents from a tiny handwoven bag of threads that match perfectly her dress and sash. Pablo's mother and his brother Lucho get waved through by a blue guard who knows them. As he passes, Lucho says, "Good to see you again, Eduardo. You remember my mother, yes?"

I say, "Hola, Señora Herzog. Of course I remember you both. Very good to see you. This is Zoila."

Lucho says, "Yes, we met Zoila outside."

"Yes, yes, good to see you. And Zoila."

We turn to find our spot. Pablo and Oso are standing nearby. Pablo and Zoila exchange a few sentences in Spanish. Then they speak in Zoila's tongue.

As we sit, I ask Zoila, "What were you and Pablo saying in your language? It sounds so different from Spanish."

"No similarity, none, between the two. I am not Spanish. I am not Peru. The books call us Inca. Pablo knows a few sentences. The regular. How are you? What is your name? Like this. Not much really."

"Can you teach me this language, your language?"

A runner interrupts us. He's carrying a basket. He says, "Perdoname, Señorita, sus cosas."

Zoila carries the basket to our bench and places it in her lap. She takes a few coins from her small colorful bag and pays the runner. He thanks her profusely and disappears into the crowd.

She explains, "He carries the things for Señora Clower, and he offered to carry my basket. That way I can walk much faster to see you and be with you longer. The visit is so short."

"Thank you for that, Zoila. My time with you is very precious." I hold her rich, thick hair back from her cheek and kiss her with the gentleness she radiates. She turns toward the basket. "I have good news for you. You go to tribunal next week."

The news makes my stomach drop.

"Here," says Zoila. "Eat. I make this bread this morning. You break open the little bread and put this cheese and this chicken on it, and then—" she opens a small jar "—you pour this on top and put the bread together and you have the American sandwich, yes? I like this American sandwich."

"I haven't had a sandwich in years. Thank you."

She hands me my sandwich and begins making her own.

"Zoila, do you want to live in America?"

"Oh, no."

She places a beautiful leaf of lettuce on her own bread. "I think we will be most happy to live in the Andes mountains above the Amazonas, overlooking our people's land from our home."

"That is what you want?

"Yes. To be happy with you."

This woman can seem so fragile. And yet she'll graduate from medical school next term.

"Soon you will choose, Eduardo, because the judges will let you go free. When you are free, you can tell to me if you will stay with me in my land and have many children or you will return to the United States."

"You want children with me?"

"Yes, and with my sister."

"Whoa! You're serious."

"Yes. She has no husband, and we need strong man to have strong babies. I know who you are. I can see your spirit. How do you feel when I speak this way? I know your cultura, your culture, and I cannot change your culture, but you must know how you feel. We are in a small time, Eduardo. That is why I say these things. I do not wish to regret someday that I failed to say what is in my heart."

"Yes, I want to go with you. I want to know you and your people. But now my worry is great because of the court. I am wondering will they believe a man could be so jealous of me that he would put thousands of dollars in cocaine in my bungalow."

Zoila looks at me with admiration and reaches up her soft hand to the back of my neck, spreading her fingers out and running them through my hair. By now my unbarbered hair reaches past my shoulders. "Eduardo, they will believe you. The women love you as soon as they see you. You are the most beautiful man I have ever seen. Your spirit is what makes you attractive to men and women."

She pushes on my hand that holds the food and motions me to eat.

The only way to prepare for trial is to study the transcripts from lower court, study them over and over.

Zoila believes the story—that Tom Dawson went into a jealous rage over his girlfriend and me. She finds it credible that a man would deliberately blow his own scam in order to take revenge on my charisma. The court will hear testimony that should put the blame on Dawson. But it is important that they believe the passion—that his woman could betray him for me, just like that, in a chance meeting at a foreign resort. But I am betting my life on the plot of a soap opera.

If things look real bad at court, the main thing I'll have to pull off is getting handcuffed alone. If I can do that, I can make a run for it in the confusion of stuffing and beating us onto the bus. I am far from suicidal. I want to live. But not in Lurigancho. Not without a fight. And the bus ride to and from the court is my only chance.

I am not saying a word to Arthur or Richard. I feel bad they are here with me. I couldn't handle it if they got killed trying to run with me. Besides that, they would talk me out of it.

The sounds of Lurigancho have changed. The all-day drumming on steel barrels has become a primordial rhythm born in the Amazon jungle. My fear of any man in the prison has fallen away. I am respected, perhaps even loved, by many of the prisoners. My hair is long but I keep it clean. The sparse hair on my face is longer than it has ever been.

I'm on the prisoners' boxing team. I box anyone in my weight class and sometimes bigger. Sometimes I win, sometimes not. Important thing is not get hurt so bad you need a doctor. One of the other inmates was a pro boxer in Lima. He helps me figure out that it takes sixty laps around the yard to equal a mile. As I train to box, I train for an escape run from the Justice Palace.

But I still don't live as free as the inmates of the Big Hall.

As I am skipping rope out in the yard, I drop the rope, go inside to the guard quarters, and tell the guard on duty sitting at the old wooden desk: "Let me out. Abre la puerta, por favor."

The guard in blue has no problem letting me out. In fact, he has a big smile on his face. He turns the huge key in the ancient lock and pulls hard on the rusted iron door. Still sweating from my jump-rope exercise, wearing a t-shirt with old ragged sweat pants and rubber flip-flops, I walk through the iron door that has protected me for years from the fear out in the Big Hall. The guard slams the door especially hard. The crash echoes into the blackest darkness, drawing the attention of every man in the Big Hall. My umbilical cord has just been cut. I'm dropping in.

With the iron door locked at my back, I wait.

To my left is the darkness at the south end of the Big Hall. In our building they talk about this darkness as the place where the most feared and evil hang out, waiting for someone to enter and be devoured. Zoila would say, "That is the devil's throne."

To my right the Big Hall seems to go on for a mile. The scene is entirely different from the one we get when we're in a bunch and surrounded by armed soldiers, when the inmates are all backed away and watching our parade. Now I'm seeing normal life in full frenzy, crowded, whirling, men running, walking, shouting. The drumming of Lurigancho is loudest here, men move in pace with it like freakish puppets. There's a fire burning in a metal drum at the far north end. Smoke pervades the cavernous room, smog for the city. Put a heavy-metal band out here, that would be perfect—except they'd shit their pants. Suddenly I get a rush. Being out here looks like hell, but it feels like freedom.

As soon as the echo of the slamming door fades, so does anyone's interest in me. Men walk past me curious but unconcerned. Out here there are no Germans, no Americans, no Peruvians. Out here, if you're anything more than merely human, if you've got something to hide or to protect even if it's just your fear or your prejudice or your false pride, someone will shank you just to get at it. You can die just because a Big Hall native looks in your eye and sees an illusion that needs to be smashed.

Across the wide hall a man lies dead. Other men are trying to lift the body and move it somewhere. I walk north through a maze of men. It's like Christmas at the mall, only there's no Santa Claus this year. At least the floor is dry. I walk past the other cellblocks and notice something strange. Many are wide open. Men are streaming steadily in and out. Our own cellblock is conspicuously locked to protect us from the truth.

A toothless man with nothing on his feet but open sores, his pants and shirt just rags held together by filth, stops in front of me and points as though he's made a strange discovery, and he yells, "Hey, el gringo esta aqui!" I look around quickly, but I can see that no one cares.

In the crowd I spot a familiar guard, one who works in my cellblock. It's been a short trip, but enough for now. The guard is walking toward our door. He doesn't notice me following him. When he gets to our cellblock, I step up alongside and say, "How are you, Jefe?"

The guard looks around, eyes wide. When he sees I am alone, he just looks at me with a straight face and then bursts out laughing. "Joo gringo loco!" he says. He looks down the hall then back at me. "Jes," he says. "Joo gringo loco." Laughing he pounds on the iron door and it opens.

Chivo finds me in the yard.

"My friend, you go out to el otro mundo?"

"The other world? Yes, it is another world out there, huh Chivo? That is your world, huh?"

Chivo is smiling and curious. "Why you want go? Here you are seguro, safe with the other gringos."

"Something to do with Zoila, Chivo. It is her freedom. She is beyond fear. And I don't know yet, Chivo."

I'm in a flow of words, more than he can understand but I don't care, some things must be said. "I want to feel what she sees in me.

I want to know what both of you are asking me. 'Do you know who you are yet?' Something has changed in me. And those drums, out there, out there in your *other world*, those drums. At first I thought my heart speeded up. Then I listened. The rhythm changed to fit the beat of my true spirit. Is it love, Chivo? That's what I'm wondering. See, that word doesn't fit anymore. The feeling for Zoila is, is…."

Chivo is shaking his head. He reaches out and taps my forehead with the palm of his hand. He says, "Tu piensas demasiado por seguro como. Ya eres Gringo Loco, my brother. You have lost your mind. You have lost the gringo mind. Now maybe you can use your brain. You must use your brain if you want to leave Lurigancho, my brother. You have become who you are. Now you must leave. I will be here in Lurigancho for all my life. That is why out there is my world. Zoila is in your new world. What you feel for Zoila is the feeling you are looking for. What you see in Zoila is what we see in you."

I look at him, amazed.

"Come," he says. "We go out in my world. Come with me. You see more better with me, come."

Chivo insists I carry a six-inch shank. I slide the shank into my waistband with my shirt over its taped-wood handle, the cool steel against my lower stomach. Chivo makes me stuff folded-up newspapers against my back, underneath my shirt, and in my pants. He will not let me walk again in the Big Hall unless I take these precautions.

With Chivo as my navigator, the Big Hall starts to come clear and reveal its order. The first time you ever paddle out into big Hawaiian surf, you need guidance, someone to point out the rocks and the reef. Chivo helps me see that the men in the hall are in discrete groups. Some are derelicts; some are bums. But others possess the features of Zoila and her family. Some are dressed in clean pants, nice shirts, decent shoes, and they live here without harassment, no one begging from them the way they do with us gringos when we're escorted through.

Walking the Big Hall with Chivo, I can see now right past his act. I can see who he is. It's the same illusion-breaking that I experienced watching him in the Mafioso cell. But out here the truth is a full revelation. I can see it reflected in the eyes around us—Chivo is a significant leader.

Out of the hundreds of men and the loud echoing, the thundering rhythms, the yelling of soldiers and the whistles blowing, suddenly emerges the man everyone calls Brujo. The Witch. Once a month or perhaps less frequently Brujo will appear on our cellblock with goods to peddle, maybe a can opener or a spoon or a pair of glasses that everyone will try on curious to find out whose eyes they'll fit. Now Brujo sees me in his world, standing with Chivo, and he laughs. "Oh, gringo, joo out here, jes? Sure, gringo, better for joo out here. Joo can walk very far—" he points to the north end "—down to there. And many peoples talking, want learn speak English, need practice joo." He pounds his chest and gives me a big smile. "Like me, I practice joo."

I see the guy who comes into our cellblock every morning to sell the newspaper. "Hey amigo," he calls, "joo come out. That's okay." I thought we were the only ones who got the newspaper. Now I am watching the real world of the prison open up to me. Where have I been?

My connection to Zoila, that's what has done it. She has changed my mind about the prison, and she has also changed the way the prison regards me. Even the guards—I don't mean the soldiers with the guns but the everyday goons on the inside—treat me different now that Zoila is my regular family visit.

If I can convince people in the Big Hall that I am not a gringo cocaine smuggler, then maybe I can change the mind of the tribunal. After all, it was Rubio at the PIP who said, "We must give the judge a reason to let you go." Zoila says her sister and brothers, her mom

---

and dad, will all be in the courtroom with her. Their presence might influence the judges' perception. Now I am balancing two choices. One choice is to run like a rabbit and likely get killed. That's my worst fear, to be shot dead like a rat. The other is to go to tribunal as planned—as planned years ago—and take the chance that I can walk out of this nightmare.

I like living in the Big Hall. Out here, bartering for cigs and candy and food, the day goes by incredibly fast. Sometimes I can even find fresh vegies in the Big Hall, a wilted, rubbery carrot or some dried out cilantro. Most of all I find a new freedom.

Back in the cell, after we're locked down for the night, Ivan announces that he's bored to death. "Hearts, gin rummy, even fucking chess! I am bored with everything!"

I lean over the side of my bunk. "Yo. Hey, you know that thing Kit has, with all the wires on the stick?"

"Yeah. That thing he made for blowing up the prison."

"No, he said it would blow the lights. Let's find out if it works. Hey, Kit. You have that ball of wire?"

"Y'all not s'posed to say anything about that tool."

"Oh, come on. Let's plug it in."

Everyone else joins in. We get Kit to go into his hiding place and break out The Tool.

Kit claims that he was an electrician before he was highway patrol. Over the months he keeps picking up wire wherever he can find it. He's got all that wire wrapped in a clotted tangle at the end of a stick. Once he scavenged a burnt-out iron from a Peruvian inmate who operated a Lurigancho laundry business. Now he's got the plug from the iron installed on the other end of the stick. With this he figures he can wreak havoc on Lurigancho's electrical system.

"Y'all sure y'all want to waste this tool on nothin'?"

Oso says, "What do you think this is—some kind of Hollywood

shit? You, Kit, are never going to use that thing to escape. Just blowing the lights out ain't going to open any doors, my man. Give it up."

I jump down off my bunk. "Hey wait. I have something to add to the show." From my small stash, I tear off a three-foot length of real toilet paper.

Ivan whistles. "That's precious stuff, man."

"Arthur, come here."

I explain my plan and take Arthur back into the cook area, where he strips naked. Over here he can't be seen from across the hall.

Then I go to the cell door and call out. "René ! René ! Venga por la puerta, por favor."

René appears at his cell door.

"Jes?" he says in his sweet, singsong voice.

"René , we have a surprise for you. Por su gusto."

"Oh, for me!"

I nod to Kit, and he plugs in the thing. There's an electrical flash like a bomb going off. Then instantly the entire prison goes black. We are swallowed by total blindness. Then I light a match, and the fire flames up the blackness. And I touch the flame to one end of the precious toilet paper strip. And now people can see that the other end of the toilet paper strip is stuck between Arthur's butt cheeks. Arthur walks slowly in front of the cell door totally exposed and lit up with a spotlight. He throws René a wave as he struts back and forth until finally I have to douse water on the flame.

Out of the darkness we all hear René cry out with a sugary shriek: "OH! For meeee?"

Every man in the cell laughs that gut-hurt laugh until we all have tears in our eyes. When the lights come on again a few minutes later, we are still laughing our asses off. Ivan is rocking with his knees drawn up, holding his stomach, laughing with tears running down the side of his face.

Not bored.

"You are beginning to look like the Indians out in the Big Hall," Hunter tells me.

In other words, I look like a hippie. This may be a problem for the tribunal judges.

"You're right."

"I can cut it."

"That's the main thing, huh?"

"No. You need to shave, too."

"I can get scissors from René."

Out in the yard we put a chair in the sun, right in the flow of walking traffic, back and forth. In one snip, years of growth fall to the concrete.

"I had long hair in Hawaii," says Hunter.

"You were a hippie?"

"No, just a long-hair surfer. But I've always smoked pot. My dad was a grower on the Big Island. For my dad, pot is the symbol of a new non-boozed-out culture."

"Hippies!"

"Yeah, I guess. But my dad did teach me to sail. He taught me to be a sailor and a surfer, not a hippie."

"How'd you get into smuggling coke? Coke and surfing don't go together. And actually sailing doesn't either."

"Money!"

"That must have been an incredible sail, Hunter. How short you cutting my hair?"

"Short!"

"Oh, fuck it. It grows back. Were you guys planning to sail back to the Big Island?"

"Yeah."

"Tony says you got popped because of some little Peruvian soldier guard at the dock."

"We tried to bribe him and gave him too much. We freaked him out. A couple grand is more money than he'd ever imagined. He got scared and pulled his gun. The rest is Lurigancho history."

"You and Tony are almost out of here. Maybe we'll meet up in the islands. Be cool to surf some fun ones together."

"There, you look innocent."

For years now I have not seen my reflection in any mirror bigger than Ivan's little compact, the one we use to see down the hall when we're locked in. The mirror attached to the wall in the cell is a piece of one-foot-square chrome steel, and it is distorted.

I decide to take Hunter's word for how I look.

4

NINA

Richard bounces out of his bunk as soon as the steel drum starts rolling. By then, I've just finished shaving. I offer him the water that I heated earlier on the kerosene burner. Arthur already has his own fire going. We drink coffee. Now we're pumped about court.

As we walk out of the cell, I say privately to Richard: "Ever think about jammin' from the court?"

"What did you say? Have I considered suicide? No."

End of discussion. And Arthur—I know already what he thinks.

"Arthur could walk today."

"It's possible. Something is going to happen. That greedy little fat bastard Ibarra can't get any more money if nothing changes."

"And changes for the better."

"Hope we actually get inside the courtroom."

The only change with the bus is that it is even more packed than usual. And we have another bus-load, not just the three. There seem to be a lot more Peruvians than usual on this trip. Another odd thing—one of the dark scrawny soldiers asks me, "De donde eres?" Where am I from? Of course he knows I'm a gringo.

"California."

The soldier points to a bullet in the clip sticking out of the gun he is holding and says: "Por California."

Arthur whispers, "Fucking animal."

The bus bumps and leans and sways, but it's not unbearable. What's unbearable for Richard is that he can't look out the window. He's in the row of seats in front of me and Arthur, and I hear him say, "I'm going to look up, fuck it." Then I hear a soldier. "Baje su cabesa, gringo." Then: *thump thump thump*—the sound of the soldier's club hitting Richard across the back of his head, followed by Richard yelling in a muffled voice as his head goes back down between his knees, "Okay! Okay! All right, I got my head down. Shit!"

With my own muffled voice I ask Richard, "Was it worth it?"

"Fuck yeah!" Then *thump*, just one but it's louder than before. Now Richard is quiet.

They think we're too scared to try anything. Where there is a will there is a way. *Today could be the day.*

At the Justice Palace, as before, the bus parks so that the door is lined up with the door to the basement—off the bus, take two or three steps, then in the door. As we cross into the lower bowels of the Palacio de Justicia, the guards remove our cuffs. The line from the bus jams up. The guards get volatile, beating men for no reason.

This impatience in the soldiers can be useful.

We regroup in the far back of the enormous basement. Most of the men are crowding forward to the bars, trying to glimpse something new—wives and babies, sisters, brothers, anyone. Friends and lawyers are yelling and passing packages of food. Every person in the mob is shouting louder than his neighbor, and prisoners crowd us begging for cigarettes and money. Others yack at us because they know some English, talking about nothing but pussy and the price of coke in America. Like most people in this sticky hot basement, they stink.

"Man, I gotta go to the head!" I say.

"Just to pee?"

"No."

"Bummer."

This monstrous cell was actually designed with humanity in mind. Up those stairs is a large latrine. But the piss stalls and squat pots are overflowing down three tiled steps and out onto the common floor, the sludge creeping eventually into huge drains that go somewhere unknown.

I roll my pant-legs to my knees and start praying that I'm not going to lose one of my rubber flip-flops in the muck.

"Get the fuck outa here you, mangy fucking rats!"

Two shit-eating rats, each one the size of a cat, are munching on whatever garbage is plugging up the hole I want to use. I wave my arms at them but they just stare at me. I swing my foot and tap one of them, and they back off, but when I start to unhitch my pants they come right back. I kick one of them in the side hard, like kicking a football, and it retreats. Another good thunk and the second rat scurries into the dark. As soon as I'm done they run back to the toilet, excited.

Arthur sees me coming and says, "How was your trip?"

"Oh, really cool. Saw some wild animals. And I always enjoy the sound of running water."

At the gate guards keep calling out the names of prisoners. Now we hear, "Los tres gringos!" Must be us. We are absolutely the only gringos in the basement.

As soon as we're outside the tall steel bars, our escorts, four of them, handcuff us again.

Richard motions with his head toward the automatic rifles pointed right at us, their big banana clips ready to rip. A soldier butts Richard. "SHUDD DUP GRINGO!" Another one stabs his weapon at me and says, "Callase su boca. Ariba. Apurase."

"You think they want us to get up the stairs?" says Arthur. For that he gets a slap across the back of the head.

Richard looks into the eyes of the soldier who just butted him and says, "Where's the elevator, señor?"

He gets another butt.

Two flights up, just to get to street level. Then another three flights to the courtroom. The courtroom is huge. The conquistadors spared no expense in its making. The first sight as I look across the awesome space are the judges, three of them, seated as if raised on thrones—the three Peruvian people who now have total power over us American boys.

There is a case in progress and we hear the poor bastard getting sentenced to life in Lurigancho for stealing. Arthur says quietly, "I wonder what the hell he stole." Richard mutters, "Secret plans for the Peruvian space program."

The soldiers are pushing us through the crowd that stands in the back of the filled theater. We have to work our way to the wall on the far side of the crowd. Suddenly my bare forearm is touched. Fingers grip with feminine softness. Zoila's face is nearly hidden within a scarf. Softly glowing in the maroon shadow, her eyes are dilated black sapphires. Her name is equal to Shiva or Kali, revered, the name of a goddess with forbidden charms.

A soldier bullies through the crowd, knocking men and women out of his way. A little girl falls.

They shove us onto a balcony. That's strange—first to be pushed forward along the side wall of the packed courtroom, then to be thrust through a side door and right out under the dull Lima sky, alone. Far below us, the honking of automobiles. Strangely, they remove our handcuffs and depart, shutting the doors on us. We are three stories up. Right away we look over the side, but there's no way to get to the street below without dying.

Lima—the gray city. Nearly every day of the year it is overcast. Some legend says the Inca put a curse on the land after the Spanish slaughtered the native people.

"Zoila is in there, in the crowd. She touched me on the arm."

Arthur says, "Why would she come here? Oh! Forget I asked that."

"That's great your ol' lady is here, but where is our fat-ass lawyer?"

The door behind us opens again, and a dark figure, a man in a white suit, steps onto the balcony. Although he's well-dressed, he reeks of PIP. He has a certain no-respect-for-life look about him, as though he's standing in the shadow even while he's in full sunlight. He smiles, and a gold tooth gleams in his shadowy appearance. His natural color is dark, but he is also sickly pale and slimy. He speaks good English, but clearly he is no American. Not even a bad one.

"Hola, my friends."

Arthur jumps at the man like a terrier. "Who are you?"

"Your lawyer has hired me to be your court interpreter."

"Where's Ibarra?"

"We can start today without Ibarra."

We look at the man. I say, "You speak good English. Are you American?"

"Yes. I am American."

Richard stands extra straight and tall, looking the dark man square face in face. "Bullshit!"

"Be nice, fellas. You need me!"

"What makes you think we need your ass?"

"You are American. International law—you must have an interpreter before you can be tried. I am registered with the tribunal as a professional interpreter. And, my American friends, I am Interpol. I am sure you know Interpol, hey?"

Is that a threat? Is this guy threatening us? Shit, now we have a cop as our interpreter.

I say, "Then let's get started."

"First you must pay me one thousand and five hundred American dollars."

I look at Richard. I know he's eager to throw this Interpol fuck right off the balcony.

"Richard, maybe we better look into this. Like, maybe we should pay this gentleman."

Richard and Arthur both look at me.

I say to Interpol, "Listen, let me talk to my buddies, will you? Give us a little bit by ourselves out here, will you, mister?"

"Sure, take some time. Enjoy the view. Enjoy being out of the hell you three live in. Remember—if you don't pay me, you have no interpreter and your trial will be postponed for another year, maybe more. It's up to you."

Moments later we are taken away by the soldiers. Again soldiers are pushing us through the crowd at the back of the courtroom. I look for Zoila, her image vibrating in my mind. The Warrior Goddess must be looking for the right instant to grab me and save my ass. In Spirit the woman has the strength, but I am trapped in the dark depths of the physical world.

What came first? The desire to live beyond fear, or Zoila? Do they go together?

Uncuffed we sit on a wooden bench in a hall with a thirty-foot ceiling. All the courtrooms open to this great hall. Gun-bearing soldiers stand on the stairs, and the crowd in the hall is laced with them. We are actually more closely guarded now than in the basement. But now we have doors and windows. And we have women. Two dark-haired pretty girls walk our way, both dressed in casual business attire and chatting in Spanish. When the young girls come close enough to hear, I say in English, "Hello, ladies. How good it is to see such beautiful faces."

One of the girls replies in very plain English, "Thank you so much."

"Are you ladies attorneys?" Streams of other nicely dressed people pass, all of them rushing.

"No, not yet. We are at the universidad to study international law. We are going to be lawyers."

"You work in the court?"

"Yes, we work in the court."

Two soldiers approach from behind the girls. They talk in Spanish. The girls get rid of the soldiers very quickly.

"May I ask your name, Señorita?"

"I am Nina, and this is my friend Maria."

"Yo soy Eduardo."

Richard and Arthur charmingly introduce themselves. They also say their names in the Spanish pronunciation.

"Oh, I am impressed. You all speak Spanish, yes?"

"No, that is our very big problem today. You may be able to help us with our problem."

"Oh, we are not able to help yet. We are not yet able to practice law."

"I'm very sorry to ask you, but do you know of Lurigancho Prison?"

"Oh por Dios. Si, I mean yes we know this is very very bad place. Casa de Diablo."

"We need your help. We are prisoners there. We are innocent, and yet we never see our lawyer or the American embassy. Please, you can help us!"

"Oh my God yes, if we can, but how?"

"We must have an interpreter. You can do this?"

"I would have to get permission from my uncle."

"Who is your uncle?"

"He is the judge in your case."

"You know which court?"

"Si. Yes, of course. I was only in my first year of universidad and I read your case in the periodical, the newspaper. Mis amigas y myself we talk about 'those gringos,' but of course we don't remember your names. But your case had many legal questions, and we also did practice debate. You see, your case has questions of international law."

"What laws are those, Nina?" I just want to hear her say she will interpret. But what she says next gives me an explosion of hope.

"Well, the most important to you could be that in Peruvian law there is no possession."

"That is very interesting. And you know how long we have been locked up inside your prison." I had to try a bit of a guilt trip. "We have suffered years and we are innocent."

"You see, in the periodical it says you had possession of the cocaine."

Arthur jumps in. Before this, he was preoccupied with Richard trying to talk to Maria, who speaks nearly no English. But now he interjects, "Yeah, but it was *put* in his possession!"

I'm a little confused at what she is saying. She sounds jubilant over the fact that the newspaper reported we were caught with cocaine. I'm thinking she's saying we're guilty.

"I am so sorry to you. Please I will explain you. In the laws around cocaine in Peru we have no law for possession. So, if my uncle— I'm sorry, if the tribunal believes you were in possession and not trafficking, they must let you go. Understand?"

The three of us look at each other with our mouths open.

"I slept for a long time," I say. "Did I miss this part? Did Rubio ever tell us that?"

"Rubio? What about our lawyer?"

Nina tells Maria what we are going through. Then she turns back. Now she is talking to all three of us in a slightly different fashion. Her voice has changed from girlish and flirty to professionally interested. "You have certainly suffered enough. You did not kill someone. You should be treated according to the laws, not according to politics of the United States' drug war. This is not justice."

I do believe we have struck Nina both physically and intuitively. She seems unable to refuse our need, and she knows exactly what we need. We need her.

"Nina, you speak English so well. Have you been to the United States?"

"Yes, I was a student at Berkeley. In northern California. The university, for only one year."

The three of us look at each other again, acknowledging the surreal event that's unfolding. We understand without speaking that Nina has been Americanized. She is different.

Suddenly a realization sweeps through me like the crash of a gong. This has been happening. This has been happening ever since I stopped hating the sound of the pre-dawn barrel being rolled up the yard. Since I found the silence. Something changed. People will come from the silence to help us.

I will not be making a run for it today.

An hour or so later, Nina and Maria come back to find us, and they have a third friend—Eva, who is beautiful and who is also studying law. Nina says, "Please talk with Maria and Eva. They must practice their English. Eduardo, for please. You can come to me?"

I realize Nina may be a little out of practice with her English, but I sure like the way she says that. Please come to me. She is already turning to lead the way. "Yes," I say. "Of course."

She stops suddenly as though she has forgotten something important. She turns to face us all and says, very business-like, "Yes, I spoke, or spoken, no spoke with my uncle. He has given his permission so that I can be the court interpreter for you gentlemens."

I punch my fist into my palm. "All right!"

Richard very charmingly says, "Lady, you may have saved us months or years waiting for another trial."

"Waiting in Lurigancho," says Arthur. He is teary-eyed. "Thank you so much from the bottom of my heart." The ladies love his performance, and he gets the hugs he's trying for. I imagine Arthur will masturbate over this one. If I recall, he hasn't been touched by a female for four years—except for Pablo's mom, who once gave him a hug for some leche asada.

I go with Nina, and she leads me through the lobby and into one of the Palace's enormous courtrooms. We leave the hubbub behind and step into a cool quietness. The room is empty except for two men.

"That man there is our lawyer," I say. "Who is the other man?"

"Yes, he would spoke with you. When you have talk to Señor Ibarra, I come back for we talk. The other man, he is a court official."

Ibarra looks more than ever like a fat pig.

"Eduardo, my boy, how are joo?"

"Where the hell have you been?"

"Oh, working for joo and the other boys, working very hard, jes!"

"Did you know we gotta have an interpreter?"

"Jes! That is why I sent to joo the best interpreter."

"Oh, you sent that guy?"

"Jes, but he says joo will not pay him. Why joo don't pay him the money I have from Mr. Chula?"

You fat fuck! I knew damn well that you were scheming to get some of that fifteen hundred in blood money from the Interpol creep. But I can't fire you. I can't even blast you. Too risky, with Murphy's case right next door. Be nice, Ed.

"Oh, I am so sorry. He never said you sent him. But now we have that young woman to be our interpreter."

"Jes, jes, how lucky for joo boys. Jes, the clerk over there he was telling me about the special circumstances with this jung girl. But I must tell you she is not a professional. My friend I send to joo, he is a professional."

"He's a fucking cop!"—I lost it there for a second—"I mean he could be on their side."

"Jes, jes, I understand."

Yeah. More like, we busted your little scam to get more plata.

Ibarra leaves, saying he will say hello to the boys and send in the young woman.

Goddamn she looks good!

She's wearing a long-sleeved black dress. A patent-leather belt with a black onyx buckle emphasizes her small waist. Her high-heeled shoes tap on the tile floor as she approaches. My eyes are drilled to her bright red toenails, which match the bright velvet ribbon that ties her jet-black hair. Her skin is like cream against the blackness.

"I know your lawyer, Tiefilo," she says. "He is a friend to my father. He was a judge."

"Yes, I know. We are very lucky to have him for our attorney."

"We have been given this private time to tell me your problem, also same with your friends. My uncle says I must listen to you and learn the way you speak. Also, I must learn to know what happen you. Will you begin?"

"Can I begin by saying to you thank you from my heart?"

"You need my help!"

"Okay, Ricardo. He is the tall one. We were staying at...."

"I'm sorry, first the judge will want to know why you came to Peru. Many people come to Peru for the coca."

"No, we came to visit the ruins and climb to the top of Machu Picchu and go to the Nazca Desert, Cuzco, and of course the Amazon. No, we read about these places and came to see them."

"And you have seen the famous places?"

"We only just arrived two days before our arrest. About all we have seen is the Granja Azul Resort out in the country. At the resort everything was being arranged for our sightseeing."

"What about Señor Arturo?"

"Ricardo and me met Arturo in Tahiti. We became friends. Arturo told us that he made his living drawing and painting famous beaches and ruins such as the Inca ruins of your country. At the resort Arturo had a separate bungalow. Do you understand bungalow?

"No. Do you mean a separate room?"

"Yes, but a small house set aside from the others. After checking in, we went for lunch, and all three of us met a couple who are American. Their names are Ginger and Tom. At night there is dancing in the resort nightclub. Ginger likes to dance and Mr. Dawson—that's Tom, Tom Dawson—Tom said he could not dance. He encouraged my dancing with his girlfriend."

"Not Tom's wife?"

I was hoping she'd bite on that fact.

"No. She, they both were very clear about not being married. They said Tom is married and has children. But Ginger, no, she is not married to Tom or anyone."

For a moment she drops the tight behavior of the interview. She puts her pen to her full, lush lips in a gesture that means herself as much as Ginger when she asks me in a lower, softer tone, "Do you think Ginger could have fallen in love with you in only two days?"

"Do you?"

"I believe that is possible. After all, you are a very handsome man, and it has not taken a long time to understand that you are an intelligent man. And yes, I would trust you."

"So that's a yes?"

The moment passes quickly. But if I can arouse her in this grave situation, then the story of our arrest becomes more palatable for her uncle. Also, I wonder if public opinion can be a force in the courtroom. Could the crowd today where I saw Zoila—*her name should be Babylon*—could those people be of her family? That could weigh heavy on our side if her uncle thinks the people want us free.

"We were having a good time until Dawson got into in a rage. Maybe the drinks of your pisco? I don't know. Tom began to act crazy very suddenly."

"What did you and Ginger do for him to be so crazy?"

"We kissed on the dance floor. It was bad, in front of Tom."

"Yes, in front of Tom." She speaks with disappointment rather than judgment. Then, tighter now, she states, "But you are not in Lurigancho for kissing Ginger."

"No, you are right. I am in Lurigancho because the police, or the PIP, found the cocaine Dawson brought to my bungalow."

"I am sorry for your problem. I must prepare you a little. I must be careful to tell you these things. I am only to get the basic facts to be a better interpreter for you and the court. But I must say to you, the cocaine is not free. Here in Peru many peoples want to sell the coca, for it is very much money for the Peruvians. Also in the United States the coca becomes very, very, very much money. Only one libre of the coca to your country for a Peruvian is enough money to buy his family a house and car and plenty of food. I tell you this because I think it is very difficult for the tribunal to believe a man would leave to you cocaine worth many thousands of dollars because you kiss his girlfriend. Because he is jealous."

"People in my country, and yours, commit murder because of jealousy. Dawson became like a mad man. He made Ginger afraid of him. She told me, and Richard, I mean Ricardo, after Tom was kicked out of the bar, she thinks he will kill her. Yes! Tom was crazy out of his mind. He brought the cocaine to my bungalow."

For the first time since our arrest it feels as though we are actually in a justice system.

Richard will tell the same story, I know. We've gone over it a few hundred times, starting at the PIP with that Interpol fuck Rubio.

Rubio was such an arrogant bastard. He really believed Ginger would jump in bed with him. His arrogance made it easier for Ginger to control him. And Del Gado became a little more human once he got his payment to play his part. Now Del Gado's part is coming up for the audition, years later. Years! Rubio and Del Gado really had us. We totally went for their bullshit. Six months, they said. The longest six months on record!

Outside the counsel chamber Nina and I find Arthur and Richard, who have four more of Nina's girlfriends around them, laughing and carrying on as if they're free.

Nina is all business. But she is not uptight. It's just that now she knows the real story. She knows in her heart, not only in her mind. She fully realizes that without her I may never leave Lurigancho alive. And Richard and Arthur could stay for many more cruel years. For a second there, while I was explaining how I came to have possession, I suddenly saw Nina as our Lady Justice symbol—the lady with the blindfold. So I gave Nina a peek over the top of the blindfold. Nina will talk to her uncle the judge, and Zoila will fill the courtroom with the Spirit.

Zoila can will the people. She is the people. The cute little girl has revealed herself to be a woman of strength, a spirit of such power as I have never felt from another human being. Beneath her humility it's all mystery, the power of a woman who knows personally the ancient gods of the Andean Mountains and the deep, enormous, life-giving Amazon jungle.

"Excuse me, I am sorry for to interrupt, but I need Señor Ricardo for to interview."

I have no problem hanging with Arthur and his small group of loveliest creatures. Their fragrances are transcendent; their voices are like sweet oxygen. Their hair—if I could touch a wisp of it or if a wisp of it ever brushed across my arm or my imagination—it wakes up a thousand memories. If I just touched the transparent cream skin, I'd have an orgasm on the spot.

I'm feeling a surge of confidence. So are Richard and Arthur. I'm getting a crazy feeling as if we've been stuck in a science experiment, a very mean one, to prove that we can still like women and that they can like us. After so much darkness….

But when Richard goes off with Nina, I get uncomfortable. I need to hear what he says and what Nina asks. I'm the one who has read the transcripts over and over knowing how crucial it is that we testify the same as we did at the PIP with Del Gado.

"I'm sorry, Nina. May I sit in the courtroom while you speak with Ricardo? It is so quiet in there. We don't get much quiet at the prison."

"Oh yes, I understand. Come. You may sit inside. And Mr. Arturo you are okay?"

Arthur stands up and says, "No problem. It will be my pleasure."

"My friends will keep you entertained." She turns to her friends and asks them to practice their English with Arthur.

Nina pushes open the huge wooden door and stands with her back against it as Richard and me walk through. Just before I enter, I glance back into the hall and see the soldiers in the hall, and a couple of them guarding the head of the stairs that lead down to the street and freedom. They have their eyes on us. They are concerned not as soldiers but as men—men who are dangerously jealous of our special treatment. They're playing right into the story about Dawson and his jealous rage.

The empty courtroom looks as though it was built for a race of giants. No escape from here. There are windows, but they don't open. Even if they did, we are too high to jump.

Nina says as she pulls the big door shut to nearly closed, "Eduardo, you may sit here, please." She points to a row of seats much like the pews in a Catholic church. "Thank you, Nina." In this empty courtroom voices carry well.

She leads Richard to a four-foot-square table—no doubt the court reporter's station—positioned at the foot of the steps leading up to an ancient slab and the tall carved chairs where judges must sit. Behind the judges' stand, the twenty-foot-high wall is draped with a blood-red velvet curtain lined with gold trim, the colors of emperors.

Just as Nina and Richard are about to sit, a soldier pushes open the door, one hand gripping the strap of his rifle, and he says, "Todo esta bien?" Nina answers as if she's irritated by the interruption and tells him in Spanish, "Yes, everything is well. I will call you if I want you." The soldier closes the door, cutting off the roar of the busy hall.

They sit at the table across from one another and Nina begins. "Señor Ricardo?"

Richard wastes no time in taking the lead. "Do you think it would be okay to say my name in English?"

"Why, of course. I am so sorry."

I am hoping Richard will control his sarcasm. No one says sorry in Lurigancho. But the word means something different out here, spoken by a woman.

"No, don't be sorry," he says. "Just, could you say my name in English? 'Richard.'"

With her great smile she says, "Richard." Then as if she's delighted to meet him she says it again.

"Richard. Is this correct, Richard?"

"Yes! That's it. A gorgeous female saying my name in English, yes! Thank you very much!"

"You and Eduardo...."

"Yeah, just call him Eduardo. I like that!"

"You two are good friends?"

"I hate Eduardo." Richard knows I can hear him. I wonder if he's still sore about the shaving cream.

"No. You are making a joke. You have been through so much together?"

"We wouldn't be in this fuh.... I mean, we would not be in this mess and in prison if he had just left another man's woman alone."

She is sharp. "But not one of you is at Lurigancho because Eduardo has been with Ginger. It is because of the cocaine. Richard, are you a trafficante?"

"Listen sweetie, I own my own home. I am a successful business-man. I make a lot of money in the U.S. I am not stupid enough to be a trafficker. I don't have to do anything illegal, hon."

"Tell me, Richard. Were you in the bungalow at the time Eduardo says Señor Dawson brought the cocaine to the bungalow?"

"Is that how it will be in the court?"

"Yes. I must warn you, the prosecutor he is a very powerful man, and he will not be kind to you or to Arturo and Eduardo. He is asking the judges to find you all guilty, and he wants you all to stay in Lurigancho for many many years."

"No! Arthur and me were waiting for Eduardo in the restaurant. Ginger was with us. She wanted to be close to us because she said that nut Dawson would kill her."

"In the court I will ask you to explain where you were at all times. But of course it will be the judge's questions. I am sure the judge will ask you these questions I am preparing you to answer. You must tell the truth."

"I got nothin' to hide, babe!"

"Do you speak any Spanish?"

"If I had to speak Spanish to go out with you, I would be fluent. But at Lurigancho there aren't a lot of Spanish-speaking people I want to talk to. The ones I want to talk to speak English."

After several more questions Nina gets to the heart of the matter: "Richard, when you entered the bungalow of Eduardo, did you see any cocaine? And please remember, this is a very serious question. It could be the difference of whether you stay in Lurigancho or be released. You must answer to me how you will tell to the judges."

Now Richard leans forward, putting his elbows on the shiny tabletop. "If that is a serious question and it makes the difference of my staying locked up in that stinking prison, please look in my eyes when I tell you—no! The only time I have ever seen cocaine was in a movie. I never saw anything that looked like cocaine, and I have never known Eduardo to use or possess cocaine. He would not be my friend if he used such a terrible drug, Nina."

Even from way back here I can see that Nina's face is genuinely disturbed. "Oh, I am so sorry. Please when you answer this question, you must tell to the judges just as you tell to me." She glances away for a moment, then meets his gaze again. "I want to say to you, you should not be in Lurigancho. Also, Richard, I am not the judges, but I must tell you the prosecutor he will have much information about you from the DEA and your government."

Richard remains charming. "Do you know what that information is, sweetie?"

"No. I am sorry to say to you no. Only the prosecutor receives this information. Now I must speak with Señor Arturo."

She turns to me as Richard is getting up from his chair. "Eduardo, could you please to tell Arturo to come in?"

Richard moves over to the pews. Without a word I get up and push open the thick door of the courtroom.

Arthur is standing in the middle of Nina's four friends. One of the soldiers is smiling curiously as he eavesdrops. With a bit of sadistic pleasure I shout, "Arthur! Excuse us, girls, but we need Arthur to come inside now."

It's a different meeting altogether when Arthur sits down. His head is bowed. He appears to be saying a prayer to himself. *God bless us, every one.* Then he and our Gift from God exchange a rapid flourish of conversation in Spanish.

Nina says, "Well, Señor, you have really impressed me with your ability to speak the language of my country. And now I will tell my uncle you do not need me or any interpreter. You understand perfectly." She is ribbing Arthur, but only because she is authentically impressed with him. She likes all three of us American boys.

"Oh, no. I think you should tell your uncle that I don't even speak good English."

"You would ask me to lie to the tribunal, Arturo?"

"Oh, no. But I...."

"I am sorry to you, Arturo. How do you say in America? I am

kidding for you."

Arthur' face turns red enough to mistake it for second-degree sunburn.

Although the questions are very close to the same ones that we got, Arthur seems to have more enjoyable answers. Nina laughs a lot more than she did with Richard and me.

She is very kind as she ends the official interview. She wishes us good luck and actually gives each of us a hug, quick and customary for Nina, but a sheer delight for us. It's as if for an instant I get to hold Zoila and feel her radiating love.

We exit the empty courtroom, the three of us walking in front of Nina. Her friends are waiting just outside the door, talking with a soldier. Their faces brighten when they see us. The soldier scowls. He turns his head toward the landing at the top of the stairs and gestures to the three guards. Two of them leave the stairs, quickly lifting their rifles from their shoulders and moving toward us with fast strides. The ladies, startled, step back. The soldiers turn us toward the wall. Nina and her friends form a half-circle in back of the soldiers and watch as they cuff us with their stainless-steel bracelets. They yell at us: "Turn around! Over to the stairs! No talking, gringos!" One soldier grabs Richard's handcuffs by the chain, and he grabs Arthur's cuffs the same way. Then he pushes, signaling them toward the stairs, using the cuffs like dog-chain for maximum control. The other soldier grabs hold of my cuffs and lifts, forcing my arms and shoulders into a painful position. Nina cries sharply: "You do not need to treat the prisoner in this way. What is wrong with you?"

The soldier only laughs and pulls harder. I cry out, "Aah! Oh wow, that hurts." Normally I wouldn't say a thing. A little theater, though, triggers large pangs of sympathy in the hearts of Nina and her friends. When we get to the head of the stairs, still gripped like dogs by the scrawny guards, I look back. Nina calls out: "Try to be strong until this is over."

Down flights of stairs we descend into the dungeons. On the

way I keep looking at the faces of the people we pass. They all look so civilized. I wonder how many of them know there is a place in their country called Lurigancho and that one of its tentacles reaches into the basement of this very building.

After the guards shove us back into the pit, they remove our manacles. As he's rubbing his wrists, Richard says, "Did you guys see the looks on those girls' faces when the guards cuffed us? They were horrified. That one Maria had tears in her eyes, man."

Arthur says, "If the judge believes that you guys never knew me and that we had different rooms at the resort, they'll probably cut me loose."

Richard says, "Yeah, me too. And Eduardo here can have visits with his little jungle woman for the next few years. Hey, we'll write you."

"Shut the fuck up. You're both about as smart as a stick. Don't talk."

"Hey, fuck you. All I said is that they believe we're innocent—because we are, dude. We are. Too bad about you."

Arthur jumps right on top. "Yeah, you're the stick, dick. We can say whatever we want. Who made you boss?"

"I wish you were both chicks. I'd fuck you both."

Arthur replies, "Oh, if the girls could hear you now! Then who'd be a dumb stick?"

"Whatever it takes. I'm not going to die in Lurigancho—with you two!"

"Yeah right! Aren't you the guy that said, 'Don't worry! Just follow my heels!' Uh huh, we did—right to Lurigancho!"

"Hey, I never told you to leave Tahiti. You were the one who wanted to come to Peru. You made your own fucking choice. Don't try to blame all this shit on me, goddamnit."

Richard backs Arthur. "No, you and fuckhead Dawson have the problem. The problem is you and Ginger."

There's no way to resolve this kind of conversation. But as soon as the soldiers start lining us up to count us and beat us all onto the buses, anything between Richard, Arthur, and me dissolves.

The next trip to court is real tense. Afterwards, we retreat to our usual corner in the Justice Palace basement, farthest from the latrine. Somehow we know that this is the day.

A soldier calls our official names: "Los tres gringos!"

We push and squeeze our way toward the gate. Richard yells at everyone in our path, "Get the fuck out of the way!" but no one budges. The men here are just like us. As we press through the crowd, I smell paste. The smell instantly reminds me of deep depression.

At the iron bars we find the soldier who called us. He is the only fat soldier I have seen since this strange sojourn in hell began. His big gut presses against the bars as he waves. He looks just like the Sergeant Garcia character in the old Zorro television show—oily hair parted way over on the side of his head, puffy cheeks, shaggy eyebrows and moustache. He keeps waving and waving till we reach the bars and then he says, "Su abogado esta aqui, gringos." Our lawyer is here. That's a new one—Ibarra, coming down here. Must be serious.

Then the fat guard smiles at us grotesquely. "Huh?" he says, and he looks at us as though we are his special little friends. "You have money, gringos? I get you out and get you good abogado, yes?"

These guards all have a cousin who claims to be a good lawyer. If they smell money, they'll kiss your ass—the same people who will shoot you in the back without a moment's hesitation.

"Oh yeah," says Arthur. "That's what we need. Another god-damn lawyer. We'll think about it."

The fat soldier agrees that we should keep in mind his generous proposition. He turns and calls Ibarra, who has been standing out of hearing range.

I say, "What do you think, boys? How could we pass it up?"

"Yeah," snarls Richard. "Peru—the land of fucking opportunity."

Ibarra is jolly today. He says the usual: "How are joo, boys?" Then, "Boys, I have good news for joo today, jes. I am bery good lawyer. I work bery hard, and I get for joo special permission for a jung pretty girl to be for joo interpreter and she is not charging monies. Yes? Joo are happy, jes?"

The three of us just look at one another. The crowd is pressing against us, everyone talking. Richard leans close to my right ear and says, "I'll be over in the corner." And he walks away, disappearing from view in the crowd.

Arthur and me turn back to face Ibarra, and I say, "You must excuse Ricardo. He's too happy. He is overwhelmed with joy about what you have done."

Arthur says, "Yeah, Ibarra, thanks."

Ibarra tells us that he will be in the court but it is not time for him to do his work and that is why he will be quiet during this phase of our tribunal.

Back in the corner with Richard, we agree to let it go. "Let him think we're that fucking stupid. He's not going to tell us the truth, anyway."

Again a soldier calls, "Los tres gringos, vengan aqui!"

This time it is a different soldier, a thin one. Doesn't matter. Their guns make them all the same size. This soldier hands me a brown paper shopping bag and a note. I take the note and give the bag to Richard. "It's Zoila," I say. "She sent us food, you guys."

Richard looks in the bag and says, "She's pretty sweet. I guess I should take back whatever shit I said about her. Thank her when you see her."

The note reads: "Eduardo, the soldier would not let me in to see you but he let me give this food to you and your friends to help you build your strength. Stay strong, Eduardo. Love, Zoila."

Reaching into the bag, Richard lifts out a metal cooking pot with a lid. The soldier at the gate says, "You eat now and give to me the pot and the spoons. Eat."

Richard holds the pot while Arthur removes the lid. "Wow, check that out. A chicken pot roast with potatoes, carrots, broccoli...."

"What's that?"

"A couple things I don't recognize but I can't wait to eat."

Hours later we are taken up the flights of stairs with all the usual harassment, but this time they sweep us right into a crowded courtroom. The soldiers remove our hardware and tell us to sit at a bench facing the raised platform. No doubt our judges will soon be looking down at us.

Zoila is back there in the seats. So are her friends and relatives. I feel as though my own family is here. Fear is irrelevant. Zoila and I are two deadly creatures letting the evil humans play their game plan, waiting patiently to see where it leads before we strike out with deadly force and fly back to the jungle.

Richard is quiet.

Arthur looks around the courtroom. "This is the real deal, dudes!"

At one end of the trial arena stands a small crowd of men and women in formal business attire conferring with each other, studying paper, moving quickly here and there. Obviously these are the ones who run the wheels and gears of this big old courtroom. Suddenly, out from this crowd steps our angel.

"Buenos dias." Today Nina is dressed in the height of formality—steel-blue dress with skirt to mid-calf, her hair pinned back severely. She's perfectly poised, but I can feel her intensity.

"I hope it's bueno!" Richard says.

I ask, "What will happen today, Nina?"

"Yes. Today will be the beginning of your case testimony. Tomorrow the others in your case will be called to testify."

"What others?"

"There is a Señor Rivera, Gustavo Rivera."

"What are they going to ask him?"

"He is the one who sold cocaine to Señor Dawson. The cocaine the police found in your bungalow. I have a copy of Señor Gustavo's confession. He says he does not know you and Ricardo or Arturo. The first time he ever saw any of you is at the PIP house."

"Nina, can you tell us what is in those papers you have, particularly what Sergeant Del Gado has said about the arrest. About the cocaine."

"I read in these documentos that the 'Sergeant'—as you call him—has reported that he entered Señor Eduardo's bungalow looking for Señor Dawson. Señor Eduardo tells the Sergeant that Dawson does not stay here. He tells Del Gado that Dawson has left two leather satchels. Del Gado opened these bags and discovered the cocaine."

Richard asks, "Why did you say, 'As you call him?'"

"Oh, yes. You mean Del Gado."

"Isn't he a sergeant?"

"No. Del Gado is no little sergeant. General Del Gado is El Jefe Supremo of our militario!"

"You mean he's like the boss of the army in Peru?"

Nina laughs a girlish sweet laugh. "No no. Only El Presidente is the boss. No, Del Gado is one of the generals of the army. But he is a four-star general, not one with the five stars. He is good friends with El Presidente. General Del Gado developed the PIP, the Internal Peruvian Police, to work closely with your American DEA."

"And Del Gado says that the cocaine was in a bag? A leather bag or satchel?"

"Yes! He has sworn it with this documento. But he still must testify this is true."

It turns out there are actually three judges on the bench, one sitting on either side of Nina's uncle.

Yeah, we know it's her uncle. But when he enters the court and sits down, the smile he gives Nina and the surrounding ladies quickly becomes a frown. When he looks directly at us, I get the distinct feel and look of a hangin' judge. The other two look like weasels, like the kids I used to know in school who would never dare to try one of our crazy stunts, but as soon as we got caught they would be right there saying "nana nana nana" as we were carted off to the principal's office.

The judges take their seats at throne-like furniture behind a massive table hand-carved with ancient artwork. The scale and ornateness are repeated throughout the room. The message is the same one I felt at the PIP station—I am a nothing, a powerless captured American boy lost here with two other scared gringos. But when I look back at Zoila, my fear evaporates. The knot in my gut disappears. The animals are restless and want out. The courtroom has filled to capacity, both sitting and standing. Zoila did this, I know. She packed the room. I whisper to Nina, "Are there always so many people? Are these people all here to see us?"

As her uncle and his cohorts shuffle their papers, she whispers back, "No, many of these people are Señor Gustavo's family and friends. But many people are curious what will happen to you. Your arrest is very big news, filled with the drama of a soap on TV. People want to know what will happen to the gringo for having the cocaine that has been indigenous to our culture for thousands of years."

"TODOS ARIBA, POR FAVOR."

Our tribunal has begun.

Arthur is called first, and he steps forward with Nina by his side. All around us people are whispering in Spanish. The crowd behind us talks continuously, like the surge of sea against the shore. The prosecutor starts reading off the charges and preaching about the evils of cocaine and condemning all those who traffic the product. Nina is talking to Arthur, going over the process. The judges are ignoring the blaring voice of the prosecutor. It's as though they've heard it all before. Instead they are concentrating on what's unique here, and that is the communication between Nina and Arthur.

A soldier brings a bible over to Arthur and swears him in. Arthur's hand shakes. It looks as though the big leather-bound book is going to burn his fingers when he touches it. But as Nina repeats every word for him in English, he relaxes a little.

Oh yeah. This is good. I can understand the question in Spanish and then hear it again in English. More time to assimilate the question for delivering just the right answer. We've waited years in Lurigancho for this.

"El Presidente de las tribunales de militario de Peru!" The prosecutor is standing behind us, and he's shouting in a bullhorn voice that echoes in the vast courtroom. I look over my right shoulder. The place looks just like a Catholic church in here except no kneelers in the pews and no stained glass in the windows. And there's the prosecutor—they should call him the executioner, the way he's carrying on. He's got his arm out with his index finger pointed, and he's waving it up and down like a boxing referee counting a knockdown. He's standing in a high wooden pulpit that rises from the other side of twenty rows of wooden benches. His face is round and ghostly pale; his long black hair hangs from the sides of his bald head over which he has combed a few strands. His pencil moustache is too small for his big, frowning face, and that ridiculous bow tie makes him look like an over-inflated balloon. His rage seems displaced, as though he got beat up a lot in school. We've never met the guy before in our lives, and yet here he is, demanding our doom as though we killed the fucking president of Peru.

"These men have lied to the Peruvian Internal Police, they have lied to their own American embassy representatives, and they will lie to this tribunal, Your Honors. They are lying, and they are drug traffickers. Señor Ar-thur Thoma-son"—he's trying to pronounce the names exactly as written in the DEA's paperwork—"will tell the tribunal that he came to Peru to paint. But he has never demonstrated any such ability, nor has he produced any work to validate his claim to be a professional artist. And the biggest lie Señor Ar-thur Thoma-son will tell the tribunal will be when he tells Your Honors he never knew his criminal partners before they met in Tahiti on the way to Peru, Your Honors. Señor Ree-chard Brew-er is a liar and will lie to the tribunal and say he only came to Peru to see the ruins of Peru along with his good friend Señor Eduardo Padilla." He gives my name the Spanish pronunciation, with a breath-like "d."

"And, Your Honors, the man who sits down there—" he points at me with his arm outstretched "—is the most offensive of all." I guess no one ever taught him that it's not polite to point. He just won't give it up. "This man will tell you that a crazy man placed a large quantity of cocaine in his bungalow, and that this man did this for revenge because Señor Eduardo Padilla is so irresistible, Your Honors, that the crazy man's wife fell in love with Señor Padilla only a few hours after they met." I hear a disturbance run through the audience. It sounds to me that the women out there are agreeing to the possibility. "Yes, the prosecution is aware of several depositions from witnesses attesting to the rage of this crazy man, his drunken tantrum at the bar the night of the arrest. The prosecution can show that the drunken tantrum by a Señor Dawson and the cocaine found in Señor Padilla's bungalow are not related, Your Honors, and that Señor Padilla is the leader of a large group of traffickers. Thank you, Your Honors."

Veinte anos, he says. Veinte anos. That gets a rise from everyone in the courtroom. *Twenty years? Did he say twenty fucking years?* Now, that is not routine. This fuck is asking the court to give us twenty years each. The audience is obviously laced with people who are cheering for us and booing the prosecutor. One person unseen shouts out, "You use the coca today?" The audience bursts out laughing.

The judge bangs his gavel, BANG BANG BANG, and everyone is quiet again.

In the quiet a baby cries. I turn around looking for Zoila. People stand to let the lady with the crying baby get out of the row, and they block my view. The mother takes her child all the way out of the courtroom. A soldier pushes open the heavy door for them.

Now I see Zoila.

We don't dare talk to each other. But we look at each other and know.

I am still marveling at the crowd. Judging by the noise, ninety-eight percent of them are on our side and willing to let the world know it. Between us and the crowd, Nina's friends all sit at a long table.

Now the prosecutor winds down. According to Nina, he'll keep quiet now until the next witness is called, and then he'll say the same thing again.

It's the judges' turn to interrogate. Nina's uncle bangs down the gavel. From his elevation he glowers at Arthur. "Is it true you came to Peru to do paintings of the Andes Mountains?"

Arthur already knows the question and the answer. That leaves him time to enjoy this beautiful lady. He watches her mouth as it forms the words. He looks into her gorgeous brown eyes as they look right into his. This is a wonderful treat after years of dodging René .

"Yes, Your Honors. Yes, I came to draw and paint the beauty of this country."

"And Señor Thom-a-son, do you have any of your artwork with you or at Lurigancho?"

"Oh, I am so sorry, Judges. I ordered new paint and brushes, but I have not received these yet."

Even though Arthur is scared, he still has his sense of humor.

"Señor Thom-a-son, did you come to Peru for the purpose of trafficking cocaine?"

"Oh no, Your Honors. That would be against the law. I am an artist. I never take drugs, it is against my religion!" The sincerity in Arthur's expression is translated in Nina's interpretation to the judges. She is working for us.

Arthur is talking directly into the eyes of Nina. Without looking, I know that Richard is laughing in his gut.

For the first time since we began this process, Ibarra enters the court by way of a side door near the rear of the room. He steps up into a pulpit that stands opposite to the prosecutor's pulpit. He says nothing and is unannounced.

As Arthur testifies, I am acutely aware the judges are watching me. I don't know for sure what they see.

"And tell the court how you come to know Señor Brewer and Señor Padilla."

"Your Honors, I live in Tahiti. While I painted the surfers on the waves in the ocean, those gentlemen and I met because they wanted to see my paintings. They are surfers from America, and we just naturally became friends."

The judges live in the upper economic class. They should have no problem imagining that an artist could have the income to afford such a lifestyle.

Now here comes the big question—did Arthur witness the fight between Ginger and Thomas Dawson? Did Arthur know Dawson or Ginger?

"Yes, I saw Mr. Dawson throw a drink on Ginger. The five of us were having a nice time talking about our different homes in the United States. Eduardo and Ricardo were telling Ginger and Mr. Dawson about life in Hawaii, and about surfing. Ginger asked Eduardo if he could teach her to surf in Hawaii, and I think that is when Mr. Dawson began to act strange and rude toward Ginger. Mr. Dawson suddenly wanted them to move to their own table. So Dawson told the waiter to move his drinks to another table. Ginger apologized to Ricardo, Eduardo, and me, and they moved. Mr. Dawson seemed very upset. At that point, Your Honors, is when Ginger asked Eduardo to dance. Actually I recall her words were, 'Would you please dance with me?' That is when I saw Mr. Dawson scrape all the glasses, candles, and a flower vase onto the floor and then yell at Ginger to come with him. Ginger refused. She came over to where Ricardo and I were standing. The whole place was standing by this time. Eduardo was trying to calm Mr. Dawson, but Dawson was getting louder. He was pushing Eduardo, calling him bad names."

"Thank you, Señor Thomason. That will be all the questions at this time. Return to your seat."

Arthur's interrogation has lasted about forty-five minutes. I get a quick look at the prosecutor's face. He looks unhappy, so Arthur must have done well.

Our interpreter repeats every word the judges say. She retains their aggressive intonation, but says it all so sweetly.

Loud and clear the court clerk calls for the next witness. Nina repeats: "The tribunal calls for Señor Ricardo Brew-er to come forward."

Time and time again I have asked Richard, "Are you ready? Do you know what the transcripts say?" Over and over I have studied what is important to remember. We never use drugs. We never had seen cocaine until Señor Del Gado opened the leather satchel.

"Señor Brew-er, do you use or have you ever used drugs?"

"Well, when I was a teenager I experimented with pot. But that's all!"

Even before Nina tries to convey his answer, she asks Richard, "I'm sorry, Señor. Please tell me what, or I mean, please tell the tribunal, what is pot?"

"Marijuana."

The rest of the few questions are the same as for Arthur. How did you meet Mr. Padilla? Did you come to Peru to traffic drugs? The difference arises when they ask Richard if he saw Ginger in Mr. Eduardo's room. Were Ginger and Mr. Eduardo romantically involved?

"Yes! I think Ginger was afraid of Mr. Dawson. She said to Eduardo and me that she thought Dawson would beat her that night. She seemed to be very attracted to Eduardo, and she needed his protection."

Being sincere about romance—this is not pleasant for Richard. And he must hate the job of building up Eduardo's ego. But the stakes are high. We must win this one. The judges have to believe our portrayal of Dawson. And Del Gado must testify that he opened the bag, that the cocaine was hidden inside the satchel. Once again our fate will hang on the whim of Del Gado.

After Richard gives his testimony, we are surprised to hear from the prosecutor. When Arthur was up there on the steps in front of the judges, the guy didn't say a word. But now he is up out of his seat, railing in his pulpit. Nina translates what he's screaming about.

"He is telling to the judges that you, Ricardo, have a criminal record. You have drug offenses in your country, and you have been in prison for attempted bank robbery. He is saying you are a known drug trafficker."

Oh shit, here it is. The one thing Richard and me have known about but never talk about. I mean, come on. Richard is in his thirties, and that little thing happened when he was seventeen. Richard told me about loaning another seventeen-year-old his twenty-two-caliber pistol, and then the kid robbed a bank across the street from Richard's parents' department store. The kid, proving his lack of genius, got caught on foot two blocks from the bank. Before the police could finish saying 'put up your hands you're under arrest,' the kid was yacking about where he got the gun and claiming that Richard planned the whole bungled robbery. The judge sent Richard to a federal prison because he turned eighteen before the trial ended. Richard served five years for his non-participation in his friend's case because—guess what—his friend snitched him off. The snitch himself served only six months, then got six years' parole.

The judges are calm. The one to the right of Nina's uncle asks Richard, "Señor, how do you answer these accusations of such a serious contradiction from your statement of not having any criminal record?"

Richard had well-educated parents, and as a boy he learned proper etiquette. Even though the federal time put some hard lines on his face, he still has a trained and polished manner when he wants to bring it on—as he does now, looking at Nina and then at the judges and then back to Nina. "I have never committed a crime in my life, judge. I work hard for my money. My mom and dad raised me to be honest and to obey the law." Richard says this as though he is asking Nina to marry him.

"Mentidas, mentidas, todas mentidas!"—lies, lies, all lies, shouts the prosecutor.

The judge reprimands the prosecutor. "Please, Señor Prosecutor, I must ask you to let me conduct this tribunal in a civilized manner. Thank you." The judge turns back to Richard. "Señor Brewer, the prosecutor he says you are lying."

I swell with pride when Richard answers: "All I have is the truth, Your Honors!" And Richard looks in the eyes of the judges, standing at attention as though he is addressing his military uncle.

Nina repeats for the judges, "That will be all for today, Señor. Take your seat."

Until I turn around and see Zoila, I'm in a very human battle of wits—international law, the courts, and politics. But when I see her I realize that only one force can get me out of here, and it's beyond wits. It is some part of almighty God, the God of Will. Will me in Lurigancho or not. Zoila is my intermediary between Lurigancho and God. She is Shiva, primitive and powerful. She emanates real peace in the silence where she was born.

We have been excused for the day. The military have been ordered to return us tomorrow, when Gustavo will testify.

As I pass the benches of spectators, I look only into Zoila's eyes. Deep inside the scarf she wears, her dark, infinitely deep eyes are sending messages from the gods. Her smile is the sun. The winds over the river spun her hair, so soft and strong and flowing. For a brief moment Zoila and I are inside the tube of a wave. No room for anyone else. Pure Mother Ocean enveloping us, allowing a contact beyond the body, beyond fear.

A soldier pushes me with his rifle. Suddenly I am aware of the sea of people who fill the courtroom. They gaze at me with calm faces. The room is unusually quiet, as if everyone feels something very powerful and right. Looking around I can see the situation now— nearly everyone in this packed room is a member of Zoila's clan.

In Peru there are no jury trials. The judges alone hold absolute power. Zoila and other Peruvians have told me that the judges look for family in the courtroom, people who have gathered in support of the accused. If there is no support, the judges assume that Lurigancho is the proper destination. By packing the courtroom, Zoila has given us dignity and a chance to live.

Once out of the bus, we walk the Big Hall escorted by several guards along with twenty-five other inmates. Gustavo lags behind. Every time I see him limping like this, I remember the scene at the PIP station—his Levi's soaked with blood, Gustavo a broken man hanging from the vicious fists of our respected four-star general.

We're all exhausted, drained of emotions. Then Richard breaks the silence.

"I was good. The ladies love me. I think the prosecutor wants Arthur!"

Arthur makes the effort of a comeback: "Yeah, well I saw Nina's uncle checking your skinny ass."

Here in the Big Hall, walking the city street at the corner of Cell-block Thirteen, I begin thinking more clearly. The rushing mobs, the men trying to bum change or a cigarette, this is familiar and somehow safer than the Palace of Justice. Over to my left is the guy who traded me some rubbery carrots for a couple of fish heads. He's squatting next to the wall with a burlap sack at his feet. He sees me and calls, "Hey, amigo." And here's Carl—his real name is Rafael, but he asked me to give him an American name, so I did. "Oye, Carl." He looks up from his pile of cigarette butts that he has heaped on a small square of newspaper.

"Oye, Gringo Loco. Como esta?"

"What's that guy doing?" asks Richard.

I call out, "Estoy bien, amigo." Then: "He's re-rolling tobacco from those cigarette butts. Then he sells them or trades them for stuff. That's where I got that can of tomato sauce we used for spaghetti. I traded him butts from you guys in our cell."

"Man, the drums are a lot louder out here."

As we get close to our cellblock door, I cut back to the prevailing issue. I say, "I think it's going to get a lot heavier."

"Yeah," says Richard. "Like, maybe our lawyer will actually say something."

"God forbid," says Arthur. "Then everything will go to hell."

"That's very funny. I'm just saying that it feels too good in the courtroom. Those judges haven't really drilled us like I thought they would."

We wait while the guard unlocks the thick rusted door of our cellblock. I am last inside. Before he goes through the door, Richard pauses to look back at the two hundred yards we have just walked.

"You fucking take strolls out here? You're fucking nuts, Eddie!"

"You should try it, R.B."

"Fuck you."

The first relief once the door closes is getting away from the Big Hall's stench. The prison is built on a slope, and the cellblocks are a little more elevated than the main building. Shit runs downhill, I guess.

Right away Arthur heads down to the yard. Richard and I start working our way through the throng of Peruvians who have come out into the hall eager for news from their friends. "Que cosas, hombre?" What happened? "Oye, tu vistas a mi esposa?" Did you see my wife? Everyone wants to hear that somebody got released—or any sort of good news. These days, it's good news just to see your fellow prisoners return alive.

For the first time Murphy is right there in the anxious throng. "Did anything come up?" he asks. Of course he means about his case. In other words, *our* case.

I brush past him. "I've got to get back to my bunk for a while. Tell you later."

Richard stops and looks right in his face. "Nothing better come up, motherfucker!"

"What makes you so high and mighty, Richard?

Murphy says this with just enough spine—maybe more spine than he intended—that it sets off a warning flash in my gut. I turn to watch.

"Hey punk, call me Pope Ricardo the First. Call me anything. But I'm no snitch, you fucking little girl."

"If you could get out of here by turning someone in, you would do it. You're no better than the rest of us."

Richard moves in close to Murphy. Now the Peruvians are moving aside. The small area just inside the iron door grows quiet. What happened to the guard, he disappeared.

"The rest of us. Who the fuck are the rest of us?" Richard sees Weaver slipping past on his way to the yard with his beach towel and folding chair. "That fuck? You and Weaver?" His voice is tight and hard.

"I ain't afraid of you, Richard."

I can feel a wave of electricity shooting through the crowd's grapevine of consciousness. People here already wonder why Murphy is still alive, especially when someone offered to kill him as a personal favor.

Chivo appears at my back, and he's poking something into my hand. He's trying to pass me a seven-inch shank, the rag-wrapped handle first. He whispers deep in my ear: "Matalo. Kill him. Kill the gringo."

In the next instant Richard punches Murphy so hard between the eyes that his head hits the concrete wall hard enough to bounce forward and meet squarely Richard's next blow, a left punch to Murphy's cheek bone. Murphy drops. His back slides down the wall. On the way down Richard catches the other side of Murphy's head with a kick. With Chivo still poking my hand and hip with the shank, I grab hold of Richard, both my arms tight around his chest, pinning his arms to his sides. I pull him back from where Murphy lies unconscious and bleeding.

Weaver pushes through the crowd. He examines Murphy up close and looks up at Richard, me still holding tight. "How could you do this to him? Man, you're fucked up, Richard."

"You're next, cop!" Richard tries to break out of my grip. His neck is bright red. "I lost five years for a fucking snitch, and it ain't gonna happen again! I'll take you down! I'll take both of you down!"

"Shut up, Weaver!" I yell. "Don't add to it. This is between us. Don't get in it. This ain't your world. Just help Murphy."

Weaver is bending down to aid Murphy where he lies sprawled against the wall.

Arthur and Ivan are pushing through the crowd, Ivan clearing the way quickly. "What the fuck happen to him?"

"Man, can't leave you guys alone for a minute," says Arthur. "Turn my back, and you're beating up Murphy without me."

Now Richard is standing in back of me, looking down at Murphy. My guess is that he's thinking he didn't have to hurt Murphy that bad. But of course he would never say this out loud.

I tell Ivan, "He fell. Can you help Weaver get him up to his bunk? I have to help R.B. He's upset about his friend having such a bad accident."

Richard and I step out into the yard where we can breathe. The

Peruvian crowd keeps standing around the scene of battle. Once we're outside, I confront him.

"You know why you jumped on him like that? Look at your hand. It's swelling up, for cripe sake."

"Shit," says Richard. "Want to walk to the Seven-Eleven, get some ice?"

"Listen. You're scared. And you're lying if you say you're not. We could get twenty years or more and you know it. Those pretty girls aren't going to save our asses. But listen, man. Something is. I believe that something else is going to save our butts. It's something I feel when I walk the Big Hall. When I look into the darkest parts, when I look into the faces of the low-lifes, the killers and psychopaths, all I see is me. Most of the time, I mean. Sometimes I'm out there and I lose it, I start seeing these people as different, and that's when I get afraid. Here's how I see it—I shouldn't walk the Big Hall if I can't see the God thing. Because without it, I'm separate, and the animals will sense that and they'll kill me. Richard, I want out of here. I don't want to be like Chivo, and I am becoming Chivo. He was trying to give me a shank to stick Murphy. I nearly took it. I want to hurt him, too. But if he died, we could spend the rest of our lives here and in federal prisons back home. I think you blew up and lost it because we don't talk enough. Understand, bro?"

"Fuck you, Eddie!" He says it in such a brotherly way that I stop right there in the flow of the evening walk traffic and give him a hug. It's a little awkward since he is so much taller. About half of the hundred and fifty men in the yard applaud, and we start walking again.

"I know you're right, man. And I know it isn't any more your fault I'm in this fucking hole than it is my own. But I'll tell ya, bro. I don't have a clue what the fuck I ever did to deserve this shit. So when you talk that God shit it just irritates me. I mean sure, we were here to party, to snort a little coke and meet Peruvian girls. For that, we get this? We came to see the spiritual ruins of the Incas. What we got was the ruins of this fucking prison, and the Inca is your new girlfriend. And, yeah, I guess I am a little hard on Murphy."

"R.B., remember what Gustavo looked like at the PIP?"

"How could I forget?"

"Remember that guy they brought in here, the PIP broke his back and still he didn't talk? Well, I ain't that tough, man. If I was beaten like Gus and broken up like our hero, I'd probably snitch off my mother. I don't know why the fuck we're here according to somebody's God. But according to Chivo and now Zoila, I will learn or stay here. I want to learn, quick. Because I think the fastest way out is to change myself on the inside so that I just don't belong here any more. And I think it's working. I mean, look what's been happening to us. That interpreter from Interpol was a nightmare devil, then Nina walked right out of a fairy tale. When I see opportunities like that get presented, I think I'm supposed to learn about the presenter."

"Man, what are you talking about. Sure, you got the little chick to interpret for us. But your girlfriend Godzoila and Nina got nothin' I can see to do with any God shit. It is just the way things are, man. What the fuck kind of God would give one shit about your nothing little ass? No, man. However we get out of Lurigancho, it won't have anything to do with God."

"Come on. Maybe Carlton has some ice stashed for your hand."

"Yeah, up his ass."

"And don't think I didn't catch that Godzoila remark."

"What's wrong with Godzoila?"

All the way up to our cell the inmates are patting Richard on the back

"Muy fuerte, gringo!"

Richard doesn't give them anything in return. He says to me, loud as if he's actually saying it to the Peruvians: "You know, these fucking assholes are just happy a gringo got smacked, that's all. Fuck 'em all."

Pelone is standing at the door of his cell, and he puts out his hand to welcome Richard into the world of sociopath killers.

"Hermano." It's a world where everybody says "brother" a lot. Just don't turn your back. Richard shakes Pelone's hand to keep peace with the delusional.

First one to say something as we walk into the cell is Hunter. "You know, if you break your jaw or need real medical attention, you may die in here."

Richard is not standing down. "Hunter, you been here a long time. You don't have any news for us except that shit. You sound like Carlton."

"Oh, don't bring me into this crap," says Carlton from his bunk. "The last time you did, it cost me a lot of money."

Kit Karson is over at the water barrels where Weaver is nursing Murphy's wounds. "Man, oh man! You really smacked poor ol' Murph, Richard!"

Stan looks over at Kit. "I heard Murphy fell down."

One after another, the other guys in the cell start agreeing with Stan. "Yeah, he fell… Sure did… Bad accident… That's how it happened…."

Oso is real quiet, too quiet.

Richard and Oso have become good buddies. They talk now more than Richard and I have in years. "Big guy, what's up? Look what Murphy did to my hand when he fell."

Oso lies on his bunk, a letter on his chest. While we were at court, the Reverend made his regular visit, smuggling in our money and mail. I see a few letters on my bunk.

"I got a bad letter, man."

"Your mom okay?"

"No, it's my ol' lady. She wants to sell my Porsche. She has no money, and her parents can't support her, they're old. I got a mortgage she has to pay or she has nowhere to live."

"When we lose our freedom, brother, we lose it all. It's like dying.

But you know what, man? Like Ballhead out there, stomping down the drain with his fucking bare feet, refusing to live in a pile of shit—dignity. Oso, we got to keep our dignity, man! She'll be all right."

From his bunk above me Tony has been listening to Richard philosophize and remarks, "Ol' brother Ed lost his dignity for a while. It really makes you stink, too."

Next morning in the basement of the Justice Palace we are talking with Gustavo. The soldier over at the gate is calling for the three of us. It is Ibarra.

On the way over Arthur says, "Boy, I wish Ibarra had to kick rats out of the way when he went to the crapper. I bet he'd shit his pants instead."

"I must tell to Ricardo," he says. "We are making joor appearance again. You make the mistake we must correct."

"What are you talking about? They all liked me."

"Jes, Ricardo, they like joo. But the judges do not like what joo say. The judge ask to joo do joo use the drugas. Joo must tell them today joo were confused and joo never use any drugas. Never, never! Do you understand for me?"

"But then I am lying from yesterday?"

"No, no, we must to change the record of what joo say before, the record, we must change what the record it says."

Arthur says, "Hey, just do it."

I remind him, "Remember what Rubio said?" I know Rubio is a lying fuck. But I think he was right when he said it. "We have to give the judges a reason to let us go! Remember?"

Richard takes complete control of himself when he is questioned again. He takes the same super-honest military stance and says: "Your Honors, I misunderstood your question and please forgive me, but no! I have never used any drugs in my life!"

Nina looks relieved when Richard makes his retraction. I am sitting next to Gustavo. The court clerk hops to the second step and turns to face the entire courtroom behind us. He's a skinny man in a dark blue suit that's way too big for him. The padded shoulders jut out, and I can see his adam's apple jiggling behind the oversized collar of his white dress shirt. He calls to the back of the courtroom: "Gustavo Rivera."

Nina will not be standing up with Gus. He is on his own, with the judges asking him directly all their interrogations in Spanish. Nina is now sitting next to me where Gustavo was. She whispers to me that she will try to tell us what is being said.

The prosecutor starts shouting behind us, his voice echoing in the ancient domed ceilings as he calls Gustavo the scum of the community, the enemy of the state, and the cause of all his country's problems.

"Gustavo Rivera es un trafficante! Este Señor Rivera hace la coca y vende la coca por los tres Norte Americanos. La gente de Peru quiere veinte anos por este hombre del diablo." I do not need Nina to tell me what the prick in the box has just said. He wants Gus to do twenty years, too

The excitement level has gone up now. Gustavo's mother and her friends and Gustavo's friends have added a lot more people to the already packed courtroom.

Different today—the prosecutor is the one interrogating.

"Señor Rivera, are you acquainted with the North American men sitting in the courtroom, Señores Padilla, Brewer, and Thomason? Did you supply the cocaine to these men?"

"No Jefe. I did not!"

Nina interprets, whispering in English. Arthur squeezes against me, trying to get close enough to feel her breath and smell her perfume. He doesn't hear a word, only the tone of her female voice.

Richard sits straight up, paying close attention to what is going on, watching the expressions of the judges as the prosecutor's tone becomes violent. He's acting as though we killed and maimed, robbed and murdered.

Nina paraphrases his tirade: "Gustavo Rivera sold the cocaine to Señor Dawson and his partners. The police discovered this crime and searched for Señor Dawson and his partners in order to arrest them. The police believe Señor Dawson has escaped to the United States. But his partners are the men you see before you. These men are housed in Lurigancho Prison so that the public and little children are safe from their business of spreading poison to our children. Señor Rivera lies. He sold the cocaine not only to Dawson but also to these other North Americans before you. Please find them all guilty, and let all the innocent people be safe from them. Let them rot in Lurigancho, Your Honors."

I hear a cry from the audience, like a doe in the forest seeing her mate felled by a rifleshot. People are talking loudly, some shouting, "Los gringos no hacen nada. Donde esya el otro gringo?" Some are chanting: "Daw-a-son, Daw-a-son, Daw-a-son."

Nina whispers in my ear, "This has never happened before. The judges have much weight toward what the people want. And the prosecutor is becoming very angry. He is looking the fool."

" Silencio en el courte ahora!" And bam bam bam bam with the judge's gavel. Soldiers around the courtroom take the attention stance. All are quiet.

"That will be all, Señor Gustavo. You will be notified of further proceedings, Señor. Thank you, return to your seat."

"Eduardo Padilla. Step up to the judges."

Nina rises with me, and we walk to the third step of four in front of the judges. They look down from their thrones of blood-red velvet and gold, the finest hand-carved wood.

"Señor Padilla, please tell the court how it is you have a Spanish last name and you cannot speak Spanish. Instead you need this very attractive interpreter." I hear giggles and murmurs. Nina's face is slightly pink. She translates the comment: "Instead you need this interpreter."

Uncle has lobbed me a softball, a perfect chance to lighten the mood. "Your Honor, I love my mother and father very, very much, and they did their best to raise me the right way. They put me in good schools; they cared for me. They taught me to be kind and honest. My father taught me a skilled trade so that I could make a good living, Your Honor. I am sure my parents meant no harm by speaking only English in our home."

Somehow what Nina says in her translation sounds so much better. The audience bursts out laughing. Uncle seems amused.

Bam, bam, bam, the gavel slams down. The judge on the right leans over to speak in the ear of Nina's uncle. Uncle's expression shifts. He looks at me as though he has just been told all the wrong things.

"Señor, we have your criminal record from the United States. You have been lying. You are a trafficante. The FBI wants you in your country. You are the member of an organization called—" he listens again to the judge on the right—"the Brotherhood of Eternal Love, a drug smuggling syndicate. How do you answer this information sent to us from your government? Speak!"

There is a low "oooooooouu" from the people in back of us.

Nina repeats what I have already understood. Her expression is steady. Her eyes are not showing any trace of belief in what the judge has just suggested.

I am calm.

"Your Honor, in my country there are many people with the same name. I can only say that is not me. I have no criminal record, and I have never heard of the Brotherhood of Eternal Love. I am a Catholic, Your Honor."

I do not want to appear to Their Honors as though I'm dumb, but I don't want them to think I am the big-time leader-of-the-pack like the prosecutor is running down. I know sure as hell that the DEA is putting all kinds of shit in the ears of these guys. I hope to God they don't push Murphy's case into this one or I'm fucked.

"Señor Padilla, tell the court how it is possible that Señor Dawson could deposit this large amount of cocaine in your room and against your will?"

"Your Honor, thank you for this opportunity to tell the truth. I met Mr. Dawson and his girlfriend, Ginger, the morning that Mr. Brewer and I checked into the Granja Azul Resort. In the lobby at the front desk Mr. Dawson overheard me speaking English and learned that I am from California. Mr. Dawson introduced Ginger and himself to Mr. Brewer and me. Mr. Thomason had already been shown to his own room."

"Until the meeting at the front desk you are saying you have never seen Ginger or Dawson?"

"Yes. That is correct. After the registering at the desk was completed, the manager, George, introduced himself and invited all of us for a Bloody Mary in the cocktail lounge."

"Please, what is this Bloody Mary?"

There is quiet laughter from behind.

"It is an American drink, Your Honor."

"Ah yes. Thank you, proceed."

"We all declined the drink and went to our rooms. Ginger and Dawson to their room. Mr. Brewer and me shared a room. A bungalow."

"I believe there is a deposition from the manager of the Granja. A man named George, as you say. The court translator will read this letter, first in Spanish so everyone will understand, and then in English. Por favor, senorita."

Uncle wants his niece to be recognized. Maybe he wants the

people to like him; maybe he would like to be El Presidente. Maybe setting us free would help his popularity.

Nina reads the resort manager's deposition in both languages. It substantiates everything about Dawson's freak-out in the nightclub. "He seemed to go insane! I had my security men take him by force out of the club, and I told Mr. Dawson to go to his room and take his things and leave the resort and never return. When I returned to apologize to my guests, Mr. Brewer, Mr. Thomason, and Mr. Padilla were leaving with Ginger. Ginger was crying, her dress soiled from the drink that Mr. Dawson threw on her. Mr. Padilla said to me that they would take Ginger to his bungalow until she felt safe. I said of course. Later one of my housemaids came to me to report that Mr. Dawson was throwing Ginger's belongings out of the second-story window. Before I could respond, he fled the resort. Mr. Padilla and Ginger met with me at her guestroom, and she discovered that Mr. Dawson had taken her money, passport, and airline tickets. Mr. Padilla offered his bedroom to Ginger. He said he could sleep on the sofa. Ginger returned to me the key for her room, and a valet took her things to Mr. Padilla's bungalow up the tram overlooking the resort. I returned to my office and called the police. The Peruvian Internal Policeman came and took a report."

"Señorita Nina," says Uncle, interrupting. "Please, Señor Padilla, tell the court what took place the next day. Especially the few hours prior to your arrest."

I get a little rush. I am overly prepared. I need to talk as if I'm just trying to recall that night years ago.

"Your Honor, thank you. I have been held in Lurigancho Prison for four years, but I can remember clearly something that changed my life and caused me and my innocent friends to be locked up. The next morning Mr. Brewer and me went to have coffee in the café. That way, Ginger could have her privacy. Then she joined us for breakfast. A few minutes later Arthur also joined us. We went to George's office and used his telephone to call the American embassy about Ginger's passport. It was the weekend, and we could get nothing accomplished.

"We spent the rest of the day at the resort. Ginger and me rode horses provided by the resort. In the late afternoon we all met over a small lunch, but we talked for hours. Mr. Thomason is very entertaining, Your Honor, and he drew our faces on the cloth napkins. Ginger told us about her life. Once it started to become evening, Mr. Brewer, Ginger, and me went to our bungalow while Mr. Thomason went to his smaller room. In the bungalow I opened a bottle of some good Peruvian wine. Mr. Brewer and me sat outside by the pool and watched the last of the sunset while Ginger showered and dressed in the room. A couple hours later Mr. Brewer had cleaned up and wanted to go down for a drink. I got into the shower while Ginger and Mr. Brewer went down to the club bar to wait for me to join them all for dinner. While I washed in the shower, I thought I heard banging on my living-room door. The bungalow is quite large, Your Honor. It has two bedrooms, a living room, and a den. With the shower on and the bathroom door shut, it is difficult to hear the front doorbell. A knock is more difficult. I turned off the shower and could clearly hear loud, hard banging at the front door. I got out of the shower, Your Honor, and wrapped a towel around my body and went to the door still wet and dripping thinking it must be some emergency about my friends. When I opened the door, there stood Tom Dawson. Your Honor, I was shocked to see him."

"And what did Dawson say to you, Señor Padilla?"

"Your Honor, he made two steps through the doorway and into my room."

"You invited him in?"

"No, absolutely not! I blocked Mr. Dawson and demanded he leave immediately!"

"Go on, please. What happened next?"

"Mr. Dawson had in his hand a large leather satchel, Your Honor, like a big old doctor's bag. He quickly set the bag down. I thought he was going to hit or punch me. But rather he stood there just inside my door yelling.

"What was Dawson yelling about?"

"He wanted to see Ginger. He demanded that she come with him. He threatened violence. I told him to leave. I told Mr. Dawson that Ginger never wanted to see him again. And that she knew he had robbed her and taken her passport and tickets. Mr. Dawson suddenly turned and quickly went away. He was headed over to the tram."

"Yes, and the leather bag? Is this the same leather bag the police found in your room?"

"Yes, it is, Your Honor."

Now the prosecutor shouts from above and behind me.

"Señor Padilla, do you expect this tribunal to believe that Señor Dawson was able to get through the resort security and up your private tram and bully his way into your room? And then leave a big bag full of cocaine and run away?"

The crowd grumbles. They don't like him. They like the judge. The judge regains control.

"Señor Padilla, how could Dawson get away like that? I mean, why did you not take his bag outside or chase him and notify security and the manager?"

"Your Honors, other than a small bathroom towel I had nothing on. I only had the towel wrapped around me. I kicked the bag aside, shut the door, and began to dress and go after him. Your Honor, he is crazy. The only thought I recall about the bag Dawson left was it might contain Ginger's belongings. Of course I had no thought to open the bag. I was only concerned about warning Ginger. I dressed as quickly as I could. As I sat putting on my second shoe, to my surprise Mr. Brewer walked in. I remember being shocked that he said nothing about seeing Dawson. Your Honor, to this day I do not know how it was possible for Mr. Dawson to slip by not only security but Mr. Brewer did not pass him either. That is a mystery, Your Honor."

Then Uncle says, "The police report states that one of the resort employees, a gardener, saw Señor Dawson crossing a lawn to the road where a taxi was waiting, and saw Señor Dawson enter the taxi, and saw the taxi drive away. The taxi driver later stated that Señor Dawson carried a large bag when he went into the resort, but that he returned with no baggage of any kind. Do you know about this taxi driver's testimony? Also, when Señor Brewer entered the room, where had you been sitting and what was said between you? Did you ask him if he had seen Dawson? And where were Señorita Ginger and Señor Thomason at this time?"

"No, Your Honor. I had not known of this taxi person until now."

Holy God! The only way that got in the transcript had to have been Rubio or Del Gado! Or who? I never said that, and it never came up at the PIP.

The judge on the right whispers in the ear of Uncle. Uncle says to the clerk, who is sitting at the foot of the stairs: "Where is that police report about the taxi driver?"

The clerk promptly produces the document and thrusts it into the air. His sleeve slides down his skinny arm. "Here it is, Your Honor."

His Honor beckons with his hand, and the clerk scampers up the three steps.

His Honor begins examining the document and says to me, "Please continue, Señor."

"My first words to Mr. Brewer were did he see Dawson. Then I wanted to know where Ginger was."

"Yes, yes. Go on, please."

The crowd in back of me is quiet.

"Your Honor, I finished putting on my shoe, jumped up, grabbed Mr. Brewer's arm, and told him that Dawson had been here and we must find Ginger right now. Mr. Brewer calmed me, saying that Mr. Thomason and Ginger had gone to the manager's office to see if

Ginger could cash a check. Dawson did not get her checkbook. I
told Mr. Brewer what had taken place. We both walked toward the
tram to find Ginger. We could tell that Mr. Thomason and Ginger
were coming up the tram from below, so we waited. They had not
seen Dawson, Your Honor. We all returned to my room. Ginger said
she had never seen the bag that Dawson had left. It appeared to be
locked, and our interest was to call George the manager and report
this occurrence to him and ask him to call the police and report Mr.
Dawson. I phoned George, and he said he would send someone
up for the bag that Dawson had left. I told the others that George
would take care of the report and the bag. We could go safely to
dinner in a bit."

"Did you go to dinner?"

"No. After about ten minutes my front door opened, and it was
Señor Del Gado coming through the door, followed by many other
men. All of them were police."

I hear the rustle of the robe as the judge to His Honor's left leans
over and whispers. Then the whispering judge speaks out loud for
the first time.

"That will be all for now, Señor Padilla. Return to your seat."

Then he gives instruction to the clerk. And the clerk calls Gustavo.

"Gustavo Rivera!"

Nina remains on the steps at the foot of the thrones. She seems
to sense she will be needed right there.

The judge on the left speaks aggressively to Gustavo: "Gustavo
Rivera, tu vendiste la coca para Dawson y los gringos verdad?"

Gustavo pleads with the judge. "No, no Señor Jefe. La coca sola-
mente del gringo Dawson. Es la verdad, Señor...."

Before Gustavo makes his next statement, he looks back directly
at Zoila where she is surrounded by her family, her tribe. Gustavo
has ancient ties with these people.

"These men are good men, Señor Jefe. I have been living in hell
with them. I know them to be of honor and great loyalty. Señor
Dawson is the man who belongs in Lurigancho, Señor Jefe."

It is good, very good, that the tribe is hearing this from one of
its own.

"You are excused. Sit down. Call Señor Padilla."

The clerk announces again, "Señor Padilla!"

Uncle returns to his role as my interrogator.

"Tell the court, Señor Padilla. Did you or anyone in your bungalow open Señor Dawson's bag?"

All right! That's the first time the judge has called it 'Dawson's bag.'
Yeah!

"No, Your Honor, no one. Only Del Gado, Your Honor!"

"That is your sworn testimony? No one opened the bag, and
none of you ever saw the cocaine in the bag until General Del Gado
opened the bag and removed the cocaine?"

For this answer I look directly into the eyes of each judge: "Yes,
Your Honors. That is the truth, so help me God!"

The judge turns his full official power toward the clerk and orders:
"Summon General Del Gado to the witness stand!"

Nina and I look at each other. I have told the same story that I
told her. She has a slight grin. She looks very, very confident.

A man like Del Gado could say anything. He could walk in here
and say that we had the cocaine sitting out in the room in big piles
on silver serving trays. He could say that Eduardo bribed him with
more money than he would normally make in a lifetime, bribed him
to tell the story that matches his testimony. He has the power to say
whatever the fuck he likes.

Just stick to the goddamn transcript!

Our day in court is moving in fast-forward. The clerk is already
yelling: "Señor General Del Gado del Militar de Peru."

He enters the courtroom from outside the huge wooden doors. Everyone turns to see El Diablo himself, the dark man whose reputation precedes him all over Peru. He is wearing a finely tailored double-breasted silver-gray silk suit, a white dress shirt with a high collar, and a black and silver tie. Even without a uniform he radiates power over life and death. Many a drug lord, cocaine cook, petty hustler, and political dissident has died horribly while looking at that face.

As he passes, he glances over at me, Richard, and Arthur. *Oh yeah! That's the Del Gado we know and love. Those eyes, black and glassy. I'll bet you made Pelone cry.*

All you can hear is the tapping of his leather heels on the wooden floor until he stops and breaks the quiet himself.

"General Del Gado reporting to the Tribunal de Peru, Señores." He clicks his heels. He has adopted the manners of a maitre d' in a nice Mexican restaurant.

Del Gado receives the judges' thanks for coming. And, as all must be, he is sworn in. "So help me, God!" says Del Gado.

Man, what God is that?

"This tribunal has one question at this time for you, General. In the transcript of this case years ago you stated that you came into the bungalow of Señor Brewer and Señor Padilla and you saw no cocaine until you opened the black leather satchel that was found in their room. Will you please tell this tribunal for our proceedings, is this statement true? Did you, and you only, open the bag to reveal the cocaine?"

He says one word loud and clear: "Yes!"

The prosecutor is furious. As aggressively as he dares, and choosing his phrases with great care, he says, "I'm sorry, General! I must ask you this. Are we to understand that it is your sworn testimony that until you opened the bag we have heard so much about you never had seen Señor Padilla or his companions with cocaine visibly in their presence or on their persons?"

"That is correct, Señor. Now is there anything further? If not, I must return to my work."

Nina's uncle is graceful in excusing Del Gado and thanking him for interrupting his busy schedule.

The three judges stand and are talking very low. Nina says, "They are going to have a meeting in private. Don't worry, we can sit. But please, we must be quiet."

The judges leave the courtroom. They are out for a mere ten minutes.

Bam.

"All rise!"

Uncle remains standing when the other two sit.

"We have reached a decision! All the prisoners will stand!"

Nina whispers, "You must listen carefully. I don't know what is going to happen."

"It is the decision of this court on this date of this year that it finds Señor Ricardo Brewer absuelto! In the case of Señor Arturo Thomason, this court on this date in this year does find you absuelto! In the case of Señor Eduardo Padilla, this court on this date in this year does find you are absuelto!"

Richard is standing next to me and asks me, "What the hell is absuelto?"

Arthur is asking Gustavo, "What the hell is absuelto?"

Both Nina and Gustavo are telling us the word means 'absolved.' "You are absolved! Absolved!"

"Is that good?" says Arthur.

It is as if everyone in the courtroom has to ask each other, "What the hell does absuelto mean?" And slowly everyone gets it, and the room becomes vivid with joy and laughter. I look at Zoila, and her face is radiating happiness and sadness at once. She is smiling so sweetly, but her eyes are sad—the way you might feel at a wedding when it's your best friend going off to start a new life. *Does she imagine I would just leave when they let me go?* People around her are hugging and jumping up and down. But no one touches Zoila. She is full of light, standing apart, waiting for the moment when the armed animals no longer surround us, the moment when our patience can be fully rewarded.

Arthur and Richard are hugging. I mean, Arthur is hugging Richard. All I can hear from Richard—and he says it loud enough for me to hear above the whooping and yahoos—is, "Yeah right! I'll believe it when we're on the street!"

Just as Arthur is making his way around the table hoping to get some hugs from Nina's friends, BAM. BAM. BAM. The gavel drops. Arthur stops short.

"Order in the court! Order in the court!"

The next words really get us. Even Richard starts to break down a little as Uncle delivers the judgment. "The military will provide transportation to Lurigancho Prison and officiate the appropriate procedure for release of these men today! This court will notify the others in the case of the next proceedings. That is all."

BAM.

5

THE REV

Everyone is happy except the prosecutor. He is still in his pulpit yelling about filing an appeal. Arthur is chattering at Nina while Nina tries to explain "absuelto" to Richard, who stares at her as though he doesn't believe a word she's saying. I'm trying to see Zoila, but well-wishers are crowding us, shaking my hand, blocking my view. Now I see two soldiers approaching. One is using his rifle to shoo people away. The other is carrying four sets of silver bracelets. He shouts, and I turn around so he can cuff my hands behind my back.

As Richard feels the cuffs tighten, he says, "This sure don't feel like absuelto." Gustavo's mother is calling out from the crowd. The soldiers tell everyone to stay back, get out of the way, and they start pushing us toward the door. I know Zoila is near. But I'm glad she's not in the middle of this chaos. We'll be together when I clear the process with Interpol and get my passport.

Although we're cuffed, we're not pinned together in pairs. They sweep us right through the basement and load us into a small armored car, like something out of a Nazi war movie. Only two soldiers, the driver and shotgun. Arthur just can't stop talking: "We're going home, you guys! American women! Hey! When I get home, I'm going over to my mom's, well, after I get a good night's FUCK! I'm going to eat my mom's cookin', and while she makes dinner I'm going to go out and lie on the grass. And then...."

Richard cuts him off. "It ain't over yet, Happy Harry."

"I don't believe this, either," I say.

"Oh fuck, get over it! Didn't you see the judge? He liked Eddie. He thinks he's going to marry his little niece. I don't know, I just know they're fucking letting us go. Well, they're letting me go. You guys might be fucked because of Murphy...."

Richard looks to me as Arthur keeps on blabbing.

What are they really up to? This is too good to be true.

It is the quickest ride to Lurigancho we've ever had, and this time we get to travel with our heads up. But there are no windows in this funny-looking little Loomis antique.

When we stop at the prison, the rear double doors rattle and shake and then swing open, and there is the scary lieutenant—the one who did our orientation on the way in, years ago. Is he here to give us our orientation out? We once watched this same lieutenant shoot two men in cold blood.

He removes our cuffs. The driver hands him the court papers then turns to shut the back of the van. After the lieutenant reads our release orders, he says, "You gringos are a long way from your home. Maybe you come back, live here in Lurigancho more time. You have friends here, yes?"

He tells us to go and get our things. "Tell the guard to take you off the count and to call up the captain for confirmation. Be back within the hour, gringos!" He barks at our two escorts, who lead us to our cellblock. As we walk the Big Hall, I am flooded with the sure feeling that we really are leaving Lurigancho. And yet the feeling is not what I think it should be. Strange to say, I'm actually sad to the point of torment. Must I choose now, whether to stay with Zoila or go home? There are as many people at home praying for our return as there were in the courtroom cheering for our release. I haven't seen my kids in years. My mother, my dad, my brothers—I have kept all these loved ones in some remote place in my emotional system, and now the system is breaking open. How can I choose? I know the pain of betrayal. I would never inflict that pain on sweet Zoila.

Maybe Chivo was right. Maybe the Big Hall did strip away my pretense and false pride. Maybe I did meet the Buddha in the guise of Ballhead. What have I learned? Simple lessons. That betrayal and betraying both hurt. That living in fear is true loss of freedom. That self-esteem is an inside job. Are my lessons done?

"We are going home!" Arthur is singing with joy all the way up the two flights: "We are going home! We are going home! Who wants to take over my business? Hey, get your leche asada!" Now he has everyone's attention. As he enters the cell, with Richard and me ten feet behind, he calls: "Hey, you motherfuckers! We are out of here—now!"

By the time we get to the cell, everyone looks stunned. The first words eventually come from Tony: "Whoa! Hey, look at his face. He isn't kidding."

Ivan pops up from his bunk, grips each of Arthur's shoulders with his big mitts, and says, "Arthur, what are you talking about?"

"The judge kicked us out of the case! We are gone with the wind!"

Weaver is the first to say it. "That's not possible! You can't even buy your way out of here, no one can. I know you guys are putting us on."

Then—except for Weaver, Murphy, and Kit—a cheer goes off. A yell goes through the block: "Los gringos son libres!"

I say, "Ivan! You have inherited my entire crypt. Do whatever you like with it. All I'm taking are my letters in this shoebox. Goodbye, brother!"

"No. Really! You guys are fucking putting us on. You're not going anywhere. Are you?" Ivan has to talk loudly because almost every-one else has got the message that we are not kidding.

Richard is putting his little girl's pictures into an envelope while he's talking with Carlton. Carlton is giving Richard his home address. Richard's hands are shaking as he tries to slow down enough to write legibly, and Hunter is giving each of us a hug. Out in the hall the inmates are buzzing. A guard comes to the cell and tells the three of us to hurry up, the soldiers are waiting.

Arthur stands in the middle of the room, his arms wrapped around a towel that's tied in a knot—his entire luggage and net personal worth. He says, "Let's get out of here before they change their minds!"

Weaver cannot help himself and says, "You'll be back. It's a trick!"

Arthur's last words: "Good luck, Murph, you fuck!"

As I walk out in back of Arthur and Richard, I say, " I love you guys. Carlton, my friend, I will never forget what you did for me. You're a great man."

Carlton crosses the cell to embrace me. "Shit howdy," he says, "I guess you really are walking out of here. Well, keep going all the way home. And you're welcome. Maybe you can do the same for me sometime, but I sure hope not."

I stop again and say, "And Weaver, fuck you!"

Ivan gets over his shock enough to say, "Wait a minute! Give me a hug. I can't believe this is happening. But if they keep opening doors, keep going until you are home. Maybe I'll see you guys in the States; we'll get drunk together, meet some girls. So long, you guys."

Richard has a last word for Murphy. "Remember, you're lucky to be alive. Maybe that will help."

Everyone follows us down to the iron door, chattering loudly. As the door to the Big Hall swings open, Chivo appears.

"I must go, hermano!"

For the first time I see tears in Chivo's eyes.

"Chivo, I do not know where they are taking me. So I tell you that you taught me how to live beyond fear. And you watched over me like a brother."

He and the others will never see the streets again. I thought they were murderers, thieves with no morals, no ethics, no love—sociopaths who belonged in Lurigancho. I was blind to the obvious. These are men with a will to survive any hardship. These are human beings. And Chivo the goat is a chief among them.

"You stay with the woman from la selva?"

"This is what I want."

"You stay with this woman!" He smiles. "Now, Gringo Loco, you have become worthy of this woman. She give you many good sons make good hunters. She good woman for you, Gringo Loco. You good man for her."

Being worthy of Zoila has been damn hard work.

A soldier pokes me with the butt of his rifle. "You go, gringo."

Chivo puts his hands on my shoulders and I embrace him. I walk backwards for a couple steps looking at what I was becoming. For a while you couldn't tell us apart, me and Chivo. Now I look back and see his world diminish as the outside world opens with its enormity.

The soldiers return us to the little armored car, and they cuff us and load us in again.

Richard says, "Man, I don't know if I can get used to no one beating my ass into the bus."

The soldiers tell us to get out. They seem to know the lone Peruvian man—a slight, light-skinned man in gray slacks and a black dress shirt—who is pointing an automatic weapon at us. He hands the soldiers three pairs of handcuffs. They proceed to unlock their own bracelets from behind and then use his to cuff us in the front. We're standing right next to another monumental Spanish-era building that's across the street from the Justice Palace. Señor

Gray-and-Black motions with his gun for us to enter the building.

He and the two soldiers take us not up the front steps but around to the rear. We go up a flight of concrete steps and walk into a dusky corridor lined with brass-knobbed wooden doors. Above each door is a foggy windowpane etched with words in Spanish, and above each of these is a transom tipped open for the air to circulate. The guards hurry us forward, and at the end of the hall we come to elevator doors.

"Push the button for roof. The top button. Push it." Arthur lifts his cuffed hands. The elevator door opens and we all get in—six men and three guns. It's a tense ride to the top.

As soon as the elevator stops, the soldiers shove us out onto the roof. They de-cuff us. Then the slight man says, "You wait here, gringos. You have money? You have food over there."

He points to a tin kiosk just big enough for two women, a pot of rice, and a pot of beans. The kiosk has a few things on the counter for sale, gum and candy. To our left, two armed soldiers sit at a desk. On the desk is a telephone.

The prisoners loitering around up here, about forty of them, look like typical Lurigancho citizens, dirty and unshaven and raggedly clothed. A few are crisp and clean as though they've just come from home. Everyone is camped out in an empty penthouse that's been stripped down to the shell, nothing but cardboard and old newspaper for rugs.

Now the elevator door opens. Ibarra steps forth in his usual brown suit, the jacket by necessity open at the belly.

"Hello boys!" he says. "How is joo? Joo will be free to go only in short time. We must wait for the Interpol to see joo can go. They must check joo have no problemas with other countries."

"Then where do we go?" I ask. "The airport?"

Arthur says quickly, "Yeah! Just take us to the airport. We'll just wait for the next plane to the USA. Anywhere will be fine."

"So what's next, fat man?" says Richard. "You need more money before we can leave this roof? Is that it?"

"Oh, no, Ricardo. Joo must trust me. I only care for joor safety and joor freedom." Ibarra is so excited his jowls bounce. He uses his hands to talk with more sincerity.

"Where's our passports?"

"Jes, that is why I have to meet joo here this place. I must tell to the major to let joo go to the street."

I catch something there and ask, "What are you talking about? The court said we could go free."

"Jes, boys, that is true. But not to worry. As soon as the prosecutor makes his appeal to the Courte Suprema, joo will have your passaportes!"

"What the fuck are you talking about? We gotta stay on this fucking roof?"

"No, no! I will tell to the major in charge, and joo will go to a very nice hotel."

Ibarra returns to the elevator.

As soon as Ibarra vanishes, Richard heads to one side of the roof and I move to the other. I find myself walking along a plastered railing overlooking the polluted rooftops of Lima. The street is six stories down. Above us there's a radio antenna tethered by steel cable. One of those cables hangs about three feet over my head. It slides on down to where it's bolted onto the building next door.

The guards up here are very relaxed. This must be just a holding place for people undergoing the international record check. When I try to talk, people tell me the only important thing about them:

"de Mexico."

"Brazil."

"Chile."

Men are sitting reading or talking or playing chess on benches. Some are lying on cardboard. One man lets me know that he's from France.

I come back to find Arthur in deep conversation with a couple of men. Richard returns from his hunt at the same moment. "What're you two idiots checking over the side for?" says Arthur. "You'd better not be thinking of jumping."

Richard laughs. "What the fuck are you saying?

"If it wasn't for the two of you, I wouldn't be in this mess and stuck on this roof when I should be somewhere celebrating. Somewhere with women."

"Arthur," I say, "don't let either one of us hold you back. Get out there and do your thing."

"Yeah," says Richard. "Just slide down one of those cables and you're home free."

"Ha ha. Very funny. I'd leave you in a second. Don't forget—I am the victim here. Can you imagine being stuck in jail because of me? Because of me? I don't think so. It couldn't happen."

The elevator door opens. Ibarra is back already. He's frowning when the door opens, but by the time he reaches us he has forced a smile on his face. We stand at rigid attention.

"Boys, I have bad news. Good news and bad news."

"Give us the bad news first," I say.

"Boys, I have bad news for to Arturo."

Arthur's voice is suddenly pinched. "What bad news?"

"Please, can you explain to me this thing in joor country 'the daft.' What is the daft?"

I say, "Are you saying 'the draft?'"

"Jes! That is the word. The FBI say Arturo is a draft dog."

Richard says, "Draft dodger? There hasn't been a draft in years. Who's saying he's a draft dodger? And so what?"

"Oh, is very serioso. Arturo must stay until joor government clears this problem. It is too late today. We must come back tomorrow. Don't worry, boys. Tomorrow we get joo, Arturo."

"You mean I gotta stay on this fucking roof? By myself? This is fucked!" Arthur looks at Richard and me, and it is the look of a little brother fighting his tears. "Hey, it's okay. I know you guys aren't going anywhere without me. You'd both get lost. See you tomorrow. Right? You two wouldn't leave me would you?

With Ibarra standing right there, neither Richard nor me will say what we are really thinking. "Oh hell no, man," says Richard. "We can't leave you."

I tell Arthur, "Yeah, like you said. We'd probably get lost without you."

Arthur's panic shows in his wide questioning eyes as we begin to move toward the elevator. He's talking fast. "Look, you guys, ah, go to a hotel and call home. Tell them to get money down here or whatever they have to do."

Richard says, "And who are *they*, man?"

"You know, Chula. Or maybe the Peruvian ambassador."

"You mean the U.S. embassy."

"Right. Or someone."

I say, "You remember just how much they give a shit. Don't freak, Arthur. We'll see you tomorrow, and then we'll go home together."

We follow Ibarra down to a large office. On the other side of the office there's a door that opens to the street and to the freedom of downtown Lima. I am acutely aware that we are not handcuffed.

"Boys, this is Señor Hector, the jefe of the international police."

It's the same scrawny fellow, Señor Gray-and-Black. We try to explain to Hector that there is no longer a draft in the U.S., and that the U.S. President gave amnesty to all draft dodgers. The Interpol cop says he will check. Come back in the morning, he says.

He tells us that we can go.

Richard opens the door to freedom and gestures with his hand. This must be the door that Rick walked through. And now me. And here waiting in the lobby is Zoila.

Zoila stands between her mother and father. Her mother is

fair-skinned with a very gentle face. The father is small and very dark with a fierce expression except when he smiles, as he does now. Surrounding them are Zoila's sister and little brother, a couple of aunties and uncles. I can tell when they glance around that this place makes them nervous. But their anxiety is overshadowed by their excitement. They shake my hand and hug me. This is like a family game show, and we won. "Please, Eduardo. You must come with us now," says the mother.

I look into Zoila's eyes and see a wonderful life. "I'm not going home yet, R.B." I take hold of Zoila's tender hand.

"Come on," says Richard. "We have to get Arthur out. Then you can go with them. Tell her. Tell her and her family that you'll see them soon. Get an address or phone number. Come on, we have to get to a phone and call the States."

When I don't respond, Richard gets more urgent. "Don't do this yet, Eddie. Not yet, man. I need your help to get Arthur, man. He's our brother, Eddie. We got no choice."

I look at him. But he keeps talking. "Have I ever, and I mean ever, said that I need you, or anyone? Well, I need you now, man."

Ibarra draws his own bottom line.

"Eduardo, I must tell to joo because joo have no papelles, no passport, joo have been released into my custody until tomorrow when we will have joors and Ricardo's passports. And I must say to joo if joo have no passport, these nice peoples they could have problem with the PIP. Everything will be well tomorrow. Joo will see tomorrow, boys. I tell to these nice peoples joor problem. I tell them in Spanish."

He speaks to them.

Zoila and I gently embrace as her family closes around us. I hug Zoila's mother, remembering her from that day when I threw the note out the window. Then once again I shake the hands of those with her.

Standing before her own family, Zoila says, "Eduardo, you are free. And you must help your friend. I am yours. Our spirits joined many, many thousand years ago. We are together always. I found you deep in the darkness of Lurigancho. Even if it is in another life, my love, I will find you again. I will give you the telephone of mi tio, my uncle. He has a bakery in Lima. He can tell you where to find me. Call when you finish your work. Get your friend. In your heart you cannot leave him. If you leave and do not try to help him, you may never have peace. Eduardo, we could not be at peace."

Fuck Arthur!

I am looking deep and questioning into Zoila's eyes. Our love grew up in Lurigancho. This is the first moment it is safe to bloom.

I take her and hold her close and say, "Please listen. My spirit is pushing me to go with you." We stand like that in a white light outside of time. When she pulls back, something rips inside me.

"Perhaps our journey of searching for one another will not end," she says." You must finish your journey. Your friend needs you. He is asking from the Spirit. We cannot refuse what the Great Spirit asks."

Before Zoila and her family can leave, I re-enter the Interpol office. I make another appeal for Arthur. The irritated agent says, "I have already tell to joo, come back tomorrow!"

Back in the lobby Zoila and her family are talking with Richard. Ibarra stands off to one side looking at a spot on his tie.

Taking Zoila in my arms, I say, "We parted too many times, but this will be the last. I will call for you tomorrow." I bring her head close and tell her softly, "We will be together. I love you Zoila, I love you."

"And I love you. I will wait for your call."

The mother's eyes are easy to read. They shine with tears. She says "Que vaya bien y que vaya con Dios mi amor. Y regresa a Zoila." Perhaps she has seen many men go off to hunt and never return. I feel a chill run up my spine with the thought I may never see Zoila again.

I am filled with fear and rage.

We all gather closely. Ibarra seems to disappear from our scene. Zoila can see that I am willing to go against my friends. I could defy the universe. But I will not put these good people into the clutches of the PIP. I will not put Zoila into the hands of Del Gado. In Zoila's embrace, for the first time since my grandmother died, I sob shamelessly.

Richard touches my upper back, his palm making a circle, and he says, "I guess I owe you two an apology. I can see this is real. And I'm really sorry, but we should get to a phone ASAP for Arthur's sake. Then you guys can meet later for dinner or something, you know?"

Zoila, tears running down her cheeks, says to Richard, "I know you are his friend. Please watch for his safety. Do whatever you must never to return to Lurigancho."

Zoila's father has been silent until now. Speaking carefully and with great dignity, he says, "I will ask our great ancestors to watch over you both. Eduardo, you know you are welcome in our home. Zoila will wait for you. She has told me of the spirit between you. Perhaps that is the spirit of your first child."

This comment gets a stir from the rest of the family. Richard says, "That would be a good-looking kid—thanks to Zoila."

Ibarra seems to reappear, and Zoila asks for the use of his pen. She writes the number of her uncle's bakery on a small piece of paper that her mother produces from her purse. Zoila hands me the paper, and I put it in my Levi's watch pocket. I know it can't fall out of the tiny pocket tight on my hip.

We walk out of the building together and go in opposite directions—us to Ibarra's car, and Zoila and her family to theirs.

Turning and walking, I say to Ibarra, "So we are in your custody? What does that mean? I can't go anywhere without you?"

"Jes, I am sorry boys but the Interpol would not give to me joor passports until the final check is completed. In the morning we can go back to the Interpol and get joor passports and Arthur, jes?"

"Okay. And then I am going with Zoila and her family and spend time with her."

"Jes, but I am afraid I must tell to joo the court suprema must make the decision."

Richard stops in the middle of the crowded downtown sidewalk, turns, and blocks Ibarra's way. He shouts, "What the fuck did you say? We have another court scene?"

"No, no, no," says Ibarra excitedly, his hands up with palms open towards Richard, his head shaking so that his loose jowls bounce and shake. "Not appearance! Only joor case on paper, joor file from the tribunal. It is the final confirmation of absuelto and then joo can leave Peru, or joo can stay and be with this girl or anything joo like."

We stop talking until we reach Ibarra's car, a late-model Lincoln, black with black leather upholstery. While I wait for him to unlock his door, I hear a honk. Zoila and her family drive past in a 1954 Chevrolet Bel Air. Zoila is at the passenger window, smiling, her slender fingers waving slowly back and forth in front of her chin. I watch the car as it travels a couple of blocks then turns a corner and vanishes from sight.

Without a shred of sarcasm, Richard says, "Don't worry, brother. You'll see her again. Let's get Tubby to drive us to the beach, yeah?"

As he starts his car, Ibarra says, "Boys, I am take joo to the best restaurant in all of Lima."

"How about taking us to the beach?" I ask.

From the back seat Richard says, "Oh yeah, take us to see the ocean."

"Smell that, man. Sea air."

Richard takes a lung-full, inhaling deeply. "It's a nice day, huh? First time I've said that in years."

Ibarra waits in his car while we go out on the sand and walk to the water's edge. We sit on the sand and just listen to everything in the free world—seagulls crying, waves pounding, little sandpipers peeping as they chase after the waves pecking the wet sand and racing back up to the dry.

"Look, isn't that a woman in a bikini?"

"Oh man, have we been absent from life or what?"

We take off our shoes and walk, feeling the sand and the water.

Ibarra leaves us at a hotel, saying that he will return in the morning to take us to visit Arthur. We check into one of the rooms. While I bounce on the bed, I hear Richard running the water in the bathroom. I walk in, and Richard looks at me. He is weeping. "Look, Eddie. Running water. Hot running water!"

"Listen, R.B. I am having a real hard time with the idea of going back and letting them have us again. They might even be watching us right now, but right now we have a chance. I'm thinking we should call this number Zoila gave me and get her to find someone to drive us to the border, any border. Ah fuck, that's no good either. If we get caught, it wouldn't take them long to beat and torture their way to Zoila."

"Even if Zoila didn't help us."

We walk back into the bedroom, and Richard starts bounce-testing the other bed. Then he stops and says, "You know what your lady said at that Interpol building?"

"You mean about Arthur?"

"Yeah. It would just kick my ass to go back home without him."

"Zoila was more than strong on helping him. It's a matter of honor and loyalty. But I have to tell you the truth, R.B. I'm having a hard time with this one. We are basically free. What do we have to lose?"

"Going back to fucking Lurigancho, goddamn it. That's what we have to lose."

"Come on," I say. "Let's go find one of those international phone-calling places and call home."

"Who's number?"

"The only one I still remember. My ex-wife."

"Joleen?"

"Got someone else in mind?"

Just a block away we find a phone-calling place. Joleen answers her phone. I explain everything to her. "Yes! R.B. and me. I'm right here with him. We think they kept Arthur for money. We're supposed to visit him tomorrow. We don't want to wait more than one more day. I'm having a real problem waiting at all. You know about this guy Murphy and his case? Well, that's a big reason we need to get out of this country. Hope you can get some help. We'll call you tomorrow."

After a few more exchanges, I hang up, feeling empty. Suddenly I have an idea. "Hey, yo, let's go see the Reverend. Shouldn't be tough to find his church. Come on."

"Don't forget the PIP. Those bastards may be right on top of us. Remember what Ibarra said. We're not supposed to go anywhere without him."

"Nothing wrong with visiting a fucking priest."

The taxi driver knows right where to go. Miraflores is the Beverly Hills of Peru. The Lima cabbies must know it well.

We pull up to a red-brick church with the stained-glass windows and a big cross mounted on the apex of the roof. Next to the church is a house; must be the rectory because it's also made of red brick with a wooden door that matches the church door. The lights are on. Night has just begun, and the street is dark.

The Rev himself answers the door. "Oh, heavens!" he cries. "Did you escape? Where is your friend Arthur? Oh, I'm so sorry, how rude of me—come in, come in. Come meet my wife and our children. We have five, you know. Oh! You two must have dinner with us! Here, sit, sit down. I shall return promptly with my wife."

The Reverend's wife is just the woman I expected him to have—

cheery, tall, with a face that would be dulled by make-up, rosy cheeks, hair in a bun at the nape of her neck, a little gray in her brown hair just like him. They are both British born and raised. They met when they were students at an Episcopal university. Each of their five children is adopted. There's one from Bangladesh, China, England, America, and Indonesia.

At the table I say, "Mrs. Robinson, this the best pot roast ever."

Richard adds, "I could get used to your cooking, Mrs. Robinson. Much better than what I've been eating."

"Oh heavens, after where you two have been, I hope so."

Reverend excuses the children from the table. He asks us, "Are you going to go and see your friend?" His tone suggests disapproval and concern.

Richard answers. "We have made the decision to go and visit Arthur tomorrow, try again to get him released, and then that's it— we're leaving Peru forever."

"Oh my," says the Reverend's wife. "I would be so terrified of what they would do once they got me back in their lock-ups. I am sorry, but I would not be so brave." She gets up from the table to settle a squabble between two of the kids and then returns to say, "If Arthur were my friend, he would have to go through his most unfortunate situation without me. Pie, anyone?"

"Pie? Oh sure. But what about Jesus?"

"Oh," she says, "I don't believe Jesus will be having any pie."

Everyone laughs. Then I say, "I mean I'm surprised to hear that from a preacher's wife. What about Jesus and loving one another and laying down your life for your brother?"

"Yes, yes, I am a preacher's wife as you say." She quickly collects dishes from the table. "But I am no saint, either. I would be much too frightened." She goes into the kitchen.

The Reverend says, "Yes, my friends, I would think long and clear before going back there tomorrow."

On our way back Richard says, "Let's get out and walk from here."

The taxi pulls over. We're about three blocks from the hotel.

"What's up, R.B.?"

"I don't know. I feel dumb. Still here. I love Arthur, man, but...."

"I know, man. I am tormented by this shit. Zoila, for Arthur? Listen. If they won't let him go tomorrow, R.B., we are gone. Come on. Let's call Joleen again, see if she got hold of Chula."

We return to the same calling station.

"Hi, Joleen. It's us. Have you been able to talk to anyone?"

There is static, but I can hear her: "Oh, Eddie. Everyone is so excited. Robin cried on the phone when I told her R.B. is with you. Wait till R.B. sees his little girl. She is so cute. Chula said he has to go into the hospital in the morning. But not to worry, he'll have his partner Mike on top of things. Chula is having open-heart surgery. He says he doesn't like the idea of you two going to see Arthur. He thinks no. He said for you guys to get to the Ecuador border. Mike will arrange for you to be picked up. Ecuador hates Peru, so there should be no problem there."

"Even if we have to walk, we will be there."

"You guys should start walking right now."

"Believe me, we are having a major problem with that, too. But we have to see him in the morning. We want him to know we didn't abandon him. Not only that—our Peruvian lawyer warned us that we're not supposed to be on the street. We don't want the heat on too soon with no passports."

From America the voice of my children's mother says, "Okay, then. We're all praying for you guys. Try to call tomorrow after you see Arthur. So we can start having an idea when you guys are going to need to be picked up."

Richard nudges me. "Hey, wait a second. R.B. wants to say something."

"Hi, Joleen. How's Robin and my little girl?"

"They're fine, R.B. Wait till you see how gorgeous Amber is. She looks like you both. I think she'll be tall like you. And R.B. I think you two should get going. Arthur will be okay. Let that lawyer and Chula handle it. There is no draft. That ended a long time ago. They're going to let him go."

"We're supposed to wait for the supreme court."

"What will the supreme court do?"

"Ibarra says two things. One, they'll send us home. Or two, they'll send us back to Lurigancho to do the trial over. That could take years."

"So you guys need to get out now."

Richard does not say another word. He hands me the phone.

"Okay! We'll call you tomorrow after we see Arthur. And hey, Joleen. I'm sorry, sweetie."

"We all love you, Eddie. Just get home. And bring R.B. He's got a beautiful little girl to take care of."

"God willing, you'll be seeing Arthur, too. Give everyone our love. Pray!"

Richard and I are quiet walking back to the hotel, noticing all the lovely ladies around us. Finally, just to talk, I say, "Maybe the embassy will type up something official letting that prick in the Interpol office know there ain't no warrant for Arthur."

"Be worth a try. We'll probably get that lesbian woman."

"Whatever! I think all Ibarra is going to do is ask for money."

We walk for while then Richard says, "What was that you said to Joleen? What're you sorry for? Getting fuckin' busted?"

"No, fuckhead! For abandoning her, betraying her. Her love and trust."

"Shit!" Richard reflects. "I'd better get started saying I'm sorry." Then he says, "Oh yeah, that's right. Diane kicked your ass pretty good, huh?"

"No! I'm a lot more like you there. I can kick my own ass better." We think about that for half a block, and then I say, "Lurigancho is an ugly fucking place. If we have to go back there, I'd rather die trying not to. What about you?"

"You might die," he says. "But not to worry. When I make it back, I'll tell all the ladies that you died trying."

"Oh, that makes you laugh? You sick fuck."

"Here's the hotel."

Back in the room we order room service—chocolate sundaes with homemade apple pie. Richard gets a brilliant idea and says, "Maybe we should get a couple of hookers?"

"Yeah, that's it. But why wait? Why not just call the PIP and tell them to come over directly? Stick to the fucking plan, goddamnit."

"Oh yeah, I forgot. You think all the whores work for the police."

"How do you think they stay on the street, Your Dumbness? Anyway that's not what we're about. We're about getting the fuck out of Peru and home."

Richard asks "What about your sweetness Zoila?"

"In memorance of Murphy's case, I think I'll meet her in Ecuador. The main thing is, we gotta talk 'em into letting Arthur out. That's it."

Ibarra shows early. He finds us in the hotel dining room having a full-on breakfast—pancakes, eggs, sausage, milk, orange juice, and good fresh coffee.

"Buenos dias, boys," says the old man.

Richard gets right to the subject we've been discussing. "Say, we need more cash. Money."

We know that Ibarra still has a few thousand for his expenses, money that Chula gave him when we all believed that Ibarra was a real lawyer. The little allowance Ibarra gave us is spent, and we're not giving up what little we have stashed.

"Jes, jes, I will give to you a loan of my moneys from Señor Chula. But first we see about Arturo. Then we can go to my oficina."

At Interpol the same cop from yesterday greets us. Today he is much different. Very friendly. "Oh si, si, Señores," he says. "Your friend is very good. I think we can contact your government today for the release of your amigo."

As soon as we step out onto the roof, we see Arthur surrounded by the detained men. Even the soldiers are in a good mood, smiling and laughing. He is telling them stories of Lurigancho, terrifying and funny. He seems to have mesmerized about twenty of them— everyone except those few who have personal experience of Lurigancho. They don't find the reminders so mesmerizing.

"What'd you guys do in freedom land? Meet any women?"

"Settle down. Plenty of time for all that. We went over to visit the Robinsons. He has a real life."

"We'll take you there when we leave here."

"Today?"

"We don't know yet. But it sounded like it, by what the man downstairs is saying."

"Thanks for not leaving me, you guys."

"Oh break my heart! Say! Aren't you the one giving me a hard time all those years? Now we can't sail without you. Now you're the fucking leader, aren't you?"

"And don't you forget it!"

"Where'd you sleep?"

"I played gin rummy all night with those guys."

Arthur points to a small group of eight or nine men, all looking at Arthur with admiration. Even the soldiers admire the fact that Arthur has survived the most fearsome experience in Peru—Lurigancho.

"Didn't you call the embassy? Did you do anything to help us get out?"

"What a great idea," says Richard. "Eddie, why didn't we just call the DEA and tell them we got loose?"

"No," says Arthur. "Don't want to do that."

Hours go by.

After a while Richard says, "Wonder what's up with Ibarra?"

"Let's see if we can borrow some cards."

"Just ask that guard over at that table," says Arthur. "He has decks in the drawer for us."

By now I'm past being worried. I have already decided that my pants would be the best thing to fling over that steel cable—slide down to the next-door building, drop to the ground about five or six feet, and take off. Figure out the rest as I go running through Lima with my bare ass flashing.

"Do you guys have any money?" says Arthur. "We can buy something to eat at the kiosk. Those two women are friendly. They gave me a free breakfast this morning."

Richard has some money stashed. "Yeah, come on. Let's eat."

The food is good, the women kind and smiling, but now my anxiety is high. I deeply regret coming back. But I still hear Zoila's words. *If you leave and do not try to help him....* I am just waking up to her total meaning. If I *did not try*, I would never live it down.

I can go to her now. Now that I've returned to the roof and taken the risk in support of Arthur, I can go to Zoila with my sense of dignity and honor intact

Richard says, "Ibarra's 'real soon' turned into hours. Five."

Finally the elevator doors open, and Ibarra steps forth in his rumpled brown suit. He looks angry. "Boys, I am bery upset with this international policemans. They say that Eduardo and Ricardo have the FBI problems, that joo may not go to the street. They say joo must stay."

"Oh man." Richard is studying Ibarra with intense suspicion.

I say, "What kind of crap are these guys up to now?"

Arthur blurts, "Did the embassy send anything? Did you tell the embassy that they're holding me on a draft warrant? Do you have any documents?" He almost sobs, "Did you do anything to help us at all?"

I ask, "Are you telling us they're going to keep us on this roof until the supreme court makes a decision?"

"I am sorry, boys. But boys, remember please to me. I am a bery good lawyer. We will work bery hard for joor freedom...."

"Listen, you fat fuck," says Richard. "Get us the fuck back on the street."

"Whoa now," I interrupt. I don't want him saying anything that might cause us trouble. "Wait a minute, Richard. What do you think he can do that would get us back out on the street, man?"

Ibarra starts talking faster than I have heard him talk before. "Jes, I understand joo, Ricardo. I understand joo are very angry. I am angry too. Bery angry." He is so emphatic that his entire body shakes. "But with money—maybe just eight thousand dollars or seven thousand dollars—we can make these police to make the bail-out. Joo understand when I say make the bail-out, jes?"

Richard gets very calm. "What makes you think we can get people to give you more money? No one will give money until we are back on the street."

He catches my eye over the top of Ibarra's shiny head. He hasn't lost control. And I can tell what he's thinking—*not another nickel for Ibarra. From now on we're acting survival-style.*

Arthur says, "Hey, are you going to answer me? Have you got any documents to show the Interpol guy so I can go?"

Richard and me look at Arthur and back to Ibarra. Call it ESP or just the fact that we've been cellmates for years, but I know what we are thinking:

Ibarra doesn't want us to leave.

He thinks, because our country won't help us, all we have to rely on is money.

He's part of the cops' plan to keep us.

But he's still useful—as long as he thinks there's more money.

The next morning they take us—cuffs and armed escort—to another jail. The following morning we go to another jail. Then another. All are branches of Lurigancho.

In one of these jails a prisoner in the cell next to us sobs as he describes the torture he suffered because he wrote a newspaper story criticizing the Peruvian government. During the beating he revealed information that led to the torture and murder of the newspaper's publisher.

In another jail a Peruvian boy with a terribly bruised face wants to know what kind of apartments you can rent in the United States. He gestures at the cell, which is nothing but a stone cage with a one-spigot concrete sink and an exposed flush toilet. He wants to know if it's possible to rent something nice—something like this.

Then, about two weeks after the absuelto verdict, a man appears at our cell door wearing a short-sleeved shirt, slacks, and a pistol. He tells us we're going to yet another jail where we will stay until the court decides what to do with us.

During our tour of Lurigancho's many substations, we have managed to wash our socks and clothes. But we possess no toothbrush or comb or brush or razor. We haven't seen the sun. We guess the time by the angle of the shadows. We tell each other, "You look good. Beard looks good, too."

Now a khaki-clad soldier appears at our steel bars, shouting and signaling with his rifle to get up. Then he stands to the side, rigid. Now here's an officer. His uniform suggests the same rank as the lieutenant in the desert who shot a couple guys right through the head. He has a light complexion and a moustache that looks drawn with a pencil.

"Abre la puerta," he commands.

The soldier shouts down the hall: "Trige la llave. Abre la puerta."

The cop with the short-sleeved shirt comes running with the key. They cuff us separately, our hands in front, and off we go.

Crammed in the back seat of a four-door sedan, we speed down the highway. The slick-looking officer rides shotgun. He lights a cigarette, takes a big drag, and slowly blows the smoke out the window. Without turning around, he says slow and clear, "Everything is still exactly as Lurigancho Prison. Make no mistake. If you try to escape, we will kill you."

The soldier drives like no rules apply to him, and I am sure that is true.

We are on the outskirts of Lima somewhere, dodging through dense traffic. The street is lined with shops and people streaming past vendors who are hawking food and clothes, toys and tools, t-shirts and trinkets. Nobody says a word. Then the driver whips left onto a side street. The street is very wide but only a block long, ending at a cinder wall. On either side of us are commercial buildings two stories high. Despite the paint peeling from their brick facades, they appear to be doctors' offices or insurance companies. The two-story building in front of us appears to be a jail. One clue is the word POLICIA above the metal-framed double doors.

Horns are honking behind us, but it's quiet on this side street. The driver retrieves his rifle then opens my door. The lieutenant opens Richard's door. Both of them pull their pistols out of their side-holsters. The soldier points his weapon back and forth at me and Arthur as Arthur climbs out. We stand close to the car doors. The lieutenant holds his gun at his side and says in a calm but intimidating voice: "Begin walking slowly to the door. Go."

I am first in the doors of our new jail. To my right is a stairway going up to the second floor. To my left is a desk with a telephone. There's a plainclothes cop sitting at the desk and another one standing next to the desk with his back to a window. Both are nicely dressed, their sport shirts and slacks accented by forty-five-caliber pistols holstered at their sides. Directly in front of me a hallway runs forty or fifty feet to the back of the building. At the far end I see bars on either side. I stop. Richard and Arthur fill in behind me. The soldier pokes Richard's back with the barrel of his pistol.

"Adelante."

We obey, moving straight ahead as ordered. As we walk into the lock-up hallway, I look back. Behind the soldier all I can see are the front doors and the small car we rode in parked at the curb. The desk is out of view.

The soldier shouts at me, "Look ahead nothing more, stupid gringo!" On the left we pass a closed door, maybe an interrogation room. After that comes a door that's definitely not an office door—it's made of steel bars and Plexiglas. Nothing but darkness on the other side.

On the right during the same interval we pass three offices in a row, all with their doors open. In the first one a cop sits behind the desk facing the door. He's dressed like the ones out front—casual but sharp. These guys don't look like PIP, not so violent and greasy and devilish. This cop is carrying on a rapid conversation in Spanish with a man sitting with his back to us, a black man of about age thirty who's wearing a green sweat suit, white tennis shoes, and handcuffs. He's saying, "No! No!" again and again. The second office is filled with two fat women in dark dresses looking down at a teenage boy who is handcuffed in a chair. Tears are running down the boy's face. The women are yelling at him. The cop at his desk looks at the boy, shakes his head, then writes something on his report. The third door is closed.

After that on the right is a cell. There are five men inside the cell, three of them sitting on the bare concrete floor toward the back, two of them standing at the door. They don't talk. Two of them have dried blood on their faces and clothes.

Across from them is one more office on the left side, and next to that at the end of the hall is our new accommodation—an empty nine-by-twelve concrete cage. It has one small barred window high on the back wall. We hear fast boot-heels coming behind us down the tiled hall floor, and we turn. It's the lieutenant, advancing on us at a fast march. Behind him, the cop from the front desk is marching even faster, carrying a ring of keys. We step back. The cop passes the lieutenant and without a miss slides the correct key directly into the lock. He swings open the door. "Entren, gringos."

He pushes me into the cell first, then Arthur and Richard, then he slams the door and locks it. The lieutenant says, "Come over here. Put your hands to the bars. I will remove you handcuffs." Speaking directly to Arthur he says, "You first, venga."

After removing our bracelets, the lieutenant tells us to come close and listen carefully. "You gringos are not free until the courte suprema says. We have international law that says you cannot be put back in the prison for now. But we are allowed to detain you until that decision. Remember, no matter what the international law says, you are prisoners of Lurigancho. My office is upstairs together with your DEA. These policemans down here have the orders to shoot you if you try anything. Do you understand me, gringos?"

"Yes sir."

The officer turns to the cop and the soldier and says, "Come, vamos por una cerveza." They all walk away laughing.

One wooden bench just wide enough for two people to sit side by side—otherwise the cell is empty. Richard says, "Lurigancho was never this clean."

"Yeah," says Arthur, "but there's no water or anything. I wonder how long they're going to keep us in here."

At first I sit on the bench. Then I look up and say, "What I wonder is what's outside that window up there. Come here and give me a boost, R.B."

Before Richard can lean down to hold my foot, we hear someone coming. Across the hall the other prisoners whisper, "Hey gringo, someone come for you."

The cell opposite is constructed so that we can't communicate easily. Our door looks straight across the hall at a blank wall. Their bars run at an angle so that they look back up the hall. They probably see right out to the front door. All we can see of them is a sideways view of their faces and hands against the bars.

Arthur presses his left cheek against the bars to see as far as he can back up the hall. "It's Ibarra, you guys."

Ibarra appears, wearing his brown suit, wrinkled white shirt, and brown tie with a big yellow flower on it. Standing with his protruding belly pressed against the bars of our door, he says, "Boys, I spoken today with Eduardo's ex-wife. I am too sorry today. I must tell to joo my friend Mr. Chula has passed away while joo boys was in transit. So sorry, boys.

After a moment of quiet shock I say, "George passed away? George died? From what?"

"Joo ex-wife says he had heart surgery and he died. I am sorry, boys."

"Jesus, man, I can't believe George died. Heart surgery?"

Arthur goes immediately to his favorite topic. "Did you find any proof about the draft so I can be released?"

Richard and me just look at each other and shake our heads. Richard puts his hand on Arthur's shoulder. "You lousy little daft dog, I can't believe we're in the same cell together."

I ask Ibarra, "Hey, you think you could go back to that hotel we were at and get our stuff?"

"Oh, jes! I will. If I can find it I will bring it next time. When I come back."

As we watch our lawyer waddle away, Richard says, "I sure hope he can find our stuff. I would definitely like to shave."

"There's something more important than shaving. There's that phone number."

"Ouch," says Richard.

Two days later our situation has improved. We now have a mattress, an old twin-sized one with black and white stripes and cotton falling out of numerous holes. I'm sitting on the bench, and

Richard is lying on the mattress. Arthur is leaning against the bars
of the cell, so he can see a little ways down the hall. Arthur says,
"Here comes our legal eagle. He's carrying a cardboard box. Nope,
now he's talking with one of the guards. Now here he comes."

As Ibarra gets near, one of the prisoners across the hall calls out:
"Por favor, Señor, tu es un abogado?" He must have overheard.

Ibarra looks at the man. The fellow has no shoes. His clothes
are rags. Ibarra says, "No, no, no, no. Solomente para estes gringos,
hombre, no mas."

The poor man spits on the floor of the hall outside his cage.

Ibarra looks at us. "They are animals. And they have no money. I
am sorry, boys, for joo must remain here in this jail. But joo are safe
here. The militario is on the second floor and also is the DEA, they
working together to catch the trafficantes de coca. Boys, I have bring
someone for joo, wait." He beckons up the hall. "I bring this nice
womans to bring every day the comida. She is very good cook. She
is called Maria, and this is her small daughter Isabel."

Maria looks as though she enjoys not only the cooking but also
the eating. She's a Peruvian, about thirty-five, and her daughter
seems to be about ten. Both have long coal-black hair. They remind
me of the women vendors from the village at Lurigancho, except
Maria and her daughter are clean and well-groomed and they seem
happy. Maria holds a tray covered with a white linen cloth. The little
girl holds another, also covered.

Richard and I smile at them, but Arthur says, "What's going on
with getting us out of here so we can eat in a restaurant?"

"Please, Arthur, joo must be patient. The courte suprema they
will move to a decision very soon. Please don't to worry, Arthur.
Now you must eat the food Maria has prepared for joo. Excuse me,
I must call to the policeman for to open the door."

While Ibarra is gone, the little girl stares at us with sad eyes.
Maria smiles and lifts the cloth to expose the delicious food—chicken
and vegetables, soup and corn bread, coffee and apple pie and a
pitcher of milk. To my complete surprise, I see silverware.

Ibarra returns with the cop, who opens the door and stands with one hand on his gun while Maria and her daughter pass us the trays. Immediately they turn and go. We set the trays down on the wooden bench.

Before the cop can re-lock our door, Ibarra says, "Oh, Ricardo and Eduardo, you only leave these things in the hotel." He hands me the small cardboard box. The cop locks the door.

Richard is already sitting on our makeshift bed reading the paperback that he brought with him from the last jail. He's waiting for Ibarra to go away, and Ibarra does.

Arthur sets up an eating arrangement whereby we can sit on the mattress and use the bench for a table. Meanwhile, I start pawing through the box Ibarra brought. I find two toothbrushes, also the new t-shirts and paperbacks that we picked up in the hotel lobby store. I grab my paperback and start thumbing through the book from cover to cover, then do it again four times and then start shaking it and shaking it, but nothing falls out. "Damn, damn, DAMN."

Finally Richard says, "What the fuck are you doing, man?"

Arthur asks, "Did you stash money in that book? Because if you did, Ibarra would have nabbed it."

"No, goddamnit. More important than money."

Richard says, "What, lost your place? I didn't think you started reading that book yet."

"Oh fuck, I don't believe this. I put that little scrap of paper with Zoila's phone number in this book. It's not here, man. It's not here."

"And there you are!"

"Hey! Reverend Robinson! How did you know we're here?"

"I went to Lurigancho for my regular visit, and your friends told me that you had gone home. I felt suspicious about that and undertook a little investigation of my own. How are you?" He remarks that our place is "a bit cramped" but expresses his happiness that we are close to his home. "Arthur, I'm sorry you were not able to come with Richard and Edward to meet my wife and kids. Well, when you leave this place you all must come for another supper. Here, I have mail for all of you. Excuse me, I will ask the jailer to open this door and let me in there with you."

A cop lets the Reverend in. We offer him a seat on our mattress on the cold cement floor. He is a big man, and it's a ways to the floor. Richard treats him like a gentleman. "How's your family, Reverend?"

"Oh, thank you for asking. Everyone healthy. However, I want to make certain you do not disappear like that again. There was quite a ruckus over you three. I personally called the American embassy. They said you had been released. They thought you'd gone home. I have your families' telephone numbers, so I called your father, Edward, and your mum, Arthur, and Richard's mother as well. No one had heard a word from any of you. Now I have them worried. However, I did have several lengthy and enjoyable conversations. You all have very lovely families."

Richard says, "Reverend, mind if I ask you something?"

"No, of course. I hope I can give an answer."

"Why do you do this stuff? Why do you go to prisons and see people like us? Even our own embassy tried to put you off the job by lying that we went home. Why do you care about us?"

The Reverend smiles. He's in the middle of the mattress. Richard is sitting cross-legged to his right. Arthur is too his left, near the door. I'm on the bench. He looks at each of us and then says, "Are you not human beings?"

Richard absorbs that for a moment. "Well, I know for certain Eddie isn't. Arthur is half." He gets his laugh. But this time he keeps talking. "All kidding aside, I'm very grateful to you, Reverend. Our families are regular working people and can't take off. Even if they could, we don't want them coming to a country like this. This government is totally crazed. It's slaughtering its own people. The natives here, I mean ones we've met in prison, tell us that the U.S. government pays the Peruvian military to kill the people of the Amazon. And these natives get lost in the prison system just because they don't have the money to move their paperwork ahead. I mean, maybe one time they stole bread or a couple of eggs for their starving families. But now they can't finish their time. Their release dates passed years ago. These are human beings, too."

At first there is silence in the cell. Then I say, "I can't believe it."

"What?"

"I didn't know you were paying attention."

Richard gives me the stink eye.

"Yes, I have heard these stories," says the Reverend. "But when I ask the Peruvian officials, they tell me that the oil companies are being attacked by the natives. They say that the Peruvian military is only protecting the oil workers."

Arthur says, "That's a fairy tale. My friends from the jungle say that the military wipes out whole villages. Then the oil people have a place to set up camp and drill for oil that actually belongs to the people who were murdered."

Richard says, "Point is, Reverend, we found a whole bunch of human beings in this prison."

"Yeah, man," I say.

Arthur says, "Amen."

"There are some animals that really should be locked up," says Arthur. "But the real animals are running this country."

"I must admit I am appalled at what I have seen. I wish I could do more. But we do what we can when we can."

The Reverend starts to push himself up. Richard is faster to his feet, and he grabs the big man's arm to help him from the floor. Arthur and me get up, also. Arthur says, "Maybe you can come back? I mean if they don't let us go soon?"

I have an idea. "Say, Reverend. You know that big map of Peru that came with your National Geographic? I noticed a few copies at your home. Do you know what I mean?"

"Why yes, I believe so. Would you like a map?"

"Yeah, I want to put it up on this wall so we can see where we are. When the supreme court says we can go, R.B. and me might take a surf trip. They have a fu... I mean, they have a terrible government but excellent surf."

Months go by. We write letters to President Carter and to U.S. Congress and right on down the line. The only answer is that Laura Schmidt comes to the jail twice. The first time, she asks us to please stop writing letters because she has to answer them all times three. The second time, she informs us that the Peruvian government has declared martial law and that all rights, including those under international law, have been suspended.

Her second visit motivates a creative response:

"Next time, let's just ignore that bitch," I say. "You know what? I'm going to beg this cop to let us out back for some sunshine!"

Whenever I look out our little barred window, which I can do standing on our bench, I see a concrete patio like something stuck onto an apartment building. Except this one is surrounded by walls two stories high. On either side I see red brick about fifteen feet high. Across the back about four strides away it's a concrete wall topped with five feet of chain-link fence and three strands of barbed wire. The basic situation is impossible. Like trying to jump out of the bottom of a wishing well.

Except for one feature.

Completely in the spirit of Peru's haphazard building philosophy, a flight of steps rises about halfway up the concrete wall. It starts in the bottom left corner, where brick meets concrete. It scales up to the level of the second floor. Then it leaves the wall and heads back toward us. In other words, it seems to be a secret back entrance for the creeps on the second floor.

But we don't want to go up to the second floor. Richard and me just want to know what's on the other side of that concrete wall. We believe that when you get to the top of the stairs, you can jump up and grab the top of the wall.

"Arthur, you tell the cop we need to get sun. Tell 'em we're surfers and it's life or death, or whatever."

"Why me?"

These cops have become so relaxed around us that I almost got my hand on one of their forty-fives. One more inch and I could have wrapped my hand around the gun handle.

Afterwards, Arthur asked me, "Why do you do things like that?"

"What?"

"You know what I'm talking about. Putting your hand on that cop's gun. Man, if he saw that, we'd be back in Lurigancho!"

"I wasn't playing, Arthur."

The mere fact that he asked the question causes me and Richard to start thinking that we might have to leave Arthur behind this time.

So when Arthur asks "Why me?" Richard replies, "Because they look at you like a cute little Chihuahua dog. You don't make them think we're up to something."

I say, "Yeah. You ask."

When the on-duty cop comes to the cell door, Arthur does his begging. "Por favor, Señor...?"

"Okay. Joo go por ten minutos, jes?"

Pueblo Libre. That's what they call this place. This is our first chance to look around, except for our trips to the latrine across the hall two or three times a day. Every time I come out of the latrine, I notice the layout—our cell, and office to the left, then to the left of the office that funny-looking door with steel bars leading into darkness.

Now the guard opens our cell door and beckons us out by extending his left arm. Then he leads us past the office to that dark steel door. He produces an unfamiliar key—it looks like an old roller-skate key, straight and simple. The cop unlocks the door, and now we are in a tunnel under the second story. To our left, toward the front of the building, the way is very dimly lit. It appears to be a storage area with boxes and a couple of old bicycles. To our right is the light of day. The tunnel opens out to the rear of the building. We walk underneath the DEA into the sunlight of the patio.

To our amazement the cop tells us that he'll be back in ten minutes. He tells us in Spanish, "Don't go anywhere!" Then he looks up at the big wall with chain link and razor-sharp wire, and at the brick walls on both sides, and I can tell he thinks he's being funny.

As soon as the cop is out of sight and back inside the station, I whisper to Arthur, "You watch the tunnel. R.B., watch up there."

I run up the stairs along the wall. No one sees me leap to grab the top and pull myself up. I look over the wall.

In an instant I am back down on the cement patio.

The three of us quickly sit in the welcome sunshine, our backs against the wall that I just looked over. I say, "The front of the building must be east and in back of us is west. Home is that way." I point to the left.

I pull off my t-shirt. Richard does the same. Arthur does not, but he is leaning back against the wall, his head pointed up toward the sun.

Richard says, "Oh man, that's good. How long have we been in that fucking little dark-ass cell?"

"Too long," says Arthur. "I lost my tan."

"Arthur, you never had a fucking tan in your whole miserable white life."

"What? I have always had a tan. And my life was never miserable until I met you two."

We melt in the sun's life-giving rays.

We are still in the noon-day sun when the plainclothes cop returns to say, "Venganse, gringos locos." Come inside you crazy whiteys.

Much later in the day, Richard asks me about the wall.

"It's a lumber yard on the other side. It's full of lumber and building materials. And then there's another wall, a brick one that's only about eight or ten feet high."

"Beyond that?"

"I'm sure it's the public street."

For the next two months we do not talk about the wall. If the subject ever arises between Richard and me, Arthur closes his ears. At other times he says things like, "If they don't let us go, if they say we have to go back and do the trial over, let's just beat it out of here." But all he really wants to hear is Richard and me planning our surfing trips.

So on this day, when we are about to have another visit from Reverend Robinson, something needs to be made crystal clear.

The Reverend comes regularly three days a week even if only to say good day. Five visits ago the guard opened the cell door for the Reverend, as usual, and then he left the door unlocked. Open. Since then, he has left the door open every time.

Mid-week during the day the police station is always busy. The offices are full of people being interrogated, arrested, locked in the cell next door, or hustled out the door to jails in other locations. It's hard to imagine walking through that wall of cops without getting shot. But one day when the door was open Arthur tested the boundaries of our freedom by cruising down the hall a few steps in plain view of a dozen of our captors.

Today, after the cop opens the door, I step out into the hallway with Arthur. Richard stays in the cell sitting on the mattress with a new paperback. Out in the hall I murmur to Arthur: "You see that front door through all these fucking cops?"

"Yeah. So?"

"Me and R.B. decided that when the Reverend leaves we're going to walk with him as far as we can. As soon as the cops say something, then bam—we hit the street and run like you never ran in your life."

As I say this, Arthur goes through a curious transformation. First he looks in my eyes. He can tell I'm serious, serious as a car accident. Then his teeth start to chatter just like fake teeth from the novelty store.

When I see this, I tell him, "Come back inside, man."

Richard looks up and says, "What the fuck—did you see Del Gado out there?"

Arthur's entire body is shaking. "You ou ou guy guys."

"Hey quit that, man," I say. "Don't fucking stutter." Then I wink at Richard. "R.B., I told Arthur our plan about running out the front door. He seems a little worried about it."

For a couple of minutes Arthur acts as though he's been locked in a walk-in freezer. Then he pulls it together and gets angry. "Listen goddamnit you guys, don't try it. You *will* get caught. Then we'll never get out and you'll fuck up my chances really good. So don't fucking do it, okay? Tell me you're not going to try anything stupid. Say it."

Richard looks up and says, "Okay." Then he looks at me. He says, "Okay, we won't do anything stupid."

I say, "Yeah, right. Nothing stupid."

"No, no, I mean it," says Arthur. "Count me out if you do, you hear? Just act like I'm not here. Because I'm not going to be any part of your death. In case you forgot, these motherfuckers will kill you."

Richard goes back to his reading. I pick up a paperback and sit on our little bench.

Ten minutes later the Reverend shows. He sits on our mattress and reads us stories out of the newspaper. Apparently there's a convention of yogis gathering at Machu Picchu. "Well, this is interesting," he says, rattling the paper. "They say that the vortex of spiritual energies in the Himalayas has moved, and now it can be found in the Andes Mountains of Peru. Interesting people."

Richard says, "If we had a map, we could see where they're going."

"Fellows, I happen to have such a map right here." He pats his chest.

"You do?"

"Of course. Months ago you asked me to bring you a map of Peru. Your request simply slipped my mind until this week, when I happened to find that old issue of *National Geographic*. Presto."

He pulls the folded map warm from beneath his shirt. We open it and lay it on the floor. It's an amazing thing to see in our bare cell.

"How will you fellows hang this up, or will you?"

"Reverend," I say, "let us show you one of the many useful things we learned at Lurigancho. Toothpaste."

"They don't call it paste for nothing," says Arthur.

"Put a dab on the back of each corner like this. And watch."

The cop on duty comes to tell the Reverend that it is time to go, and he sees the big fold-out color map. "Que cosas, gringos?" he says. "Why you have this mapa?"

We tell the cop that we're planning a surfing safari. He lets us keep it. And the next day, to our amazement, the cop brings us several more maps of Peru.

Richard and me use these maps to see where the fuck we are. But we spend little time studying the coastline. Our attention is concentrated in the east, looking for the jungle. We memorize the routes of the rivers—Urubamba, Ucayali, Yavari—that flow into the Amazon and head where we want to go, into Brazil.

Tonight while Arthur snores on one side of our mattress, we sit at the other playing yet another game of gin rummy. Richard says, "So how do we get to the river? And what are we going to do without papers or passports?"

"When we get to the street, we're going to disappear. We have money stashed for taxis. These taxis aren't all radioed to the cops, not like at home. Once we get to the river, we'll catch one of those water buses. Collectivos. I never took one, but I know they exist and no questions about papers. When we get to Brazil, we find the American embassy, get temporary passports, and go the fuck home."

"Go over that wall in the back? And then get a taxi?"

"Yeah. Got a better idea? Bust out the front door?"

He picks a card from the deck and searches for a discard.

"I'll tell you, R.B. I know in my gut that these fucking assholes are not going to let us go. Ibarra and the PIP are on top of us. They think if they hurt us more, we'll pay them more money. Take us back to Lurigancho, and we'll really start shelling out."

"Agreed. They're not going to let us go."

I pick up his discard and rearrange the fan of cards in my hand. "I'm not going back to Lurigancho, R.B. And if you go back, you're gonna die there, man."

"I ain't going back."

"Once we're on the street I think we should split up and meet back at the Reverend's church. Remember where it is?"

"Muddy Floors. It's on one of the maps."

"But really, man, don't you think it's better—we go separate ways?"

"Sure. That way when you go down I can tell them at home all about it."

We finish that game. I win. So I shuffle and deal again. After we look at our cards, I say, "So what about Arthur?"

"One true thing. If he knows the plan, they'll beat it out of him after we're gone."

"That's it then. We do the wall. You and me."

Richard takes three of his cards and lays them face-down. Then as he adjusts his hand he glances up and catches my eye, and then he looks down and shakes his head as if to say no.

"What are you shaking your head about?"

"You ever jump fifteen feet to the ground and live?"

We are sitting at each end of the mattress cross-legged. I lean forward and hiss, "Listen, you have to really fucking want it, man. Don't hesitate even for a second. Even if they start shooting, I'll see you at the Reverend's. Don't look back or stop for anything."

We play in silence for a while. Then I say, "When you're over twenty feet away, those forty-fives aren't worth a shit."

"Is that right," says Richard.

A few thousand hands of gin rummy and several thousand games of solitaire and a zillion paperback novels later, Ibarra comes to tell us that the supreme court is close to its decision.

I beg him. "Tiefilo, Señor, por favor. Please! Please! Promise me! Please promise me you will come here and tell us what is to happen, what they say, whether we will go back or go home. Say you swear you will do this thing. Say it, please."

"Jes, jes, jes! I promise this to joo, Eduardo. But please, boys, do not to worry. Even if joo must return to Lurigancho, it will be bery short time, boys."

"Just swear you will come as soon as you know."

"Jes, I swear. But tell me why this is so important to joo." Never before have I half-believed anything about this man. But now he seems completely sincere.

"Because I want to be able to write a letter to my mother. And if we have to go back to prison, maybe you could get these people here to let us call our families in the States. You know we have no phone at Lurigancho."

Ibarra seems to be convinced that I have given him a good reason to keep his word.

Arthur is talking at the door with one of the guards. He tells the guard that today is Richard's birthday.

"Este es el dia de su cumpleanos?" says the guard. He tells the other cops.

Later three of them show up at the door. One is carrying a small brown paper bag. I'm sitting on the bench and I look up, and the one with the bag flashes me a peek of its contents. I say to Richard, "Hey man, this guy really has a bottle of Smirnoff. And he's opening the cell door. Stand up. It's for you."

Richard places his paperback face-down and rises from the mattress, using the wall for support. He says, "No shit?" He steps back as they swing open the door. The one with the bag pulls the bottle all the way out and hands it to Richard. Maintaining a professional demeanor, he hands Richard the bottle with his left hand while he shakes Richard's hand with his right. "Feliz cumpleanos, gringo," he says.

Richard grabs the hand and the bottle at the same time and says, "This is real?"

The three guards look pleased with themselves. One of them says, "You drink slowly, amigo."

Richard stays at the door while they walk away. Then he turns and holds up the bottle, reading its label.

"There's no proof on this."

I take the bottle out of Richard's hand. "Hmmm. Remember, in Peru they don't need proof. I wonder if this is real. You think these cops would really give us booze?"

Arthur says, "Give the man his bottle; it's his birthday. Open it, R.B."

I hand back the bottle. He screws off the cap takes a small sip. "It's real, all right." Gasp. Cough. "Whew, man, maybe too real. Jeesh. Here."

Richard hands the bottle to Arthur. Arthur says, "You guys are wimps. Watch and learn." He puts the bottle up to his nose. "First you have to let the fumes enter the nostrils. Then you have to hold your breath and swallow, like this."

We watch the bottle at Arthur's lips, the clear liquid draining out two good gulps. Taking the bottle away from his mouth, he looks at Richard and me with a grin. Then his lips form a small opening. "Ou." His eyes water up, and he pushes the bottle at Richard. Now he's squeezing his face tight to keep from puking. His cheeks puff out like Dizzy Gillespie's. His eyes bulge. He turns and bounces off one wall, then takes three steps to the opposite wall and stands there with his hands out, looking at the floor, shaking his head and blowing out a long breath.

"Man, that is some strong shit."

Richard puts the bottle to his lips and says to Arthur, "Told ya." He swigs. "I've been drinking this shit since my babysitter used to put it in my bottle. After I went to sleep, she could make out with her boyfriend."

I take the bottle. "Yeah, I had a nanny she used to put whiskey in my bottle."

After the alcohol numbs us, we feel pretty good about downing the whole bottle.

Later Arthur stands up from the mattress saying, "Well, I can tell you guys this. We are not going back to the prison. We are going from here to home. I can see it all now. The court is going to give you two a fine. Then it's gonna give you another really big fine for getting me involved and fucking up my life. And then we are going to go home. I shink I finally figured it out."

Arthur uses his right hand to grip a steel bar of the cell door. I say, "Are you holding that bar to keep your balance?"

"What makes you shay zhat?"

Richard says, "Because you can't talk straight. You're fucked up."

I say, "Wasn't that you who was teaching us how to drink this rocket fuel? Because you just pronounced 'think' wrong. And you're looking kind of pale, man."

Richard and me both laugh at Arthur.

Arthur is still holding the bar, but his face gets flushed and his eyebrows make a frown. "I've had it with you two laughing at me. You two assholes who got me in here in the first place laughing at me. Me. That's really good. Me, who has held you both together through all these years. I'm the one who got a job and went out in the world and worked while you were lying around reading intellectual comic books and you were sleeping and hiding and playing with Pelone. That's all this has been to you guys is fun fun fun laughing at Arthur. Well, when I'm at home with all my women, we'll see who's laughing."

"Jee, man," I say. "What will I tell René ? He'll be broken up when you don't come back."

"Hey. You know, I could have had Zoila. She was checking me out before you saw her. I mean really checking me out. I just let you have her. Because she's not my type."

"Well, thanks, Arthur."

Richard has the bottle in his hand on the mattress. I'm standing nearby. Arthur says, "Here. Get up and give me that bottle, R.B."

Richard stands up with his left hand on the wall, but I snatch the vodka. I tip it for another sip, and Richard grabs it back. "Hey! What the fuck's wrong with you?"

Richard butts up to me with his chest nearly touching me. He looks down his nose and says, "It's *my* birthday, Eddie. You think it's all about you!" And he taps his index finger hard on my chest.

With my right hand I knock his left hand finger off my chest.

He throws a right-hand punch. But he has to aim downward at my jaw. I move, and the blow glances off my forehead. As I duck, my left foot slips on the mattress. I go down to my right knee. Arthur gives a cheer. "He knocked you down!" he shouts. "Oh! You're not so bad. R.B. knocked you down, Eddie!"

Still down on one knee, I raise my head. All I can see are Richard's

Levi's from the knees down to his rubber flip-flops. Suddenly I feel a rush of violence surge through me. I grip his ankles and yank his feet toward me. Richard drops to the cement. I have my left-hand fingers around his esophagus. He's choking. And he can't move because I have my knee deep in his gut, knocking the wind out of him.

Arthur leaps onto my back. With my free arm I grab Arthur by the head and neck, and I flip him over my shoulder. He lands on top of Richard on his back, his feet and legs sprawled out toward the cell door. Arthur flips over and pushes himself up from Richard's chest. I yell, "I could kill you both in a minute!"

He looks shocked.

Instantly the cops come to my mind. I release Richard's neck and roll onto the mattress. I grab Richard's paperback and pretend to read.

A cop comes to the door and asks, "Que pasa, gringos?"

We all start laughing that teary gut-hurt laugh. The cop leaves us again with no more investigation. Every time we look at each other, we go from almost crying to laughing. Richard is trying to stop laughing. He struggles to speak through his tears, " Eddie, you still don't scare me!"

"He sure fucking scared me!" says Arthur. "Did you see his face? Man, you looked like crazy Juan. Don't do that again."

"I won't. I don't know what happened. I love you guys. But you gotta admit, it was good."

Arthur says, "Give me another drink. You're crazy."

"It's empty. Anyway, shit, we don't need any more of that fucking rocket fuel."

Across the hall the men in the other cell are at their door.

"Oye, gringos. Que pasa?"

Arthur goes to tell them everything is okay.

Nearly six months have passed since we first came to live at Pueblo Libre. We have become the gringos who live at the back of the jail. We have even gained some weight, thanks to Maria and her daughter Isabel, who bring our one meal for the day then go sit with the cops while we eat. The cops gave up checking Maria's trays months ago.

Today when the mother and daughter are getting ready to leave, I ask, "Maria, you have tortillas?"

"I am so sorry, Señor. We have no tortillas in Peru. That is more of a Mexican food, Señor."

We chat while Richard acts helpful, gathering the dishes and silverware. Then Richard hands Maria the tray with the dishes stacked neatly, and we say our regular goodbye. As we watch them walk down the hall toward the front door, Richard whispers to me: "I got it!"

Arthur asks, "Got what?"

I look at Arthur and remind him. "You do not need to know. Remember?"

Richard says, "Oh, fuck it. He asked. We think a spoon handle will open the lock on the door to the back, okay? So don't ask any more, okay? When they find the fucking spoon, we'll be gone. You still have time to change your little mind, Arthur."

"You two give me a real weird feeling in my stomach."

"Arthur," I say, "you get that same feeling when you take off on a fifteen-foot wave at the Pipe on Oahu. Or make a clean drop down the twelve-foot face of Honolua Bay in front of the Cave. Or sail in a storm with sixty-foot groundswells thousands of miles from land. It turns into the biggest adrenaline rush of your little life. But if you're not ready for it, if you're afraid, you just might drown choking on your ego."

"I don't surf," says Arthur in a low tone. "And nothing will make me change my mind about doing something you're out of your mind to try."

"Lurigancho is like never coming up for air. You drown."

Richard says, "If I get a chance to go sailing, I'm not going to care how bad the weather is. I'd rather go down with Mother Nature than spend another day, minute, or second back in Lurigancho. Even if I have to go sailing with Eddie."

Now the cops come and empty the cell across the hall. No one has stayed over there more than a day or two, and they are always told not to talk with us. They do talk with us once in a while, but mainly to ask for cigarettes. Every so often I ask one of them if he knows anyone named Zoila. But never does anyone say yes.

It's Friday night, and the three cops who always do Friday nights are very kind to us. They have a little tradition now of bringing us barbecued chicken and a couple of beers around nine o'clock, when the people upstairs are mostly out in the field busting and torturing their victims.

Arthur goes to the latrine, so we grab the moment for a quick talk. Something's bothering Richard. "Man, I know it sounds wimpy but I'm a little concerned about having to take one of the good cops' guns away and shoot 'em."

"If it happens, shoot him in the leg. Besides, we're going on a Saturday or a Sunday. You know it can't be a weekday. Too many people around."

"We'll figure it out."

Arthur re-enters the cell. "Man! Sure would like to go out on the town. It's Friday."

On Friday and Saturday nights, the honking and roar of town get a lot louder. Men and women are out there having fun, dancing, being with friends, and making love.

Later that evening Richard and me sit on our mattress playing yet another game of gin rummy. I put down my cards to stretch, and suddenly I feel melancholy. I go and stand next to Arthur at the cell door, where all we can see is about twenty feet down the hall. I bump his shoulder gently, as if to say without words, "What's up?"

The cell across the hall is empty again. The iron door is open, giving me more of a caged feeling because ours is locked. The light from the front lobby casts a warm glow in the peace of the police station. No cops here other than the three downstairs. The DEA agents upstairs sure as hell aren't working on the weekend. Tomorrow night is the big soccer game, Peru against Venezuela. It will be on the radio and TV. The cops have offered us a radio for the weekend, but we said no thanks.

Arthur and me hear the sound of leather shoes with hard heels walking toward us. Cops wear rubber-soled shoes.

Arthur sees him first. "Hey, R.B. Ibarra is here!"

"No shit?"

Ibarra's face is somber, almost sad. Arthur looks into his eyes and says, "It don't look good!"

Richard stands, and Ibarra tells us: "Boys, the courte suprema has reached the decision in joo case. They say joo all must return to Lurigancho, and joo must do the entire tribunal from the beginning. I am very sorry to joo boys. We will need a little money for the tribunal and for your food at Lurigancho."

"When do they take us back?" says Arthur grimly.

"Lunes. Monday, in the morning, joo will go to the Justice Palace and ride the bus back with the other prisoners. Please, boys, do not worry. Joo will be at Lurigancho maybe six months, no more. Trust to me. And to Murphy, we will get joo free before his case go to tribunal. Do not worry. I will come to see joo in Lurigancho next Saturday. I'm sorry, boys, but I must go."

Richard says, "Yeah, sure. Thanks for stopping by."

"Tiefilo keeps his word, jess? Good night, boys."

We can smell the barbecued chicken down the hall as the evening breeze comes our way. One of the cops is smoking a cigarette. The smoke travels on the breeze down the hall, through our cell, and out our little cell window.

When the food arrives, we go through the motions of being

thankful for our regular Friday-night party of chicken and beer. Everything's on automatic. Of course we say nothing to the cops about our horrendous news. In fact, Richard makes sure Arthur hears it out loud: " Do not, I repeat, do not let on to these people that we know what Ibarra just told us."

As I sit back down on our mattress, numb, I say, "I'm just not too emotional about this shit anymore. You know what I mean?"

Richard, sitting besides me, says, "Yeah, I know what you mean."

"Well, I feel pretty fucking emotional!" Arthur says in a forced whisper.

"That's okay, just don't show it."

Behind Arthur's back Richard holds up his paperback novel. Across one of the pages he has written one word: "SUNDAY."

That night we go to sleep staring straight up at the chipped paint on the ceiling. Next morning, Saturday, we get one of the cops to call the Reverend, and he comes right over.

"Oh heavens, no bother, please," he says. "Glad to come. But is everything okay? Is there something I can do for you?" One of the cops unlocks our door for the Reverend.

"Reverend," I say, "would you take these letters and this other stuff? It's just a pair of Levi's and a couple t-shirts and this shoebox of letters."

"Well, yes, but why? I feel you're not telling me something. Something has happened. Please, what is it?"

"Oh, no, nothing. We just have so many letters, and the weather is changing and we don't need this many clothes. Really."

He looks concerned. But we don't want him indicating to the cops, however unwittingly, that we know our fate. We don't want to be treated any different. Most of all, we don't want anyone to think of putting us in the military brigade for the weekend.

We are putting our stuff together for the Reverend. He sits on our old mattress, watching us. Suddenly he says, "Ed, what will you do when you get back to America?"

The Reverend is a big man and sitting cross-legged is an effort for him, but he does not appear to be uncomfortable. The only thing he carries with him is a small leather case that holds car keys attached to the zipper on the outside and a bible on the inside.

"Reverend, the first thing I'm going to do is see my kids. And then I'm thinking about going back to school, to college."

Richard loses the mask he usually puts on for the Reverend. "Whose brain you gonna use?"

"Why, Richard, I don't believe I have ever heard a negative remark like that from you. I think Ed would do well in school. Are you saying you do not?"

"No, I'm just kidding. Arthur is the college boy here. He studied art. Excuse me, Reverend, that's a little joke between us."

"Arthur, what will you do when you're back home?"

"Sorry, Reverend, but I can say it in one word if you really want to hear it."

"Oh, I'll take a chance. Go ahead, tell me this word."

All three of us answer together in harmony, "Women!"

The Rev laughs, then he drops a quotation: "'Humor is a prelude to faith, and laughter is the beginning of prayer.' That's Reinhold Niebuhr—a countryman of yours, by the way. I have tremendous respect for anyone who can remain sane through the experiences you have known at Lurigancho. To be honest with you, I wonder how can I do God's work in that place."

"Oh, you do more than you think, Reverend," I say.

"All I can do is ask God's help when I go there because I am so helpless to do anything on my own."

Richard remarks, "We don't really have anything to complain about. I mean, look at Arthur. He's not going to get a good-looking woman after what Lurigancho has done to him, but he might become the richest leche asada maker in America."

"Then I could give you two bums a job," says Arthur. "Maybe."

I say, "As priests go, Reverend, I've only known the Catholic kind. None of them were quite like you—in other words, somebody I could relate to as a God person."

The Reverend scoots his butt back toward the wall and leans against it. "What is a 'God person'—someone who works for a church?"

"Not at all. The truest example I've ever known is Zoila."

"Oh yes. The young girl from the jungle. What became of her?"

I give a sorry laugh. "I don't know. She came to the prefectora and we talked. Her family came, too. She told me to take care of Arthur first, and then her and I could take up together. I had a number for her, a bakery, but now that's gone. She probably thinks I dumped her and went back to the States. She is truly a God person."

"She is, Reverend, she is," says Richard. "It took me a while to see it. At first I thought she was just using Eddie to get to America. But she doesn't want to go to America. She wants to take him to her turf and make babies. And I watched this guy let his woman go in order to help Arthur, who doesn't deserve it. And now he has about as much chance of finding her as a chicken growing lips."

"Is this all true, Edward?"

"Reverend, you can find God persons inside Lurigancho where you least expect them. You probably never saw the man we call Ballhead, who cleans up the filth. The prison administration doesn't even know he exists. At first I thought he was mentally ill. Now I believe he's a kind of holy man. Maybe it's me that flipped."

"Flipped is right," says Arthur. "Reverend, you remember what Eddie looked like when the Peruvians gave him his special name."

"I'm sorry, I do not know this name."

"Gringo Loco. Even before he met the lady from the jungle, he was running around out in the Big Hall with the rest of the psychopaths. And that lady from the jungle was making him worse."

I get up from the bench. "Listen, you. If it wasn't for Zoila, you'd be rusting your ass off here without me."

The Reverend observes, "You three have been through so very much together. It would be difficult for me to imagine any one of you would abandon the other."

All three of us look at each other and laugh.

Richard says, "Reverend, we've been trying to get away from each other for years."

The Reverend consults his watch and starts to get up from the floor. We stand with him. Arthur yells out the door to summon the guard. Today the door is locked.

"I am sorry to go. I am curious about your God observations, and I would very much enjoy hearing more sometime. Okay, gentlemen, see you Tuesday—unless you've gone back to the States before that."

Arthur gives his honest opinion: "Fat chance, Reverend."

One of our regular weekend cops is at our door a few minutes later. "Mis amigos! Ustedes quieren cervesa, y whiskey, maybe joo likee more vodka, jes? Maybe gringos likee radio por joo can listen to the futbol. Toda la gente de Peru listen to this championship of the whole world soccer players, jes?"

Arthur jumps up to the iron bars. "Cervesa?"

Richard says, "I could go for a little cervesa, but I'll pass on the vodka. I might hurt Eduardo."

I agree, "Yeah, si Señor Jefe! Cervesa si, pero no vodka. No radio, gracias. Pero nosotros no tenemos dinero."

The cop insists on paying and leaves.

The cops have a television turned on somewhere up in the front lobby. They're watching the World Cup. The television is loud and the cops are cheering and the noise echoes throughout the jail, mixing with the roar of Saturday night traffic.

Not twenty minutes pass, and the cop returns. He unlocks the door and gives us a bottle of Johnny Walker Red, a bottle of vodka, and three quart-bottles of a Peruvian beer. With the chicken remains still on a torn-open shopping bag and this booze, it looks like a jail party. Arthur cracks the Johnny Walker immediately. He tips the bottle and drinks it like water after a two-hour racquetball game.

I gently take the bottle away. "Hey, you're out of your mind. You're going to get sicker than shit."

"GOAL!" shouts the TV set, and the cops go off.

Arthur has tears in his eyes. Those huge gulps of whiskey are already getting him bent. "Fuck, man! I don't want to go back to Lurigancho. I've had enough." He makes a slight sob, almost undetectable.

I take hold of Arthur's shoulder and turn him to face me. I put my arms around him and in his ear I whisper: " I love you with all my heart, brother."

Richard feels the seriousness of the moment. He stands up from his game of solitaire and also puts his long arms around Arthur. "Hey brother, I love you, too. Everything's going to be fine, dude. Take it easy."

"Hey, let's get civilized." Arthur pulls himself together.

"What do you mean?"

"Let's get some glasses from the cops."

The cop brings us the oldest looking glasses I have ever seen. Looks as though they've been washed only with beer or whiskey for years. Arthur sits on the mattress and pours a glass full of imitation Johnny Walker.

"Arthur, you really got me going now," I say. "I feel like we lost all our appeals on fucking death row."

"So?" Arthur holds up his glass.

"So give up some space. Move to the end of the mattress here, goddamnit. I want to lie the fuck down. I don't feel too good. I wish they would turn that fucking TV down."

Arthur seems to have acquired a calm courage from the whiskey he's guzzling. He pours another full glass of amber liquid. "Hey, look at it this way. You'll get to see your wife. You know? You'll get to see her again every Wednesday. Not to worry, man. Take it easy. Here, have a drink of this."

I take the foggy glass and sip. This stuff is the color of whiskey but tastes like pure grain alcohol. "Whew, wow, that really takes your breath away. Here, no more for me."

I've thought about that wall and every step it would take to get over it. I've thought about the razor-sharp wire at the top. That's why I once asked the Reverend to bring us some towels, saying it would help us wash and dry ourselves. So now I fold a thick terry-cloth towel as a pillow. I lie back between Richard and Arthur.

"I guess that's one way of looking at things. I wasted my time coming back for your daft-dogging ass, and that's the only way me and Zoila can be together. I don't know. But I do know you've got some strong shit in that bottle, and you're drinking it like water. Hey, wake me up if those girls from Puerto Rico show."

I fall asleep right there while Arthur gulps his Johnny Walker and Richard sips a beer.

I wake barely a moment later.

Now Richard is on his knees over me, looking down into my eyes. I start to ask him what's up, but he puts his hands together in front of his chest, like prayer, and he says: "Please, brother! Let's go now!" He looks as serious as any man could. His eyes are welling up with tears.

I sit up and look around the cell. The door is open. Suddenly I am wide awake. I can hear the sound of a typewriter in the office next door. The soccer game is still loud in the background. But something has changed, or has become. There is a soft glow in the light of the cell, and there's the feeling of another presence with us. *Is it that little bit of alcohol I drank?* I feel somehow unattached to anything of this place or time; I feel that I can get up and walk out. Six months in this cell and four years at Lurigancho—suddenly I feel that I have finished my sentence. At the same time, I'm mindful of the dangerous ground that I now must cross or die.

"Where's Arthur?"

"He drank all that whiskey. He's in the head throwing up."

I am still on the floor. I can hear Arthur across the hall barfing his guts into the toilet. Richard is on one knee, ready to run a race.

"R.B., if you can open that door, we're gone, brother!"

Richard scrambles to his feet and heads over to where he hid the food-lady's serving spoon—inside the lining of one of his tennis shoes. He hasn't worn them since Ibarra brought them from the hotel. Now for the first time in six months he kicks off his flip-flops. He slips on socks and the tennis shoes faster than I have ever seen him move.

With the flattened spoon in his hand, Richard looks over to me. I'm ready. He nods his head and takes three steps to the door. I'm right at his back, thinking, *Holy shit, we didn't plan on a cop being in the next room. We have to cross in front of him.*

Suddenly—divine intervention. The phone rings up front in the lobby. Its ring cuts through all the other sounds.

We freeze at the open door. The soccer game is going strong. Arthur's ugly song from the bottom of the porcelain bowl has its own independent rhythm. A cop shouts down the hall: "Oye, Alfredo! Venga al telefono. Es su esposa!"

The cop next door stops typing and exits the room for the front lobby. I whisper to Richard from so close behind that my chest is touching his back, "That's two of 'em. Where's the third?"

"He went for more chicken. Come on."

When the typing cop rounds the corner at the end of the hall, he creates a blind spot. We can't see them, and they can't see us.

Richard steps out one foot at a time. I walk over to the mattress and grab our towels, then move out into the hall two steps behind Richard. We pass the empty office. Now Richard is in front of the steel door. He wedges the spoon handle into the lock. We both know the lock is spring-loaded and is going to make a loud noise. Just as Richard turns the spoon handle, Arthur pukes again and the television explodes: "GOOOAAALLL!"

"Bam!" goes the lock.

Out we go. I close the door behind me. We pass through the tunnel and stop at the edge of the patio. Carefully and slowly Richard looks around the area. Then he dashes over to the wall and ducks into the shadow. He's almost invisible. He's craning his neck to see up the stairs, looking at that doorway on the second floor. We can hear voices coming from up there, but we see no one. He waves me over. In a flash I'm next to him, handing him a towel. Everything feels right.

I grab my towel in my teeth and scale the four steps, just enough to grab the top of the wall. I pull myself up enough to throw my left leg up onto the top of the wall. Then with both hands gripping the chain-link I pull myself farther, till I can get my left knee up to the top. Then I haul myself up the rest of the way and stand at the top of the wall facing the chain-link.

With light from the open second-story door hitting my back, I begin side-stepping to the left, out of the light, toward the brick wall at the corner. I stop and look down at Richard. He flings his towel up to me and then hoists himself up. I put both towels around my neck and continue side-stepping until I reach the corner. Now I hear the chain-link jangling. Richard is on top of the wall. I hand him his towel, then start scaling the fence. At the top, gripping the chain-link with my right hand, I throw the towel over the barbed wire strands. Bracing myself with my left foot against the brick wall, I pull myself gingerly up over the wire and slide carefully down the other side of the fence. Now I'm standing on the lumberyard side of the fence. I tug to get my towel back, but it rips. So I leave it there, hanging like an old battle flag.

Carefully and slowly I turn my body around so that my back is to the chain-link and my face is staring out into—nothing. Dark-

ness. Void. There is one bright floodlight shining below. It illumi-
nates about a ten-foot circle of the ground in the center of the yard.
Fuck, this is a lot higher than I thought!

Now the fence I'm holding onto shakes, and Richard slides over
the barbed wire. He thumps onto the wall-top to my right. Now he's
in the lead because we're both side-stepping back to the middle. We
want to jump into that lumberyard's pool of light. But the closer we
get to it, the more we're backlit by the second-floor cops. In fact I
can't tell what's right below me.

We hear loud voices erupt from that second-floor door. They
don't seem to be coming for us yet, but the sound makes me nervous as hell

Richard whispers, "Jump, man."

I can hardly make out his features.

"Shit. You jump, goddamnit!"

Without another sound, Richard lets go of the chain link behind
him and leaps forth. With his long legs he springs into the night like
a six-foot cat. I see a dark blur as he falls. Then I hear the scud and
oof of him landing. He hits the ground hard, right in the middle of
that pool of light. The jangling and wobbling of the fence echo in
my mind.

The instant before I jump, I watch Richard get up on his feet
and start racing across the floodlit patch. He's running toward a ladder that he and I can both see leaning against an old wooden shack.
The sight of him carrying that ladder to the outside wall, the wall
between us and the open road, inspires me to give it all away. Suddenly I'm dropping straight down like birdshit through the dark.

I land on a lumber pile.

The banging and crashing of my collision make enough noise to
wake Ibarra. I do a great log-roll, running backwards as fast as I can
like a drunken lumberjack. Then I go down like a folding accordion.

Once I stop falling and rolling and look for Richard, he is at the top of the ladder. I catch a glimpse of him disappearing over the wall.

I try to yell, but pain is paralyzing me. Nothing comes out because I have my teeth clenched tight, grimacing. I have to stand up. So I do stand up, using the wall I jumped from as support. I try pushing up with my foot. It isn't working at all.

I can't seem to get any support from it.

I try to get upright again. Pain shoots through me as though I'd been struck by lightning. I fall back onto the loose pile of lumber.

I try three times before I realize that I can't stand and I can't walk.

6

LUCHO

Pain knifes through me from the ground up. I start spinning. Concentrate! Did that when I was a kid—spin, spin, then stop and don't fall down. Center on one spot. I look at the floodlight. But it's going blurry. Could be the tears running down my face.

I hear my dad telling me how to take a hard punch. "Breathe from your stomach. Fill your brain with oxygen. Never let yourself go out. If you get knocked out in a street fight, you could get killed or crippled."

I take a deep breath and roll my body off the woodpile. *Richard jumped into the light. Not darkness.* The lumber pile tumbles and bangs as I slide into the dirt. I sit up and reach down for my foot. *Don't scream!* The ankle is twice its size. I tear at the laces of my tennis shoe, completely loosening it, but the shoe is tight on my foot, it will never come off. I'm breathing fast, too fast. Pouring sweat.

If shock sets in, I'm dead.

I hold my breath and look up at the top of the wall between me and the police station. Nothing, no sound, no indication they know. I'm conscious of everything. Intense fucking pain. Cars honking. Some have no mufflers; some have loud ones. A ladder jutting a foot and a half above a brick wall—the only thing between me and the street. The smooth, even line of the top of the wall. They'll shoot me if they....

If it comes to outcrawling them, then....

Oh Jesus, that hurts.

I shake my head hard.

That's smog, man, smog. Smell it. Only in the free world do you get to smell smog.

Holding my ankle with both hands, I take a quick last check up toward the jail. Then I drop to the dirt on my belly and start pulling with my arms and pushing with my good foot. Crawl to the ladder, man.

Crawl! Crawl!

The lumberyard ground is thick with filth, and I choke as I climb like a wounded worm across the floor. Finally reach the old wood ladder. I grip the bottom rung with both hands. Then I pull my body up to where my chest is on the ladder. I can reach up again, gripping the higher rung, then pull my body to nearly standing. Holding tightly onto the rough wood, I lift my bad foot and set it on the first rung. Then I pull up.

"AHUGGGGG Shit!"

Get up the fucking ladder! A bullet will hurt more than that!

I flip the bottom of my t-shirt into my mouth and bite down hard on the cotton. Pull. Then hop with the right foot. Pull and hop. My arms and legs are trembling like a dryer during spin cycle. I forget where I am. Then, like the moment of death itself, I clear the top of the wall and stare into a hallucination of headlights and taillights.

I look away to clear my vision, then look back.

This is what we've been hearing for the past six months, this honking and engine-racing. It's a fucking roundabout, a two-lane traffic circle with cars entering from all four directions and squealing around narrow corners to exit. Richard is out there jumping into the Saturday-night traffic waving his long arms trying to stop somebody.

Thank God he panicked and didn't run away before he started flagging cars.

Placing both hands on top of the brick wall, I negotiate my butt onto it with my back to the street. With a terrible effort I grab my injured leg and pull it over to the other side of the wall. Then I'm straddling the wall and I have to go through the rest of it, keeping balance, spinning, the traffic spinning. *Ah! Ah, shit!* A bullet in the brain would be a relief. But I have to do this. I have to take the next fall.

I wobble and start to slip. In a panic I clutch the brick-wide wall-top. The cold breeze snaps me alert. Don't want to die falling onto a bike rack or a fucking Vespa.

Below me, a teenage boy and girl are embracing. I am about to die and fall on them while they are perpetuating the fucking species. The rest of the sidewalk is empty. With one last look back at the chain link, I aim my body to land only a couple feet to the right of the teenagers, hoping to hit the dirt between the sidewalk and the street, and I push off the wall. As I push, I throw my legs out in front of me. For the terrible moment that I fall, I make myself keep my legs high so that I will land on my butt.

Slam!

I'm dead.

The teens next to me are startled. Not breaking their tight embrace, they stare down at me. I'm trying to catch my breath.

Richard's out there waving his arms, yelling at the cars: "Taxi! Taxi! Taxi!" Cars, not slowing down, drive around him like a lamp post.

"Richard!"

I yell as hard as I can. The traffic is louder. It's the fucking Indy 500 out here. Nine p.m., and everybody is out on the town. Even us.

"Richard!"

He doesn't hear me.

He wouldn't ignore me.

Typical South American teens. They've seen it all. Man falls out of the sky. They go back to kissing, wrapped in their warm llama ponchos.

I grab a pole—it's a bus stop sign—and pull myself up. "Richard! Richard!" It takes a couple seconds for him to adjust his sight and see me hanging onto a signpost waving my arm. He dashes to the sidewalk and runs to me. He's breathing hard, as though I stopped him in the middle of a race. He looks right past me and nods to the teenagers. "Hola."

Then he looks me up and down. "How'd you get so fucking dirty?"

"I can't walk!"

"Jesus! Okay, come on. I'll carry you." He bends his shoulder to me. "Let go the pole." He drapes my body over his shoulder and hauls me away from the jail. Thirty feet away there's an alley, and he takes me in there. Then he leans me against a wall. As a car flashes past, I can see the sweat running down his face and neck.

He runs back into the street and manages to stop a car directly in front of us. Cars are speeding around the stopped vehicle, honking and shouting. Richard looks into the driver's window, waving his arms. He points over to me, leaning in the dark of the alley. It's a little sedan, and it zips into the alley, stopping about eight feet away with Richard running behind it. The young Peruvian in the passenger seat is smiling; he waves me over, then reaches back and pops open the rear door.

Again Richard bends down low enough for me to fall forward over his shoulder. He stands, quickly checks back toward the jail, then drags me to the car and dumps me into the seat. He dashes to the other door and jumps into the back with me. The driver is studying a map.

"You don't know Miraflores?" I gasp.

"Oh you want Miraflores?" he says, folding up the map. "No problem. We go." I close my door, and the driver blends instantly with the chaotic traffic.

"What'd you tell him?" I say to Richard.

"Never mind! Mirrored Flowers, what's the difference—we're going, aren't we?

The two boys are in their late teens. "Miraflores," I tell them, "Church of the Good Shepherd."

"So what's wrong with you?" says Richard. "Why can't you walk?" He's staring at me. "Quit making all those faces. Jeesh, what happened?"

I ask the boy in front of me to turn on the dome light. With the light on, he studies my face. I can see my own grimaces reflected in his. He pulls his seat up as far as he can. I reach down and pull up my pant leg. In the dim dome light it looks as though I've got a cantaloupe inside my sock.

"Holy shit, look at that," says Richard. "What the fuck am I supposed to do, carry you all the way to North America?"

"I know you can't carry me, dumb ass."

At the stop light the driver looks back and sees my foot. He sees how dirty I am. "I take you the hospital," he says. "I know the way. Oh my God, look your foot. It is very bad, Señor." The light changes, taking his attention back to the road.

Richard rips the thread at the hem of his flannel shirttail as he gets out our money stash. He shows me. We have six U.S. twenty-dollar bills.

I say to the driver, "No, no thank you, amigo. You're a good guy. Just the church, the church. We will get help there. And if you could please hurry because I am in a lot of pain, man."

Richard taps the driver on the shoulder then slides a twenty-dollar bill into his shirt pocket. "You guys have a good time tonight and don't think about us again. My amigo will be fine once we get to the church. If he needs the hospital, the Reverend will take him."

There are more cops outside than I've seen in any other ten-minute drive in my life. We come to an accident at an intersection, and there must be a dozen of them. One cop is directing traffic, and he looks in the back window of our car before he waves us on. That gives us a thrill.

The boy in the passenger seat is sitting sideways, his back against the car door and his head turned toward me. "What happened to you? How did you get like this?"

I wonder what he would do if he knew the truth? I'm sure he's heard of the PIP.

"Ask him," I say, tipping my head. The boy looks expectantly at Richard.

"Ah, well, he was dancing with five women, and, ah, he fell off the dance floor. So now we're going to confession at the Church before any more bad stuff can happen. How's that?" He looks at me and back to the teen.

The kid scratches his head and says, "Okay, I understand. Sure."

The driver says, "We only have a couple more kilometers before your confession. Maybe when we come to the United States we can call to you by the telephone? You have?"

The numbing of my own natural painkillers is wearing off. I look right at the kid in the passengers seat and say, "Oh my fucking God this fucking hurts. Are we almost there?"

"Oh, I am so very sorry," he says.

The driver says, "Yes, yes! Only one more minute. Look, you can see the top of the church, the big cross with the light."

"Richard, the Reverend could get in a lot of shit over this. Remember how worried his wife was?"

He doesn't have time to respond. We've stopped now, and now Richard is opening my door and starting to pick me up. "No," I say. "Just help me walk on this one foot. Don't make a scene. If you carry me, someone will get suspicious. Come on. And we gotta get out of here fast and go somewhere."

Richard lifts my arm across his shoulder. "You're right. The PIP and everybody else will be coming right here. But I don't have any idea where we're going."

"But we will make it! Ah! Ah, God!"

"I guess God wanted us to stop by one of his pads on our way out." Richard bangs on the car a couple of times as way of saying goodbye, and we start toward the rectory door.

"You said God? You, man? You think God is in on this?"

"I mean my God. Yours fucked you up. Look at you. I want to hear you say you need me." We're halfway to the Reverend's big oak door. He stops. "Tell me you need me."

My foot is fucking killing me. "I need you, goddamnit. But I hate your guts." We stumble ahead like two drunks. Just before the door I say, "Do you think Arthur will miss us?" Now we both start howling with laughter, and I'm crying and laughing and crying, and Richard knocks with the brass doorknocker. When Reverend Robinson opens the door, I believe I see God in his eyes.

He's not surprised at all. The look on his face is: "What took you so long?"

He shouts into the house, "Dorothy! Come quickly, please."

Richard says, "Sorry we're late, Reverend. It's hard to get a taxi when you're carrying around a broken body."

"Come in," says the Reverend calmly. "Come. Bring him over to this settee. Put that foot up here."

His wife enters the room.

"Dorothy, please get those Ace bandages. I think we are going to need two or three."

"Do you think it's broken?" says Richard.

Mrs. Robinson returns, and the Reverend says, "You're the nurse. What do you think?"

All she needs is one glance. "Oh, dear. Almost certainly you will need surgery. This swelling indicates serious injury, I'm afraid."

I have less pain now that my foot is elevated. "Don't be afraid," I gasp. "Screws up your life."

"Oh, I know," she says. "I'm so very sorry you are hurt. I am assuming you two have escaped or something in that category? That's not important. But it is important to get some ice on that wound." She leaves the room again.

Richard looks at me and I know what he's thinking. I say it out loud: "Can't walk. Can't even crawl good."

"You need to come with me," he says. "I can carry you somewhere. Thing is, we both need to get out of the Reverend's house in the next few minutes. They're gonna come here for sure!"

Mrs. Robinson returns with a plastic bag full of ice. She's carrying a clean sport shirt. "Darn sorry, Reverend. Sorry, Mrs. Robinson. But Richard is right. We have to go."

She answers, speaking quickly, her British dialect making her words very clear and strong. "You are covered with red dirt. I am going to wash your face and hands. This will only take a minute. Then you can change into that clean shirt. It is my husband's, but it will do."

With speed and skill she wraps my foot with three Ace bandages and then stretches a white sweat-sock over the thick wraps. She cleans my face and hands with loving care. It's a mother's touch. The warm cloth is very soothing.

"I can drive you somewhere," says the Reverend. "But where will you go?"

"Yeah, we don't trust our lawyer," says Richard. "We think he's in on this whole tribunal decision. We think they're trying to extort more money from us."

"Oh! Wait!" I say. "R.B.! Do you remember Pablo?"

"Yeah, sure. We can go to his house. He lives in Lurigancho."

"No, man, do you remember his brother? What's his name? Remember Pablo's mother, and the food, and we met them in the yard?"

"Oh, yeah. So what about him?"

"Reverend, do you have a phone book?"

"Yes, in here, in my study with the telephone."

Richard holds me by one arm and the Reverend grabs my other, and they help me into the study. I sit at the Reverend's roll-top desk. Mrs. Robinson brings the directory over to the desk. I thumb through to names beginning with H. "Herzog. Bingo! Here it is. Lucho Herzog."

I dial the number. After two rings a voice at the other end says, "Hola. Quien es?"

"Lucho? Do you remember me? This is Eddie. You met me at the visit with your brother Pablo."

"Oh my God! Eddie! Yes, of course! How are you? Yes, that was over a year ago. Are you in Lima?"

The time pressure is pushing against my throat. "Lucho, I need your help. I just escaped."

"Oh my God, Eduardo! Yes, yes, of course! What can I do?"

"Remember Ricardo, the other tall American you met that day? He is with me. We both need your help. Can we come to you? I cannot walk, Lucho. I'm hurt bad."

"Yes!"

"Lucho, please tell this man where to go." I hand the phone to the Reverend. "Here, Reverend. You could drive us to this man's house."

When the Reverend hangs up, he and Richard begin helping me up. Mrs. Robinson hugs both of us. With great sincerity she says, "God is with you men. You have suffered much. Time to go home."

Richard and me lie flat on the floor of the Reverend's VW bus. We drive forty minutes. We can see out the windows, high-rise apartments all around us. This is an upper-income area of Lima.

The Reverend slows way down. He keeps looking straight ahead as he talks to us, not wanting to alert anyone to our presence in the back. "There doesn't seem to be anyone around except two men on the sidewalk. Perhaps one of them is your friend. I'll drive up to them and ask directions to a another part of town." He stops the van. "Hello," he says. "I seem to be lost. Can you direct me to Lucho Street."

"Hello, yes I am Lucho." The voice is familiar and pleasant. "Pull over here by the curb. I will open the side door, correct?"

The Reverend parks and gets out. The sliding door opens, exposing us to the outside world. Speaking very softly, Lucho says, "You can get out. Alvaro and I will take Eduardo. There is no need to talk until we are upstairs. Come." Lucho reaches in and takes my hand, pulling me to a sitting position. Gingerly I lift my injured foot toward the door and follow with my right leg. Once I'm sitting, Lucho lets go of my hand and places his left arm around my back. He pulls my right arm up onto his shoulder. The man called Alvaro does the same from my left side. They lift me off the ground. Quickly the Reverend slides the door shut and gets back into the driver's seat. The little bus hurries off into the night, the fluttery Volkswagen engine the only sound in the empty street. Lucho and Alvaro hustle me into the building. The elevator is open. Richard is already inside, holding the door. "Push ten," says Lucho.

As the elevator door slides shut, Richard says, "You guys have a nice place."

Lucho whispers, "Thank you, Ricardo. But please. We should not talk until we are in my apartment. We don't want people to hear you speaking English."

All this excitement distracted me from my pain. But now that I'm upright again, my heart is pumping and my foot is throbbing. As the elevator rises, the pain starts to climb my shinbone almost up to my knee.

At the tenth floor Lucho sticks his head outside the elevator. No one in the hall. "Come now. Quickly. The apartment is just there across the hall."

Lucho puts his body against the elevator door. Richard says, "Here, get on my shoulder again." He picks me up like a big sack and drags me out and across the hall. Alvaro steps in front with the key and he opens the door and we are inside.

Richard carries me to a couch and lowers me slowly onto my right foot, then eases my butt onto the cushion. Alvaro comes out of a bathroom carrying a brown plastic pill bottle. "Here, take two of these. In twenty minutes you will have less pain, I promise. They were for me when I broke my arm in a soccer game."

Richard asks, "Did you win?"

Alvaro has the look of an American tennis pro or maybe a surf champion. He seems to be a few years younger than Lucho. Both are very handsome men who speak excellent English. Lucho says, "You must stay in this apartment until we can find a safe way for you to return to your country. Ricardo, I see you looking at the telephone. Please remember always that the PIP can tap any telephone. They are above all the laws."

I am panting and breathing the way I saw my ex-wife do it in her natural childbirth classes. *Hoo hoo hoo.* It's not working.

"So you guys know Del Gado?" says Richard.

Alvaro had been the quiet one until now. Now he says, "Every person knows Del Gado. Del Gado will one day be the president of Peru, and it will be a very sad day for my country."

That comment gets me past the knife-like stabs of pain. I lift my arm from my forehead and say, "Are you serious—that scary mother-fucker, president of Peru? That would be a sick trip, man."

Richard and Lucho go into the kitchen to make some drinks. By the time they return, I am feeling the helpful effects of the pain pills.

Richard and Lucho sit in matching leather chairs. The apartment is spacious. Richard has a glass of Seagrams VO and Seven-up; the ice cubes ring against the glass. "You look more relaxed now," I say. "All you need is a paperback and a bunk."

Richard says, "Now he's making jokes. This is the guy who insisted we jump the wall. Lucho, do you have ideas, brother? We had a plan, but my leader here turned into a pill-head." He swigs some whiskey. "Hey, maybe Eddie can just live here permanently with you guys."

Alvaro laughs. Lucho says, "You will both have to live here, of course. You must not go out for any reason. I must repeat this strongly. Del Gado has people everywhere."

"Why is everyone so afraid of Del Gado?" says Richard. "I thought he was only scary to cocaine traffickers." Then he adds, "And stupid fucks like us."

"We have many rebels in Peru. In Spanish we call them revolutionarios. To buy weapons, they traffic the coca. By fighting them, your country is protecting our corrupt government."

Alvaro speaks up. "You call it a drug war. But in Peru it is the revolution of the people, just like your own war of independence."

"The situation is very complex," says Lucho. "Even if you are not willing to give your life to the revolutionary cause, you may have a family member involved. You may not know. Then one day they will arrest you and torture you to learn about your cousin, or your cousin's brother-in-law. Then it is either death or Lurigancho. That is a small example of why my people fear Del Gado and the PIP."

Richard says, "Sorry for your country, man. But the police are a problem everywhere you go...."

"They are not the police," says Alvaro heatedly. "They are the P-I-P, the Peruvian Internal Police. They are the Gestapo. Your country is helping the Nazis."

"Is the PIP winning?"

"We are not sure," Lucho says. "Certainly the government officials are making money—money from the United States and from the people who take the oil and other resources from the people of the Amazon."

"Because of Del Gado," Alvaro adds, "many people have disappeared. Some of them were American smugglers."

The painkiller is wonderfully effective. I say, "Lucho have you ever heard of a lady named Zoila? Her family is from the Amazon."

"Alvaro, let me see that pill bottle." Richard studies the label. "Hey, no wonder you can think about Zoila. This is morphine."

Alvaro turns to me. He's sitting at the opposite end of the couch, and my injured foot is next to him, elevated on a dark blue velvet pillow. He says, "May I unwrap your foot? I am a professional soccer player. I have seen a great many injuries. Maybe we can do something. I am sure you do not want to go to the hospital."

"No, man—no hospital, no doctors. Go ahead."

After unwrapping the bandages, Alvaro says, "This is very bad. I am going to have to cut it off." He watches my eyes open wide. "Oh, I am sorry to make a joke. Please. I will get some ice for your foot. If we take down the swelling, you will have less pain and it will heal faster. But I don't think you can put weight on this foot for a while, I am sorry."

"Where did you escape from?" says Lucho.

By now Richard's had four or five drinks, so he does most of the storytelling. They are spellbound—these two noble men. How unconditionally brave they are, to help us at the risk of their own freedom and possibly their lives.

"I have a plan!" Lucho announces.

For ten days we have lived in the apartment night and day. The newspapers and the television have broadcast our pictures. "They do not believe you have left Lima," Lucho told us. "Mostly they believe this because you have no passports." We realize an unexpected benefit of years spent in Lurigancho— the photographs in the media no longer look like us.

During the ten days, I've been working hard to regain the ability to walk—carefully, with a cane. And I'm off the pain pills now. So when Lucho says he has a plan, I welcome it. "It's time to leave," I say. "I can travel now."

"Yeah," says Richard. "You're faster than a snail."

"You are welcome here no matter how long you must stay," says Alvaro. "You must not let them catch you."

"Well, let's hear the plan."

"Yes," says Lucho. "I have many friends working in the airport. You know I am a professional travel guide. For example, I only just returned from guiding the Russian Ballet through Bolivia, Brazil, and Peru. In fact, I was in Russia only a few days before you called. Here is the plan. My friend, a lady, who works at the airport, is coming here tonight."

Richard is uncomfortable. "We have to meet someone?"

Alvaro asks, "Gabriella?"

Lucho nods.

Alvaro says, "Ricardo, I understand your concern. But we know this woman. We have known her from kindergarten. She is our close friend. We trust her, and you can, too."

"What's you're plan, Lucho? You have our full attention, brother."

"Gabriella will work to make you look different."

"You mean a disguise?"

"Not exactly. Ricardo he has blond hair. She will color his hair. And then he will shave the mustache."

"How about let's make him shorter, too?" I say.

Richard says, "I wouldn't make jokes right now, Eddie. This is getting real scary."

"Sorry. Lucho, go ahead."

"She is going to be here soon. How is your foot today, Eduardo?"

"I took a few laps around the indoor track." From the kitchen to the front door and through the den back into the kitchen, that's a lap. I can do several laps before it throbs like hell. No pills. I need to be alert, goddamnit. Alvaro has dragged my crippled ass around this apartment so I could bathe and use the bathroom.

Richard mutters, "I've had this mustache since I was seventeen!"

"So that is very good," says Lucho. "There are no pictures of you with a clean-shaven face."

"I don't think my own mother would know me without this brush."

I say, "Okay, Lucho. Let's get it on. I guess you want us to get on a plane?"

"Yes. A domestic flight. You will not need to show your passports, and Gabriella will be your ticket agent at the counter."

Gabriella shows up ten minutes early. She is five foot nine, but she looks like an Amazon to me—my posture has been reduced to stooping over the cane. Bending helps the muscle spasms that keep clenching around my left hip and lower back.

Lucho holds the door open, and Alvaro greets Gabriella with a squeezing hug. "Hola, Gabriella. Como estas?"

"I am okay. Tired. Twelve hours at the ticket counter. And I took reservations over the telephone. You know how that is."

She is a beautiful woman with coal-black hair put up in a bun. Her airlines uniform is red, matching her lips and fingernails. By contrast, her creamy skin looks white. Her eyelashes are so thick that she seems heavily made-up, though that's not the case.

Richard says, "All of you work at the airport?"

"Yes," says Lucho, shutting the door. "Even Alvaro, who is getting old for playing soccer, must work for the airline. Most of our friends who can speak English get hired easily. And we get to visit your country a lot. We like that very much. Gabriella, this is Eduardo—Eddie. And this man, Ricardo, is called R.B."

"Oh, mucho gusto. I'm happy to meet you both."

Richard responds charmingly. "You're a good-looking woman."

I answer her with my free hand out for a handshake.

"Oh, yes, a handshake is your custom."

Suddenly I realize how stiff I am, nervous about this stranger. But I look into her face and for an instant, I see Zoila. "I'm sorry. I feel a little uncomfortable because of our situation." Gently I brush aside her hand and extend my right arm for a hug. Her fragrance is nothing short of divine. Lucho helps her with her coat and asks her to sit on the couch. We all sit.

"I want you and Ricardo to know that the PIP killed my brother," she says. "They beat him to death."

"The PIP said her brother was a big trafficker of cocaine," says

Lucho. "He sold a small amount to a PIP working with an American DEA man."

"Twenty American dollars—that was the value of the cocaine. My brother did not know any big cocaine people. But the PIP said that he knew of a secret laboratory. They beat him until he died. He was good person. He and his wife have two little girls." Gabriella says these things without tears, proud, like Zoila. "The PIP called our mother and father and told them to come to get the body. They said, 'Your son was a gangster in a cocaine Mafia.' When she saw the body, my mother could not tell that this was her son. We were told later by our friends that the killer was a man called Del Gado. You have met Del Gado?"

"Oh, yes."

"He created the PIP. At first they called themselves the Vigilantes. Then your government gave them millions of dollars to make war on our people."

"Anything to stop the coca."

"No, no my friends. The coca will never stop. Coca is our number-one resouce, shipped by the tons to Germany, where it becomes pharmaceutical. In every dentist office on earth is Novocaine, for example. And there is Lidocaine, even Solarcaine. In exchange, Germany gives weapons and tanks to protect the border. The PIP does not wish to stop the coca, only to control it. I am talking a lot, I'm sorry, you probably do not care to hear all of this. But you asked."

Gabriella crosses her leg, her dress riding up to mid-thigh. My mouth waters. Only God could have shaped such a beautiful sight. And those sheer black stockings magnify the work of the divine. Richard and I are sitting in front of her, paralyzed. She reaches down and loosens the red strap of her high-heeled shoes from around her small ankle. "Oh, my feet," she says. "I must take off my shoes."

"Sweetie," says Richard, "you take off whatever you like."

Gabriella removes both shoes, then looks at Richard with one eyebrow raised. "How long you were in Lurigancho?"

"Too long, I guess."

"Gabriella," I say, "please forgive my friend. We have been locked in cages for over four years, and you are a beautiful women. We thank you for coming here. What do you want us to do?"

"No problem, Eduardo. Ricardo, please." She hands him a pair of scissors that she withdraws from her purse. "First, you cut your mustache. Then I will make your hair black."

She places the scissors on the kitchen counter. Taking a chair from the dining table, she places it against the kitchen sink. After Richard barbers his lip bare, she sets him in the chair so he can lean his head back over the sink. Then Gabriella washes his hair, massaging his scalp with her fingernails and long, gorgeous fingers. Richard keeps moaning and growling. Playfully, she slaps him on the chest. Suds fly.

"I'm not hurting you, am I?" But when she leans over him and touches his hair again, he groans.

I'm leaning on my cane in the kitchen doorway. Lucho, Alvaro, and me are watching the transformation. Richard's arms have relaxed at his side; his legs stretch out across the kitchen. And now that he's removed the brush, I can easily see the ridiculous smile on his face as Gabriella towel-dries his hair.

"You must be still," she says. "I am going to dye your hair and your eyebrows to match. I promise you will look very different."

Richard lifts the towel off his face and says, "Good enough to take you to dinner?"

From the kitchen door I say, "R.B., you are a fool."

Alvaro and Lucho are both laughing. Alvaro says, "You are very fast, Ricardo. But I understand. Thank you for your offer to my fiancée."

Gabriella pauses in drying Richard's hair and looks down at his hazel eyes. "I am sorry," she says. "I am sure I would have enjoyed the dinner very much. Come. Sit up in the chair. I will apply the color to your eyebrows. Cover your eyes or keep them closed."

The result is amazing.

"R.B., you look a lot better. It's very Guy Lombardo.

"As long as I don't look like you, bro. Who the fu—I mean who the heck is Guy Lumbago?"

"Without the brush you look a lot like Arthur."

Gabriella looks at me says, "Oh, that is something I forgot. I hear that you left a friend in the jail?"

"He made the choice," I say. "If Arthur wanted to come on this trip, he'd be here right now." I catch a look from Richard. "Or maybe not. I barely made it myself. I hate to admit this, but if it wasn't for Ricardo, I would have crawled around till the cops got me."

"Yeah, crawling in traffic without a license. Back to Luri, Eddie."

Gabriella says, "I think you two love each other."

"He was just a dirt-covered cripple when I found him and brought him here. Yeah, he loves me. But I don't love him!"

Alvaro says, "You must have had a very hard time leaving him. But of course you could not help him if you two were taken back to the prison. And Ricardo, you have a little girl. Eduardo has two children."

Gabriella looks lovingly at me and says, "Eduardo you have been in so much pain. I wonder if after those years at Lurigancho you will look different to your friends and family?"

I wonder if Gabriella knows Zoila? The possibility seems so remote I don't ask.

"Oh yes!" says Lucho. "He looks very different from when I saw him at the visit a year ago. With the cane no one would know him from pictures taken years ago."

Richard can't resist. "Yes, Lurigancho really beat him up, Lucho. Not like me. Gotta stay strong, man."

"You're funny, Ricardo," I say. I can clearly remember when he was all bones and skin, no muscle, no folds, his knees bigger around than his thighs, his Abe-Lincoln cheeks. But he always kept shaved and always managed a cold-water bath. I turn to our three hosts. "You guys will never know how funny he is."

"Get up," says Richard. "The plan is on."

I'm lying on a pad on Lucho's living-room floor. Richard is already dressed and standing. I raise myself up on my elbows. "Who else is up?"

"No. I said the plan is on. Lucho and Alvaro left. We let you sleep."

"Thanks," I say, struggling. The foot makes it hard to stand. "I couldn't sleep. I was still awake when you guys started sawing logs."

Richard hands me my cane and lends me his hand. "Without those guys here I feel strange, kind of jumpy."

I call a taxi. As the phone rings, I remember once again that I have lost the number for Zoila. "Yes, por el areopuerto, por favor."

After I order the cab I say, "Okay. You're gone first. I'll call another cab for me twenty minutes after you go out the door. If I make it to the airport, I'll see you there. Good luck."

"Oh, fuck luck. I thought you said it's God. All I can say is, you'd better show." He starts reaching out to give me a hug, then he rears back.

"What? I smell bad?"

"It seems dumb giving you a hug goodbye. I'm going to see you at the airport in just a few minutes or so. When you get there, act like you don't know me." He starts to walk away then comes back. "Shit, yeah, give me a hug. If they spot you at the airport, I won't be able to do anything and you won't be able to hobble away from a duck."

"A PIP duck."

"A really old PIP duck."

We hug each other with the pounding-on-the-back routine.

"But yeah, you do smell bad."

When my time comes, I go down the elevator and out to the street. This is the longest walk I've taken on my crippled foot. I have the break wrapped in three bandages and three white athletic socks. In my free hand I have a small carry-on bag with one pair of pants that Lucho gave me, a couple of shirts, and more socks. I'm wearing Lucho's dark-blue sweatpants because these are the only pants that can stretch over my swollen foot-plus-wrappings. I'm wearing one shoe, but I have the other in my bag. We have all agreed for safety reasons that Richard and I would walk a few blocks away from the apartment building to meet our taxis. In case something happens, we don't want to be noticed in front of Lucho and Alvaro's place.

On the sidewalk I see people, the first ones in over ten days. This is a weekday. No kids around. Just a few old folks out for a walk. Cops come out mostly at night.

As I turn the corner, I see a white 1959 Chevrolet Impala coming toward me with a yellow plastic sign on top of the roof. The black letters say TAXI.

I open the back door. But the driver says, "Wait, Señor." He jumps out and comes around to my door, talking as he rounds the rear of the Chevy. "Please allow me to hold the door for joo."

From here to the airport there is very little chance of something going wrong. I feel a weird freedom. Sort of like sailing on a seventy-foot yacht. *In the hands of God with total freedom—but only seventy feet of it.*

As the taxi pulls up to the terminal, my gut starts tearing into itself. *Damn! I hope I don't have an ulcer now, too.*

The door of the old Impala is opened by a teenage boy, one of many kids with dirty hands begging for money. Some of them carry water in old paint buckets and crumpled newspaper to wash car windows. The fare is eighteen dollars. Still in the seat, I hand the driver one of my twenties. "Keep the change, gracias."

As I stand out of the cab, the beggars all turn away. Some tourists down the taxi line are giving handouts. No one even bothers to ask me. I take this as a good sign. My image works—a cripple with no money.

Image, hell.

The terminal is busy, people all preoccupied with their own taxis and luggage, talking fast, saying hello or goodbye in many languages.

Man, when's the last time I was around regular people? No one is paying any attention to my broken ass. Cool.

None of the porters approaches me. I have the strap of the small flight bag over my right shoulder and a Spanish newspaper in my right hand. I must avoid opening my mouth. I can tell now the accents from different parts of Latin America, but I can't replicate even one of them. Not even Carlton could conceal his American accent.

I enter the terminal. I can spot the PIP hanging around—one over by the elevator, another by the ticket counters. Even in their slacks and sport coats, they stand out, scary and sinister. Lucho pointed out that they wear a metal scarab around their necks, like a badge of dishonor. Gabriella said that the Nazis wore scarabs.

I have no choice. I have to go to the counter where the scary scarab man is standing.

The terminal is packed with travelers. But through the crowd at the counter and the distraction of the dark dude, I spot Gabriella. Her eyes are fixed on mine. I feel her confidence. Everything is okay. When it's my turn at the counter, Gabriella greets me and talks to me as though I have a reservation. The cop at the counter isn't interested in my broken self. He is looking for two gringos. Not a dark-skinned, crippled Peruvian. "Oh si, Señor Chavez. Aqui estan sus papelles. Muy bien. Muchas gracias."

If Lucho wanted to turn us over, it would have happened by now.

We're getting on the flight to Iquitos, a city on the Amazon River about six hundred miles north of here, where Lucho will meet us. He left on the first flight this a.m. to make arrangements. The plan is to disappear down the Amazon then sneak out of Peru by the back door.

I'm limping bad and my foot is pounding in pain. The concourse is teeming with people, but even out here I can hear Richard's voice and his laugh. When I get into the waiting area I see him immediately, standing tall with a drink in his hand. VO and Seven-up with ice. He's yacking it up with some other tall gringo. I limp past, and Richard lifts his drink and calls out to me, "Salud!" The other guy does the same. I'm the wretched Peruvian, and two jolly Americans are wishing me good luck and laughing. Richard is loving every second. I ignore them totally and ease down into a soft chair. There's the relief I badly need. *Fuck, I hope I don't lose my goddamn foot.*

The plane is a 727-twin jet, and it's full. Richard sits to the front of the plane, and I'm four seats in back of him. I've got a window seat. A plump grandmotherly woman sits in the middle seat next to me. We get the seatbelt check and the mandatory crash debriefing. Then engines start their full whine, and our wheels start to roll.

Oh man, yeah! We go home.

As the jet airliner gains speed, I am rushing all over my body inside and out. After so much confinement, I am finally pinned to my seat traveling hundreds of miles an hour, sitting among free human beings, finally going north where we belong. And then we fly over the Amazon jungle. I had no idea how vast and beautiful it is. As I lean toward the window, I dream that the plastic pane is Zoila's beautiful face, her mouth whispering to mine the secrets of her untamed home. We're flying low enough that I can see clearings with villages carved out of the jungle forest. Many of them look abandoned, the roofs caving in. She knows I'm not dead, she must. She knows, somehow, that I escaped those bastards and I could not come for her. She knows I would have found her if I could. Now, with my longing for Zoila tearing me exactly opposite the velocity of this necessary airplane, I rest my head against the window and cry.

The lady sitting next to me puts her soft hand on my wrist and says, "Oh pobresito estas injurido." She thinks I'm crying about my foot. She turns to her husband sitting next to her in the aisle seat. He calls the stewardess and asks me what I want to drink. He is buying. I accept a VO on the rocks. "A double, por favor!"

Alcohol is a very powerful thing. It works quickly to take the knot out of my stomach and dull the pain in my foot. The amber drug enables me to relax and enjoy a freedom appetizer, even if it is twenty thousand feet up.

The captain announces that we are coming in for a landing at the Iquitos airport "Favor de sujetar su seat belts, gracias." Outside my window is the largest river I have ever seen, and it runs a great distance out of my range of sight. This is the same river we thought so hard about while we studied the map at the Pueblo Libre jail. And the city of Iquitos, right there. The map said over seventy-six thousand people. Central for trade of all resources. The river runs along the edge of town like a trucking highway for the exploitation of the jungle. I can see roads that come from very far off to Iquitos. The plane descends, and I begin to see giant birds sailing among the high treetops. We scream down the runway toward the terminal. The stress of what remains of our journey slips upon me again like a chronic disease.

As we taxi to a stop, I see dozens of soldiers and armed plain-clothes cops waiting for us.

My heart immediately begins pounding so hard that I can feel my chest pulsing against the inside of my shirt. My mouth goes dry. No one else cares. Richard can't see because he has an aisle seat.

How did this happen? I kept my mouth shut. All I said was muchas gracias to the people next to me. And a couple of words in Spanish to the stewardess. The stewardess, did she radio the cops from the plane somehow? Or was it that gringo Richard was

yacking with back in the terminal? It doesn't matter. The only point
is that we're trapped. And Richard doesn't even know yet.

Grabbing the seatback in front of me, I pull myself up and yell,
"R.B.! Look out there!"

People are reaching for their carry-ons and over-heads, but they
stop to look at me when they hear my voice. I must be one of the
only two English-speakers on the plane.

Richard bends to look out the window. Then he stands up—the
plane is still rolling—and he rushes back to me. Reaching over the
heads of the Peruvian couple who bought me the drink, he pulls me
close and says, "Brother, nobody ever made it this far! Fuck 'em if
they can't take a joke!"

Then he returns to his preordained place.

I turn back to my window. As the plane stops, the ground crew
drives its ramp up to our jet door, and the armed men begin to line
up in two rows at the bottom of the stairs. This is a gauntlet through
which all of us must pass. I study the soldiers—fifteen of them, all
in full dress uniforms. The other men are wearing coats and ties and
weapons. *Fuck, are they all dressed up because of us? Jesus, where are the
TV cameras?*

Passengers are now packing the aisle. I suppose they have forgotten my outburst. We all now take our unchangeable places in the
ritual of debarkation.

People move aside to let me go first. I don't request it. But I'm a
cripple. Besides that, I shouted crazily in a foreign language. They
want me out of here right away. I end up at least a dozen people
ahead of Richard.

Oh fuck it. What are they going to do?

I start remembering what Del Gado did to Gustavo's leg.

Shit, what a thought. Ow.

I approach the stewardess at the exit door and smile at her. She smiles back. Nothing seems to be happening here. Nevertheless, I look down at my foot. This attitude serves the purpose of hiding my face. I concentrate on walking down the steep stairs using my cane. My knees are weak. The cane handle is slippery with perspiration. I hobble off the bottom step looking at my horrendously swollen ankle with its Ace bandages and socks and throbbing pain. I see the legs of the first soldier, his pants dark green with a perfect crease and tailored to meet his spit-shined dress shoes.

I look back to see Richard stepping onto the ramp. He's staring at me, hesitating to see what's going to happen. He looks confused. By now I've passed a few of the dress pants and shined shoes. No one has made a grab for me. I keep limping down the entire line of soldiers and cops. Suddenly at the end of the line there's a soldier who shouts a loud order.

"Attention!"

Everyone around me looks up to the top of the ramp. Filling the door of the plane, a four-star general of the Peruvian military stands in a posture of over-fed but humorless grandeur. He was on the plane with us but unseen—perhaps in first class, or maybe in the cockpit with the captain. With his big black moustache and his bristling eyebrows, he looks like a cousin of Del Gado. The extravagant panel of medals on his chest glitters in the mid-day sun.

While he stands there saluting his gang, I limp into the terminal feeling relieved that I didn't shit my pants. No one around me seems to care about anything except claiming their luggage and connecting with their next transportation.

Richard joins me without a word. We are simply members of a crowd standing outside the terminal. No Lucho to be seen. We gawk around. Then Richard sidles closer. "You disappointed?"

"Well, yeah. I was all ready for a beating."

"Come on, let's look inside the terminal."

Richard is taller than just about everyone and sees over the heads of the crowded terminal. "There he is. Lucho! Over here!"

Lucho, smiling with the suave ease of an experienced travel

guide, greets us both with brotherly hugs. We are safe in a throng of travelers and tourists and families and luggage. I feel an artificial surge of relief and immediately reject it. Don't want to let my guard down just to take a sucker punch.

"How are you gentlemen?" Lucho asks in a cheery voice.

Richard does the old-friend act. "Hi. Hello. We're good. Thanks for coming to pick us up."

"Yes, yes, we must hurry to our taxi. Everything is ready."

We have no clue where we are going. Lucho wouldn't tell us. He knows that the PIP can torture information out of anyone. They might have picked us up at the aeropuerto in Lima. Or any one of the soldiers in the general's gauntlet could have woken up to notice the escaped gringo criminals walking under their noses. Maybe we would finally scream out the names Lucho and Alvaro, but we certainly wouldn't be able to say where we were going. We are simply helpless in Lucho's hands somewhere in the Amazon jungle.

Lucho guides us through the crowd to the waiting taxi. The driver is an old native who appears to have lived in the sun all his days. His face and hands are dark reddish brown like a Pueblo elder. He has laugh lines about his mouth and at the corner of his eyes. His car, a 1956 Ford, has been a cab for many years, judging by the multitude of permits obscuring the windshield on the passenger side. Lucho introduces us as his close American friends.

Traffic is a free-for-all to get out of the airport, and soon we're driving on dirt roads with patches of pavement. The driver seems to know exactly where he's going without a single direction from Lucho. Instead, Lucho is talking to us excitedly from the front seat. "How was the flight? I am so worried about you leaving the apartment. I remembered that I left you with no key. Okay, good, everything is okay."

Richard asks, "Where we going, Lucho?"

"Onto the river. We have a speedboat waiting."

"I remember seeing that river on the map we had in our cell. It runs all through the jungle of Peru through Brazil and out to the Atlantic Ocean."

"The same!"

"Lucho," I say, "what about...." I jerk my thumb toward the driver. "Does this guy speak English?"

"This guy, as you say, he is my father's friend. He has known my father from a boy, and me from the time I am born. I trust him with my life!"

"Sorry, Lucho. No disrespect, man. Just being cautious."

"Paranoid is more like it," says Richard. "Man! I thought Hana was the jungle. Wrong!"

"Yes, I have been to Hawaii and to Hana on Maui," says Lucho. "No, this is the real jungle. This is also a very dangerous jungle. In the water of this beautiful river is two thousand variety of creatures. The smallest creature can enter any orifice of your body and it will find its way to your intestine and feast on your organs. Also are many land creatures that are deadly."

"More than Pelone?" Richard asks with a straight face.

"Who, I'm sorry?" Lucho looks at Richard then to me.

"Never mind him, Lucho. He was thinking about a pet dog he used to have."

"Yeah, vicious fucking animal!"

We drive through a maze of old buildings and run-down housing, two-story homes with banana trees growing on the street. Kids and teenagers are playing street games, mostly soccer.

"Is this the town?"

"Yes. This is Iquitos."

A multi-colored parrot flies low across the road, as natural as a sparrow flying across Wilshire Boulevard. People are making bonfires and cooking food on open fires.

"Iquitos is old," says Lucho. "Maybe three or four hundred years, maybe more. Here the children of Amazon natives mixed with the merchants who came from all over the world. They are light-skinned and dark. In town they speak Spanish. In the jungle the language is Quechua."

"Say, Lucho. You ever know a girl named Zoila?"

"I am sorry, but no. Is she your friend? That is a name of the poor people of the Amazon. You will not meet anyone from Lima with that name."

"Yeah, she is my friend. She is from this jungle. I want to see her, but I think it might be impossible now."

"Oh yes, Eduardo, there are many, many tribes of this jungle. To look for her could be an unending task."

"She gave me the address of her relative's bakery in Lima, but I threw the paper away. I wouldn't want any connection to her found on me if we were caught."

I just hate to admit that I lost such a precious item.

"Here we are!" The taxi stops, and Lucho steps out and opens my door. As I struggle with my cane, he lends me his hand.

We're standing at a boat ramp by the edge of the river. The dense jungle crowds the river, and the river goes so far into the distance that it has a horizon.

Lucho pays the taxi driver and gives him a hug, like family. They exchange words in Spanish. We turn to the boat that is waiting for us at the ramp, an eighteen-foot speedboat. Lucho is very friendly with the driver. We do introductions, and then we are gone into the Amazon.

A wild macaw flies overhead, throwing gold and scarlet across the big sky. The river is clear and blue. Richard and me both have tears in our eyes. Freedom combined with the natural beauty—we can't talk, and this is no time for talk. Once again we are receiving the undeserved assistance of honest people. This boat driver, just like Reverend Robinson, Lucho, Alvaro, the taxi man—God knows who else—all accept the unbearable consequences of helping Richard and me. At thirty-five miles an hour our speedboat slices along the glassy water.

"Look, R.B.! Dolphins in the river!"

"Wow," he says. "First time I've seen those. Heard of 'em. Look over there! Lucho, are those parrots? I've only seen those in pet stores and in Lahaina. The tourists take pictures with them."

"Yes of course those are parrots," says Lucho. "But no one will ask to take your picture. These birds are wild and free."

"Just like everyone on this boat."

"Yes," says Lucho. "Just like everyone on this boat."

After an hour we come to a small dock on the river's edge.

"This is my friend's lodge. You can stay safely here until we can think of how to get you out of Peru and to your country."

"Sorry, Lucho," I say, "but how well do you know this man? He owns this place?"

"I have known this man from grammar school. Our parents grew up together."

Richard says, "You and your parents sure grew up with a lot of people who live far apart."

"Please do not be alarmed when I tell you that my friend—his name is Oscar—once was a PIP."

"Holy shit!"

"Whoa! What?" says Richard. "He quit the PIP? Can you do that?"

"Why did he quit?"

"Why did he quit?" says Lucho. "All the murdering and corruption, raping women, beating people nearly to death—could you be a PIP?"

"Me?" I laugh. "Hell no! But Ricardo could."

"Hey, it's just a job," says Richard. "Don't be so judgmental."

"Okay, I understand the jokes. No, Oscar could not be a part of the PIP once he saw what they do. At first Oscar thought it exciting to work with the American DEA. But soon he quit. Then he asked his father and the Bank of Peru to lend him money to build this resort. He does very well, and he respects that you have paid any dues you owed. He wants to help you escape. Remember, my brother Pablo never imagined he could be beaten and tortured by his own people and then thrown into that filthy prison for all those years. Don't worry. You will like Oscar."

"Like?" says Richard. "He wants to help us get home. I love Oscar!"

"Sorry about Pablo, Lucho. Ricardo will never be the same, either."

Several eight-foot-long canoes are tied to the dock. The water line of the river runs along the roots of enormous trees. Dark-skinned people come out to greet us—natives, I'm sure, of the jungle that stretches farther than the imagination in every direction. I hear them speaking in familiar sounds.

"Lucho, these people are speaking the language of the lady I mentioned, Zoila. Does that mean she could be from this part of the Amazon?"

"No. It is a language spoken by millions of people all through the Amazon and the Andes mountains."

A couple of men in white uniforms come running to help us secure the boat. I can see the lodge waiting for us just a short distance inland. There's nothing else around here. Just the river, the jungle, a few main buildings, and a couple dozen cabins of various sizes. The building style is very Tarzan—palm-thatched, screened-in, one-story, hand-hewn. If you want to drop out, this is the place.

Lucho tells the driver to wait for him. "I will be back soon."

"You're leaving us here?"

"Yes! Don't worry, Eddie. I will come back. I must be at work, and we must figure out how to get you out of Peru and to the United States."

An athletic man steps forth from the lodge. Another soccer player, light-skinned like Lucho with brown eyes and reddish hair in a baby afro. He's taller than I am. Lucho introduces him with an upbeat flourish: "This is Oscar."

He shakes our hands vigorously, as though we won a big prize. "You are very brave men. Please, Lucho has told me some details of your journey home. You can confide in me. No one here will question you because they all know you are my personal guests."

Oscar is carrying a backpack. He seems to be ready to go somewhere.

"Thanks, Oscar. We're more interested in being free than being brave, but thanks. We will repay you anything we cost you."

"Please make yourselves comfortable. This worker will take your things and show you your bungalow."

"Not things." Richard hoists our one little flight bag. "Thing."

Lucho says, "When Oscar returns, he will bring you a few changes of clothes. Oscar is Ricardo's size, and you are mine."

Richard looks to Oscar and asks, "You got any good whiskey up there?"

Oscar smiles. "Only the best. Yes, up there is the bar and the restaurant. I have given instructions that you may have anything you want and as much. Don't worry. We will get you to your country, but it will take a little time to make preparations." As he steps into the speedboat, Oscar says, "All the guests are making a tour of the jungle. A few of them are from America. You'll meet them at dinner. Ciao! See you in a few days."

We watch the speedboat disappear around a bend in the river.

"Well, it's getting better. Right?"

"Way better!"

Our bungalow is at the back of the resort at the edge of the jungle. The room has two beds, nice beds with sheets, and it is real clean.

"Come on, let's get a drink and meet some free people."

"Americans."

As we walk through the compound, the maids flirt with us. They are young native girls who speak Zoila's language.

"Hey, slow down goddamnit!" I'm limping behind Richard.

"Come on, hop-along." Richard has two things on his mind that erase everything else—whiskey and women. He walks faster.

"You're a jerk! You know that, don't you."

"Tell me again at the bar. See you there."

When I finally hobble into the restaurant, I see a few of the guests who have returned from the tour. A big man sits at the bar. He's white and reminds me of an Irish bare-knuckle boxer with his handlebar moustache, cut-off Levi's, and a Penney's Towncraft t-shirt. He's carrying a large Bowie knife strapped on his side. He looks to be about forty. Next to him are two teenage boys, fifteen or sixteen.

Richard already has his drink in hand as I open the screen door with the end of my cane.

"Bring another one of these for my friend, bartender!"

The big guy turns to Richard a few feet away and asks, "Oh, hey! What's up? You guys American?"

"You bet!" Richard sticks out his chest and raises his glass in the air like a toast and adds, "From the top of my head to the tip of my foot. God bless America!"

When I finally travel the ten feet over to the bar and hold my drink up to the sky, I add, "America the beautiful!"

The big guy says, "Hi, guys. People call me Doc, stuck since Vietnam."

"You were a doctor in Vietnam? I'm Ed. That's Richard, but he can't help it."

"No, I was a medic. But now I'm a chief of neurosurgery. This is Joshua and Mike, the bored twins."

Richard asks the kids, "You guys are bored? Shoulda been with me and him the last couple weeks!"

The Doc looks down at my foot and asks, "Too much excitement?"

Richard answers, "No. He kicked himself in the ass so much he finally broke the damn thing."

"You'll learn not to pay any attention to his remarks. Have another drink, Richard. Say, Doc—you think you could take a look at this foot? All I been able to get to was a little jungle clinic with a nurse and no doctors."

Richard says, "I will have another. You want one?"

"Yeah, sure."

"Yes, I can look at it. Come over to that chair and take off all the padding and socks."

When Doc sees that there is not as much wrap as he thought, he says, "Holy jee! That is really swollen. You need surgery. Richard, ask that bartender for some ice in a big bucket."

The bartender is quick to bring the ice. The swelling goes down a lot in only twenty minutes, and the ice turns my foot numb. Between the ice and three whiskeys I feel better than I have since we jumped the walls.

Other guests enter the chow-hall. Everyone is thirsty. They've all taken a long walk through the jungle to see authentic natives of the Amazon. They shriek out images of topless women and old men in loincloths. Someone says, "It just all seemed so put-on," and several people agree.

While they yammer, I watch the old servant who pours water into our glasses. She very much resembles Zoila's mother. The young girl serving drinks at the bar could be related to Zoila—her high cheeks and her thick curly hair with the same auburn sun streaks. And though she's a servant, she walks with her shoulders back and her head up, showing an unbroken spirit.

Doc introduces us. "Ed, Richard, this is my wife Helen."

"Happy to meet you both. Did you just get to Peru?"

"No. We've been in Peru four years."

"For years, or four years?" She holds up four fingers.

Both Richard and me hold up four fingers.

One of the sons asks, "You guys surf here?"

"We were planning to, but stuff happened." Richard gives the boys a once-over. "You guys surf?"

One twin says, "Oh man, yeah! Been surfing since we were little. Last time I surfed was at Blacks in La Jolla. Dude, I got so lipped, so barreled!"

The other twin bursts out, "Oh, dude! The drop is so freaking steep at Blacks!"

"Hey man, how'd you hurt your foot anyway?"

"I went off a fifteen-foot wall and ate shit."

"So you hit bottom?"

"Yeah, bottom."

"Was it a coral reef?"

"No, just the floor. It was dark. Not sure what I landed on."

"You were surfing in the dark?"

"Well, let's say if it hadn't been for him, I would have drowned. That's why I put up with him."

Richard lifts his glass high and says, "Here's to surfing!"

Doc says, "Hey, let's eat."

Helen breaks away from talking to the lady next to her and asks me, "What have you and Richard been doing in Peru for four years? That's such a long time away from home. What about your families? Have you seen them?"

I answer, "I'll tell you this. We haven't had sex in four years."

"Oh, so you're missionaries?"

"Hey everyone! Couldn't wait for me, huh?" It's a blond American man—young and fat. One of the workers shows him a seat at the end of our table. Richard is hard at work trying to talk to some French people. As blond man sits, he looks to me and Richard and says, "Are you guys from the States?"

Doc says, "They are practically from here. They've been in Peru for years. Missionaries."

Blond serves himself from a tray. "Well, it's a beautiful country. Missionaries? So, are you on a break here, or are you gentlemen working in the jungle?"

Richard answers, "Yeah, right—a break. But so far the only break has been Eddie's foot."

"Actually, we've had more breaks than that," I say. "But one thing is for sure—I won't be taking any long walks through the jungle to visit the natives."

"You won't have to walk," says Blond. "Somebody with the lodge will take you out there in a canoe. Your buddy here can walk with us. We're going in the morning."

Everyone agrees that Richard and me have to go see the indigenous people. After all, we're on vacation.

The canoe ride provides me with a closer feeling of the jungle. It's so still but filled with natural sounds of the prehistoric land Zoila was born in. Why she is who she is. How she can be so very soft, gentle and fragile, but at the same time so very strong. Always true to her spirit. Now she is no mystery. Here, you understand the mandatory lessons of the struggle to live.

My guide is placing his oar in the water without a splash. Our small boat cuts silently along. The others are walking to the native village.

I hear a sound from some creature in the distance. When I turn around in my seat at the front, the native paddler rests the oar on his lap. Putting his index finger to his lips, he makes a shhh and cups his hand to his ear. We listen to the daytime creatures of the jungle. I contrast these sounds with Lurigancho, the snoring, screaming, drumming, yelling, people dying or wounded, coughing up blood—and that fucking barrel rolling. The wild jungle is a safer and much more desirable place.

To my right a snake's head pops up out of the water, the brightest lime-green color I have ever seen. Suddenly it whips its body, matching the length of the canoe, and swiggles away on the surface of the river. Weaving through a maze of water-rooted trees, we reach an intersection with a far littler river. We dart up that side route to a small stretch of beach. The native paddler puts down his oar. As we run aground, he jumps out and pushes me and the canoe high onto the beach.

We are at the front yard of the native village.

He helps me out of the canoe and holds my cane until I am on my feet, balancing with his help. We walk into the village. The young man knows all these natives. They are his relatives. They live open-air, no privacy, under one thirty-foot roof. Women and girls are gathered at one place, where there is cooking and conversation. I hear a young voice that sounds a lot like Zoila's. The women all wear sarongs that cover them modestly from the armpits to the knees. Many of the little kids are naked or with ragged shorts. They're playing, like any kids. The men of the village are dressed in different types of pants and shorts. They generally appear to be happy and free. I see no sign of a generator or any source of electricity. I find a place to sit and am left to myself apart from these peoples' lives. The kid who paddled me here smokes something from a long, skinny pipe with other boys his age and the older men.

Suddenly the village gets word that the tourists are coming. The men start getting together at the far end of the village. Some of the women call to the younger native kids. Now the women and girls are pulling their tops down, exposing their breasts, and the men are trading their pants and shorts for loincloth wraps. Men and women use their fingers to paint tribal marks on their faces with a black ointment. The men have fetched their blowguns and drums from their huts. There are about sixty men, women, and children in this village.

One thing that catches my attention is the large wooden bowl being spit into by nearly every adult in the village. They all look like baseball pitchers, their cheeks filled with wads of chew.

Off in the distance I can hear the women of the tour group laughing. Richard can be very entertaining for the ladies, and this is his first chance in years. Now everyone from the lodge appears through the trees. The villagers are wearing their full dress, or undress. The show begins. Blow-dart exhibitions. Dance to the beat of the tribal drum—a sound very familiar, a Lurigancho beat.

Richard heads my way. I say, "See that bowl?"

"Yeah."

"Do not drink out of that bowl. I don't know what it is they spit in it, but that bowl is full of spit."

"I like the taste of spit. I've got some in my mouth right now."

For a few minutes we just watch. The village women are trying to sell their handmade cloth, the same fabric that they are wearing around their waists. Helen and the other tourist women seem to be intimidated by their naked breasts.

"How long do you think these people are going to last?" I ask.

"Oh, come on, man. A little swig of spit now and then never hurt anybody. You just don't want to get hooked on the stuff."

"That's not what I mean."

"I know," he says. For a moment he actually seems to be thinking. "Well, they'd probably last a lot longer if the Gringo Loco moved in and started producing a lot of little Eduardos of the Jungle."

"I'm not so sure."

Every morning I wake to the sounds of roosters, jungle birds, and a donkey. The ocelot cat has a growl like a lion, and some of the birds sound as if they can carry off small children. Every so often we hear something else out there in the jungle, something that makes us stop everything and say, "What the hell was that?"

One day we walk down to the river and find the twins, Mike and Josh, pointing under the dock. Richard asks them, "What's up?"

Josh says, hands on his hips, "We don't see any reason why we can't go swimming!"

"Me neither," says Richard. "I'll be right back."

Me and the boys stay on the dock. Richard returns wearing a pair of cut-off Levi's and stands at the top of the stairs to the dock. He tells the servant standing nearby to bring him a whiskey. Richard downs the whiskey and tells me and the boys: "Let's find out."

He jumps off the dock into the chest-deep water. Then he dunks himself a couple of times. The boys and me are waiting for something bad to happen. Richard climbs back onto the dock and says, "It's cool. Jump in."

Just then we see two of the lodge workers waving their hands and arms to get our attention.

They want us to sit at a table near the stairs while they go to the edge of the dock, one with a fish net on a pole and the other with a machete. They catch two small fish, each no more than six inches across, and dump the silver, wiggling things at our feet. The man with the machete sets the large steel blade near the fish's mouths, and the fish attack the steel, chomping viciously.

The native with the net says: "Piranas muy peligroso."

I look at Richard.

He's looking at the spot where he went dunking. Then he turns around and yells toward the bar: "Dos whiskey y dos Coca-Cola!"

"Listen, you guys," he says. "No need to tell this yarn to anyone. Your mom would freak."

"Don't worry about us!"

Then Richard nudges me with his elbow and moves his head in the direction of the river. A speedboat is approaching. Richard and me have kept an ear and eye out for whomever those speedboats bring to the lodge. Should the boat have cops or soldiers, we have well established between us that we will take to the jungle.

"I think it's Lucho and Oscar. It is!"

"Weird how my gut starts flipping around when one of those boats comes here."

"I could puke."

"The PIP still believes you are in Lima somewhere," says Lucho. "They are threatening to arrest anyone helping the escaped Americans."

"Any pictures of us?"

"None, not on the TV or the newspaper. I do not know why."

"We going to live here forever?"

"Oscar and I have arranged a plan to get both of you to Colombia. A place called Leticia, on the Amazon River north from here. We must go through Brazil."

"Sounds good. Are you going to make us invisible?"

"In the morning you will take the early speedboat to town."

"Shit! You want us to go back into Iquitos? Man, we're so safe here."

"This is better. It's the way to your home, to your country."

"Okay. Tell us what to do, brother."

After a very pleasant dinner and evening with all the guests and Oscar and Lucho, Richard sits with me under the stars for a bit. We are both quiet.

"Christ! I feel like we're going to a gunfight tomorrow."

"We'll make it, Eddie. That guy Oscar has it wired."

"All these people helping us. I mean, I appreciate the fuck out of what they are doing. But don't you wonder?"

"About what? Wouldn't you help someone get away from the PIP or from Lurigancho? Yeah! You would, I know you would."

"Yeah, maybe you're right. But why would they help you?"

We don't even stop for coffee the next morning before getting in the ready speedboat and shooting the fifty miles back to Iquitos.

At the small-craft harbor up on the road we wait for the same taxi and driver who brought us to this spot. Now we get in the taxi. The only communication we have with the driver is a smile all around.

He drives us to the town square. We get out and walk thirty-five feet to the center of the park, and we sit at the fountain. I can hear Lucho say it: *"Near the fountain you will see many men with cameras to take pictures of the tourists."* Right on cue an old man with a box camera asks in Spanish if we would like our picture taken.

"Only answer si!"

"Si."

The old man sets up his box camera in front of us about five feet away. He covers his head and camera with a black velvet cloth, takes a picture of Richard, and shoots one of me. Flash, flash.

We make the silent trip back to the lodge without incident. Amazing.

Richard says, "Hey, how about that? No police, no PIP, and no military. I sure feel free, riding in this boat."

Lucho is carrying a large brown envelope. In our bungalow Lucho closes the curtain.

"Okay, here look. You are Peruvians!"

Lucho pulls some official-looking papers from the large envelope. "How do you like your new names? Ricardo, you are Enrique Domiguez Baptista. Eduardo, you are now Fredrico Antonio Chavez. Here are your documents for travel. You are leaving today."

Now Richard goes into the bathroom and pukes.

"Is Enrique all right?"

"Don't let his weak stomach fool you. He's all right. We're both a little nervous. These pictures of us came out pretty good, huh?"

Richard comes out of the bathroom with water splashed on his face. He stands tall with his chest out and says, "What's the plan, Stan? I'm ready!"

"In one hour you two will leave in the speedboat. You will take the same taxi at the dock; the driver is waiting for you. His son will be with the old man. We need two people for this to work."

"You mean it could fail?"

"Just stick to the plan we have made."

Richard's nervous humor: "Guess we better start packing our luggage. We only have an hour."

Lucho says, "The taxi driver and his son have a pass from the military to take passengers to the naval base."

"A naval base?"

"Yes. You are Peruvians going to visit your family in Colombia. A small amphibian plane leaves from the base twice a week. The plane only seats twenty passengers. The people who use this plane are the poor people of this region. All the passengers must have the papers you have in your hands."

"What if...."

Lucho smiles and begins again. "Look. At the bottom you will see that the Ministario de Peru has signed the papers. Oscar has the best connections for documents."

Richard says, "Cops meet all the best criminals."

"In this case," says Lucho, "it is the cops who are the criminals. Okay, we must get going. Listen, when you get to the base, the driver and his son will take these papers into the terminal and they will give the names, your new names, to the agent inside. When papa and son come back to the taxi, where you will wait, they will give to you the boarding pass only. You get on the plane. The first stop, you stay on the plane. You understand me? Do not get off the plane at the first stop. Wait until the next stop. That is where I will meet you. Ready?"

Richard says, "Fuckin' A!"

I say, "Let's go!"

7

REYNA

There are no goodbyes.

The speedboat trip seems very quick. As we arrive at the dock in Iquitos, the taxi is waiting right where Lucho said—the old Indian driving, a frowning man with graying shaggy hair sitting shotgun. The frowning man wades out into the water to help me. Richard comes around to my side. The two of them carry me to the shore, keeping my bandaged foot dry.

"Hola," says the old man. "I am Pancho. This is my son Phillip. We go."

Sitting in the back seat, Richard and me are quiet. Now the son drives.

I am thinking ahead, trying to imagine all possible bad jumps that could await us. I say, "Pancho, por favor, will you please write a note for me? The note should say that I had had an operation on the inside of my throat and I cannot speak."

When we reach the parking area at the military base, Richard and me wait in the cab. Father and son go together into the terminal. We are out of sight of the plane or where the plane might be. Then Pancho and Phillip return to the cab. They get back in the front seats and reach back to hand us our boarding passes. They shake our hands. We are all smiles, men with nothing to fear. Pancho points the way to the boarding area, between a couple of buildings.

Richard and me know better than to say a word. I move slowly along with my wooden cane. Between the administration buildings and the terminal we can see the river. A small gunship is anchored close to the bank. In front of us is a small dock, to which a twin-engine amphibian airplane is tied. About fifteen people stand on the dock. Some of them load cargo into the belly of the plane. Two uniformed officers walk past. They have loose collars. All the passengers seem to know each other.

Richard is carrying our one piece of luggage, a small gym bag. Inside the bag is some bathroom stuff, a pair of pants rolled up on top of a couple shirts, and a couple pairs of underwear. The clothes Oscar and Lucho provided were too small, so we have been hand-washing every day. Our forged documents lie on top of everything.

Now the plane's cargo is stowed away. The twenty passengers are sitting in their seats. I'm in the middle of the plane; Richard is two seats closer to the pilots. The engines rev up, and a man on the dock unlashes our rope. The amphibian plane begins to slide a few feet away from the dock.

Then out my window I see a thin, light-skinned man with a pencil moustache. Around his neck on a gold chain hangs a scarab pendant—the mark of the PIP.

"Richard!"

He looks back to see me pointing. Then he looks out the window and sees what's coming. It's the real boogieman, the terror under the bed. I know this feeling. It can paralyze a gorilla.

The PIP is waving the plane back to the dock, and the native who untied our plane to freedom is looping the rope back onto the cleat, securing us to Peruvian soil.

The two pilots get off first. We see them out there on the dock chatting with the deadly cop. They order all the passengers off the plane, and the cop wants to inspect all the cargo.

I am the last off. I lean hard on my cane. Fear makes me feel as though I weigh four hundred pounds.

You know this feeling. It's just like dropping down the face of a big wave, man. Do you want it, or do you want to drown?

The cop is joking and yacking with the passengers, his back to me. Off the short ramp, I walk over next to Richard and whisper: "Swim!"

Two natives are unloading the cargo—crates of vegetables, a couple crates with live chickens, another with a huge pig's head. No one else has heard me, but Richard is sure what I said. I start to step toward the edge of the dock, but Richard grabs hold of my arm and squeezes tight. He has such a death-grip around my upper arm that I abort my swimming event.

The PIP cop turns and takes two steps over to us. He looks me up and down, then delivers a spew of Spanish faster than I can figure it out. I shrug my shoulders, reach in my shirt pocket and hand him the note written by the cabdriver. He reads the note and hands it back, looking at me as though I'm the most pathetic thing he's ever seen. He looks Richard in the eye. They are the same height. He glances down at Richard's feet, at the little gym bag.

"Esta es su bolsa?"

The PIP's tone is violent. Looking back into the cop's eyes, Richard fearlessly and aggressively says: "Si!"

The skinny PIP bends down. Without lifting the bag, he unzips it. Then he straightens back up to eye level. He reads our documents. How glad I am that the jungle is so humid because I am dripping sweat.

He studies us. "Los dos Peruanos?"

Richard answers with one syllable. He delivers it violently, right back into the eyes of Death.

"Si!"

The cop hands Richard the documents and tells him to move aside. He starts to inspect the cargo between us and the belly of the plane. After that he jokes and laughs some more with the pilots and a few passengers. Then we all get back onto the plane and the cargo gets re-loaded, and then we are in the air.

This plane is a death trap.

Lucho told us to get out at the second landing. He's going to pick us up there in a motor launch, and from there we'll boat to Colombia. But the first stop of this plane is also an option—also in Brazil. If we get off at the first stop, no one will know where we are, not even the PIP. Then if the PIP pick up Lucho and torture him, he will be able to say with all honesty, "I don't know where they went."

Our plane hums just a couple hundred feet above the jungle tree-tops. For a while I notice every detail, but soon it drives me crazy to try. Now we circle over the wide river. Paddlewheel ferries line the shore near a small harbor. Having swooped over a vast body of water, we splash down facing a floating dock just a couple hundred feet from shore.

Sternwheelers. Rollin' on the river.

As the plane cruises up to the wooden float, I'm up out of my seat and making my way to the front door to disembark with the other seven or eight natives getting their belongings out of cargo. As I start past Richard, he grabs my arm, trying to prevent me a second time from deciding my own fate. This time I jerk away from his grip, get out the door, and get down the steps into the jungle sunshine.

Richard is behind me.

The plane takes off.

"Why the fuck did you get off? We were supposed to stay on the plane until the next stop! What's wrong with you? Where the fuck are we? Do you fucking know? No! You do not know!"

"*You* didn't have to get off!"

"Yeah, right!"

He's trying to keep it to a whisper, but he's so irate that other people on the platform start to listen. Two women next to us look at each other and then look back, giving us a disapproving once-over.

"Look! Here comes our ride."

We're standing on a floating platform outside of a harbor on a river wider than any river I ever imagined. Now that the airplane has ski-ed away on the river and leaped into the sky, all sorts of little boats are approaching the platform.

I point to an old native man in a tattered straw hat who's motoring toward us in some kind of rowboat that's been souped up with a five horsepower engine.

"Come on. We're here now!"

The harbor has a good feel to it. The main feature is the row of ornate, Mississippi-style sternwheelers lined up along the shores. I see restaurants and lots of diverse-looking people walking about the shops. Everything is good except that I realize now what an asinine, suicidal move I just made—to get off the plane and get off the plan. To be on the lam. I don't know this country, I can't speak this language, and I don't even know the name of this fucking town. Before, I was merely frightened. Now I'm going nuts with terror compounded by pure embarrassment.

Once we're on shore, I start limping fast and sweating profusely. "Look!" I say, controlling my voice with all my willpower. "Those two are Americans." A man and woman are strolling purposefully along the sidewalk, checking their watches—white, well-barbered, excellent shoes. "Come on, let's ask them where the embassy is at."

Richard hangs behind and lets me approach them first. "Hi, hey—are you guys American?"

"Yes," says the woman. "Are you?"

I completely lose my cool.

"We escaped from prison in Peru. If they catch us, they are going to beat us to death. Please tell us where the embassy is so we can get a temporary passport or something to get home, to get on a plane."

She says, "Listen, slow down."

She's very commanding, with severe hair and no makeup.

She says. "My name is Susan. This is my husband John." He's a serene-smiling, dome-headed guy with a good tan. "You're a mess. The way you're acting, the Brazilian police will take you to jail. Come on, let's get a beer on this ferry."

Richard is cool. The husband is both calm and cool. She's right. I'm undone.

What she means by a ferry is one of those paddlewheel boats—floating saloons with scarcely a customer. The design is right out of Mark Twain. The interior is all wood siding or cream-colored paneling trimmed in dark mahogany. The staircase to the top deck is made of fine hardwood with hand-carved banisters. The bar upstairs commands a fine view of the river.

The lady orders four cervesas from the waiter.

"Now!" she says. "We've been here years researching the rain forest. We know a lot about the government, believe me. We have had our share of problems dealing with the police and government officials. What are your names?"

I take a sip of beer and try to calm down. I'll let Richard lead.

"I'm Enrique. This is, uh, Eduardo."

"Hi," says John. He shakes our hands. He says, "Sounds like you guys need some help. What part of California you from? You are from California?"

"I have a house in Dana Point. Eddie lives full-time on Maui. Except neither one of us has been home for a long, long time."

"How long have you two been in a prison?" she asks us, looking around. Fortunately, this town has more ferries than tourists. We are alone except for the waiter and bartender, and both of them are out of range. They don't care anyway.

"Four years."

"What is your sentence?"

I tell her what's in store for me: "Forty-two years, sweetie."

She gawks. John says, "Who'd you guys kill?"

"No, no, not me. I only have to do a little over twenty years."

Susan regains her composure. "Listen, you two. The American

embassy will return you to prison in a heartbeat. And the governments of Peru, Brazil, and Colombia have signed an extradition
treaty. If you two don't have passports—and I doubt you have—
you'll be arrested and thrown in jail until they find out where you
belong. Then you're back in Peru, my friends."

"And now what's the bad news?"

Susan softens under the influence of Richard's sarcastic humor.
"Look, I don't know anything about Brazil. But in Colombia, in
Leticia— It's on this river about fifty or sixty miles from here, less
than two hours by fast boat. If you can get to that town without
going to jail—and I can almost guarantee you're going to jail here or
Colombia—then find a man named Walter Thompson. He can help
you get home. I'm not saying that he will. But he can. That's the only
thing I know to help you guys. Sorry. I truly hope you make it."

The sound of a speedboat in the distance catches my attention.
I turn my head toward the river. A red speedboat is shooting into
the harbor, leaving streams of white. A handsome, athletic fellow is
standing at the passenger side clutching the top of the windshield
and scanning the shoreline. I stand up and shout, "Look."

Now I'm sure what I see. "Look, it's Lucho. No shit! It's Lucho!"

We hug the lady and shake John's hand.

Lucho jumps up onto the dock and says, "I am so glad to find
you. The pilot told us you got off the plane at the wrong place."

"Sorry. My fault. Enrique tried to stop me."

"No problem. Come, let's go. The driver is taking us to Leticia to
visit my good friend."

This is a far different boat from the little taxis out to the lodge.
Twin forty-five engines thrust the first four feet of this fast-moving
haul right out of the glassy water. Our rooster-tail as we spin out of
the harbor is ten feet high.

I have to yell to Lucho above the engine and wind. "We were

told by a lady, an American, that someone in Leticia can help. His name is Thompson. Do you know him?"

"Walter Thompson? That is my friend! That is who you are going to meet."

Lucho tells us that Thompson is the owner of three hotels around Leticia. He is from New Orleans, but he has been in Colombia for twenty years. He owns a game refuge for the Amazon's critters, and he runs a good business selling birds and animals to zoos and private buyers all over the world.

The three of us are squeezed together in the back seat, which is built for two. Richard's mouth and mine are close to Lucho's ears. The driver can't hear us.

"Lucho, do we have to tell your friend Walter the truth?"

Richard says, "Tell 'em we got robbed on the ferry."

"Yes, the ferry," I say. "We put our bags on the bottom floor and went up to get a beer, and when we returned we couldn't find the bags with our passports and travelers checks. But here's the truth, Lucho. We should tell you. All we have is about a hundred dollars."

Then Richard shouts, "As soon as we get to a phone, we can get money sent to us."

We reach Leticia Harbor about two hours before dark. The jungle has not broken, not for an inch of the way. We're sliding out of Brazil next to Peru and into the narrow toe of Colombia, but the jungle is the same jungle in every country.

At Leticia Harbor the men all look as if they escaped from the Big Hall. Most of the boats that are crowded in here look as though they should be flying the Jolly Roger. Lots of these old crates have been hauled up into drydock scaffolding. Men are scraping the bottoms. Men and boys fish from the stinking harbor's edge, garbage floating. What few women we see are looking at us like whores hoping to pick up a drunk.

Lucho jumps out and ties us to a slip and tells the driver to go. Lucho pays him.

"Come on, there is no customs here. We must hurry. We are getting a taxi up on the street."

Lucho tells the taxi where to go.

"Yes, I will tell Walter only that you and Ricardo have been robbed. I cannot promise he will help, so we better pray."

Walter's door is open. He sits with his back to the door. When he hears Lucho say, "Hey, old friend," Walter swivels his chair around and stands. He is a big man, taller than Richard. But he outweighs Richard by at least sixty pounds. Like many gringos living in the Amazon, Walter has sun-bleached hair and a sunburned face except for the white skin that has been protected by sunglasses. His smile reveals good teeth and a genuine welcome for Lucho. They hug, lots of slaps and pats on the backs.

He says, "Yes, of course I'll help you! These goddamn police here, the DAS, are some brutal sons of bitches I'll tell y'all. Here, let me set y'all up with my ham radio set here, only takes a few. Got to get an operator first. Give me a sec."

The file cabinets are stuffed so that the drawers won't close, and the tops are stacked to the ceiling with official documents and who knows what else. Walter was a zoology professor in New Orleans. After twenty years of teaching he came here and built this business, including this pile of paperwork that he has to stretch his legs to get around. He speaks fluent Spanish on the radio set.

"Here you go," he tells us. "It's the operator in the States. Tell her the number y'all want to connect with over there."

I only know one number by memory.

"Hello, Joleen?"

I explain to my ex-wife that we are here in Colombia and that we need four or five grand immediately. We agree to call her back in an hour.

After one hour and three cups of Walter's coffee, Joleen is on the phone telling me that the money will be coming tomorrow morning on the first plane from Bogota. Walter makes Richard and me promise that we will not leave the hotel grounds until the money comes.

Lucho comes with us. The old one-story brick and tile-roof jungle hotel has screens, no glass. There are palm trees all around and a swimming pool in the center of the brick bungalows. We have two comfortable beds.

In our room Lucho explains to us—looking at me most of the time—"Listen to me. You are safe here as long as you do not leave the hotel. Stay away from the front desk. The DAS police like to flirt with the girls working at the front desk. If they see you, they might want to see your papers. It is a crime to register at a hotel before you go to the office of the DAS and have your bags inspected and your passport and visa stamped."

"What visa?"

"The visa given by the DAS after the inspection."

The hotel has a restaurant and bar. But once again our world is confined to one room, and Lucho brings food to us. We sit at a small dining table eating rice and beans and fish from cleaned-out coconut shells, using small corn tortillas that are thick like bread. Lucho tells us, "You scoop out the food with your spoon onto the tortilla." Even though night has fallen, the air is thick with humidity and ninety-degrees hot. But our front wall and all our windows consist only of framed window screens, so we are bathed in a cool breeze.

"We need to be at the airport before seven forty-five," says Lucho.

At just after dawn Walter comes around in his own car, and we go with him.

The airstrip has been carved out of the jungle, which looms over the flatness ready to reclaim the earth at the first opportunity. An airliner from Bogota lands on time, and an attractive American stewardess walks off the plane ahead of the seventy or so passengers. She seems to have a good idea what she's looking for. She walks right up to Richard and me—the tall one and the guy with a broken foot who walks with a cane.

"Hi," she says. "Anyone here named Eddie Spageddy?"

She hands me an envelope containing five thousand dollars.

Walter drives us back to the hotel. Before we get out of the car, he says, "Now don't be too hasty, boys, about goin' ta see them DAS rascals. Don't worry about payin' me 'till y'all know what you're going to do about your papers. But I guess you're going to have to check in with them guys sooner than later. Let me know."

Once we're inside the hotel grounds, Richard says, "I'm going over to the bar. I'll bring back some drinks."

Lucho and me are tired. "All this walking around is a big deal with this foot, Lucho. I'm going to lie down."

Lucho and me both doze off.

Richard wakes us abruptly, announcing that he's met some Americans at the bar. "Get up. You got to see these ladies. They already have boyfriends, but that's all right. We're not asking them to marry us. Come out by the pool. I told them we'd rather be outside because we're wanted criminals."

Lucho looks at me with his eyebrows raised. "Don't mind him," I say. "He's had a drink. See how much bigger he is."

"Come on," says Richard. "Walter said that we should make ourselves comfortable. We don't have to hide from the other guests. Just act natural, Eddie. But try not to drool. The girls are gorgeous." Then he adds, "Of course, ever since Lurigancho every woman we've seen has been gorgeous.

The youngest is Reyna, a seventeen-year-old sweetheart. The other young lady's name is Julie. The boyfriends are Charlie and Billy. All three of them are twenty-one years old. Very healthy looking, very upper class. Reyna is Colombia-born, and she has brought her friends to visit her country.

The two girls are fellow students at Rollins College. Reyna says that her roommate at school is the daughter of a former U.S. president.

The company of these young, intelligent, sensitive, gorgeous people from America fills us with good spirits. A servant builds a fire for us in the big hearth some thirty feet away—no need for it here at the equator, but the flames cast a pleasant illumination. Firelight emphasizes the rich, healthy glow on the sunburned faces of our new acquaintances. The ladies snuggle up to their athletic boyfriends while the lads trade soccer stories. The sight of it brings on the stark awareness that we are far from completing our mission.

Lucho excuses himself and returns to the room. Now the girls want to know what Richard and me do.

"I have never played soccer, but we both surf. I live in Hawaii, on Maui."

Reyna exclaims, "Oh yes, Hawaii is so beautiful! My uncle took our whole family to Hawaii on his private plane once. We only went to Honolulu. But it was so nice. The ocean was so clean and clear."

Richard has had a few drinks and so have I, and we are about to fade.

"Thank you very much for your company, you guys. Really, you have no idea how special this is for us. Thank you."

"Yeah, we really can't tell you," says Richard. "Thanks again. Really good to meet you all."

The Colombian girl says: "We are going back to Bogota in the morning. Are you going to be in Bogota?"

"I can't say how long, but we are going through there, I guess."

"Please take my phone number and call us if you get to Bogota. It is a beautiful city. Have you been there?"

"No. But if we can, we will call. Good night."

Our plan is to go to the DAS first thing in the morning, report being robbed, and get a visa. Walter says we can fly home on the visa alone.

Healthy fear can save your life, but paranoia kills. The worst is when you can't tell the difference any more. Cocaine drives you right to that breaking point, and that's where you find Lurigancho. This pleasant evening has brought the stench of Lurigancho sharply to my mind.

It is barely first light. Richard and me are ready for some breakfast. Lucho gets it.

"This is it, Lucho! We love you, brother. Thank you. This is a grand for you. Here is another for Oscar. And this thousand is for Arthur. You must give this money to the Reverend, Lucho. Arthur will need it."

"Oscar will appreciate this. And yes, poor Arthur, he will need this."

"Do you think the DAS will be a problem, Lucho?"

"Come, I will go with you just in case."

"One more obstacle."

"What will you do when you get back to the United States?"

I tell Lucho the facts. "Lucho, my brother—it might be a while before either one of us can call you up and let you know that we're home. But you know what, Lucho? We are looking forward to that. Federal prisons—we call Club Feds. Beyond that, who knows. I'm fucking crippled, Lucho. Ricardo is a mental case. He won't admit it, but we know he needs help. Right, Enrique?"

"Lucho, listen man," says Richard, ignoring my dart. "No one ever did anything like you have for me. You saved our lives. Eddie's right. We are expecting to be picked up at customs. You know what, Lucho? In federal prison we can have visits, food, water hot and cold, clean sheets on our bunk every few days. I can work out and be healthy. And I can see my new little girl without looking like I've been in Lurigancho.

"Plus, they have school, college. I can learn something. So what we're telling you, Lucho, is that we don't mind going to prison in the States. Not after Lurigancho."

"And we'll have a court hearing and a real lawyer. We won't wait years for a trial."

Lucho is flabbergasted that we are not going to be free, finally, after all this work to escape our horrendous fate. He sits down hard in the chair and puts his face in his hands. Suddenly he gets a new idea, and he pops his head up.

"If you think you are going to prison in the United States, why do you want to go there? Maybe you should live in another country, like Holland or France."

"Because we're Americans, Lucho."

At the DAS shack a fat, dark Colombian man in khaki shirt and pants tells us we must go to Brazil and report the robbery to the police there and bring back a copy of the report.

Lucho and Richard perform this last cross-bearing adventure. They go back into Brazil, saving me more painful hobbling on my melon-sized foot. I'm distressed at the thought of staying crippled all my life, but that anxiety is balanced by my relief that I still have a life to stay crippled in.

Our four young friends leave early for the airport. Just before they leave, one of the boyfriends pops his head in our door to say goodbye for them all.

Lucho and Richard are gone all day. I sleep through it. For some reason I need that long sleep.

Richard is first in the door. "Man, we almost had to come back for you. Anyway, come on. Let's go see the DAS before we miss the last flight to Bogota."

"Oh man, I'm for that."

Lucho comes in: "Did Ricardo tell you?"

I look at Richard. He doesn't seem to be as lifted as he was a second ago, before Lucho came in.

"No, not yet."

"Tell me what?"

Butterflies fill my gut.

"The cop at the DAS office is the chief of police here. He gave us this piece of paper. It is a document signed by him, the chief."

"What the hell does it say?"

"We have seventy-two hours to get a passport and leave the country, or else we go to jail."

"I'm ready!"

Lucho stays behind for a later plane and to be near just in case. We part at the gate.

Our flight to Bogota seems fast. The airliner is full of locals and tourists. I still feel trapped, but I'm trying to relax and be friendly with people who are curious about my foot. I tell them all the same story. "Hit a rock in the river when I jumped from a high cliff." That seems to end the conversation because my injury is self-inflicted. Out of sheer politeness nobody wants to ask me for a detailed account of my own stupidity. Mostly what I get is, "Oh, I see." Or, "Uh-huh, gee!"

At the terminal in Bogota we move unnoticed along with the other passengers. Although I'm subdued, Richard seems to be getting all jacked up with a feeling of freedom. He says, "We got some bucks. Let's go to the finest hotel we can find."

The taxi driver says, "Si Señor, the Tacendama Hotel is the finest hotel in Bogota."

Our taxi pulls up to the front of the hotel. Richard says one word: "Luxurious!"

"Where's the king and queen?"

A valet opens our doors.

At the desk we are told that with no passports we cannot register. We are turned away. The document signed in Leticia has no value.

"Don't worry. Let's get a cab to the Hilton. There are probably more Americans there."

Same thing at the Hilton.

We go right down the economic ladder until both of us are limping along the weary sidewalks of Bogota. By now the thought of being stopped on the street—a local cop or one of these foot-soldiers we keep seeing—has sunk in our hearts from the level of anxiety to downright despair.

"Shit, shit, shit," we keep saying as we stump down the streets.

"It's getting dark, R.B. At least two patrol cars have seen us. No telling what the hotel employees did when we left—could have called the DAS or something."

Richard looks up. "Okay, this place is only sixteen dollars a night, American. They'll let us in. We just been trying to get into the high-priced places, that's the problem."

"You think? I don't. The last place was only twenty bucks." We step inside the sidewalk hotel under blinking, ugly fluorescent lights. In the glum lobby a dark-skinned man stands at the shabby desk. This looks like one of those places that rents by the hour to the working ladies.

"Oh no, Señores, no!" says the clerk. "No passport, no rooms. Sorry, Señores. I give you the room and you have no passport, the police put me in jail. Jail is very bad, Señores."

I ask him, "Can I sit to rest here?"

"Si, Señor. No problem."

I remember having put something in my back pocket, and I get it out. As I'm reaching, Richard gets the same hit. "You got that chick's number, huh?"

"Hey! Let's call this lady. Reyna! Let's call Reyna."

I ask the man behind the desk to dial the number.

He listens for someone to answer. He speaks rapidly, identifying himself, then he listens. As he listens, his eyes flick up and lock on Richard and me. He says that he has two gringos with him, Eduardo and Ricardo, who would like to speak to you, Señorita.

Then his eyes widen with shock. He straightens his posture, then straightens it even more until he comes nearly to military attention. "Si, Si, Si," he says, then he hands me the phone.

"Hola! You remember us?"

Reyna invites Richard and me over to her residence. She tells me to give the telephone to the clerk, that she will give him directions and he will call us a cab.

After he hangs up, the clerk looks at us with an entirely new picture in his eyes. He says, "Would you like a room, Señores?"

We already got rid of those documents that claimed we are Peruvians—we threw them over the side of the speedboat to Leticia. So our one little bag has no reason to stay with us. The clerk calls a cab and gives directions to Reyna's. Then he takes our bag and gives us a key.

"Wow, should have called her hours ago."

"Didn't think of it. Only thinking of home. Of Amber."

"You never talk about your kid. I didn't think you really gave a shit!"

"Let's not talk about her now, either."

"This part of town reminds me of Miraflores."

"Does, huh? To me it looks like the Hollywood Hills."

"Great imagination."

The cab driver seems to know exactly where to go.

We motor into a spacious horseshoe driveway in the front of a ten-story condominium. There are four units on each floor. Richard pays the driver.

"Look for the elevator," I say. "My foot's killing me, and I don't want any more of those goddamn pain pills. They remind me of Lurigancho."

"What floor?"

"She said they—her and her mother—live on the tenth floor. At the top.

When the elevator opens at the end of its ride, we can see at a glance that they really do live on the top floor—the *entire* top floor.

This is the penthouse.

"Who are these people?"

"Push the bell."

Reyna herself opens the double wooden doors that lead into a cool entry cavern lined with rare woods. Richard looks at the paneled ceiling, which glows in shades between cognac and gold: "Looks like koa wood from Hawaii."

Reyna is cheery and answers, "Yes it is similar to koa, but it comes from Peru. You like it?"

We both answer, "It is beautiful."

Reyna yells a girlish call: "Mama! Come meet my new friends."

Julie and Charlie and Billy are also in the living room. The penthouse is huge, like a mansion. The mother has the bearing of a movie star, or maybe a queen. But she is gentle and caring. Her mothering response goes right to my wounded left foot. "Oh, por Dios, que es la problema."

"Mama! That is Eduardo. He will tell you in a moment. And this is Ricardo, Mama."

Richard reaches his hand out and gently shakes Mama's hand. He turns on that charm that women love about him. "What a lovely home you have, Señora. It is a pleasure to meet you and to be in your home. I apologize for my friend, he is a mess."

"My daughter says you were diving or jumping in the Amazones?"

"Yes, playing a game and not able to see what was below when I jumped."

I hate lying to good people. Like not telling Zoila the extent of my part in the drama at the Granja Azul that day we were arrested.

"Please come sit down. Take your weight off your foot. I am going to leave you young people alone. Enjoy your visit. I am very happy to have met you both. Come again the next time you're in Bogota. Maybe then you can go dancing, Eduardo. Good evening."

Reyna tells Billy to put a record on the turntable—Fleetwood Mac.

"What's the name of the album?" asks Richard. "Never heard it before."

Reyna look at him with disbelief and says, "You never heard 'Rumors?'"

"How long has this been out?"

"Years," she laughs. "I believe it's one of the best-selling records of all time."

"I guess I was just wasn't paying attention. Eddie here probably knows it. You ever heard of 'Rumors,' Eddie?"

"Nah, not me. Who is this, the Andrews Sisters?" Everyone laughs and believes that we are very comical.

We spend a pleasant evening lounging in the luxurious living room with our hostess and her American friends. At one point we ask about her father. She says that he is out at the ranch, the seventeen-hundred-acre ranch.

"My father goes to the ranch to be with his brother, my uncle."

"Your uncle is a rancher?"

Reyna giggles and says: "No, my uncle is the President of Colombia."

Ever since Pueblo Libre we have been led by grace. That is the only word I have to express what has happened whenever paths opened where there was no path. The cell door left open. Richard's imminent knowing that it was time. The cop in the next office, his phone ringing. The World Cup game timely distracting our guardians. All these incredible people who came to us out of that grace— Lucho, the Reverend, even Pelone who knocked me awake when I was too blind to see. Some greater power has been running this escape. Perhaps this greater power also opened the clear path that got me to Lurigancho in the first place, I don't know. But I do remember my sessions of solitude in the pre-dawn cell, moments of total contentment listening to the silence. Perhaps it's ridiculous to talk about following the trail of silence. But our escape has been littered with evidence of this trail, which I now believe is leading us home.

And Zoila. Zoila is the essence of all I have learned. Perhaps grace has allowed me, unworthy, simply to learn that such people exist. So that I could aspire to be one of them. Perhaps some day I will find a way to let that grace flow through me to others—to people in dark places who need to find their own way into the light of real freedom, which lies beyond body, beyond fear, and ahead into the deeper mystery of one's own life.

No, we could not get a fancy hotel room. But now here we are, desperado fugitives in the company of the country's presidential family, drinking their Chivas Regal and listening to rock-and-roll.

The next morning we awake at sunrise, and we call the U.S. embassy as soon as it opens. I explain to the lady on the phone that we have lost our passports and want temporary ones. The embassy worker says, "I'm sorry. You can take the pass that you have, go to the airport, and go home. But buy your tickets first."

"Come on, R.B. Let's go buy a ticket home." Saying that gives both of us a smile and a sudden burst of energy.

Only a block away we find a travel agency and buy two tickets— Bogota, a stop in Mexico City, and then into LAX.

Three hours later we are standing in line arguing with the immigration officer. The line is backed up and the airport is buzzing with travelers. This immigration officer is stressed to the max already. People are pushing and shoving. This is a big, busy place.

"You must have a passport!" The immigration cop doesn't want to bother with anything unfamiliar.

"But if you will look at this document from the chief of the DAS in Leticia."

"No! Passport only!"

"Listen, please look at the paper!" I let him see me plead with him.

This time the cop looks down at my foot and into my eyes, and then a quick look at Richard. "This is for you both, this paper?"

"Yes."

He quickly looks at the signature. "Okay. But you must fill out a visa over there." The immigration man points to a counter where other travelers are filling out the form provided.

Back in line, and we are passed through.

Once through all the checks, we're in the boarding area. "Hey man! This plane lands in Los Angeles."

Richard can't quite get the feeling. "I hope we make it," he says.

Richard clutches his stomach and bends forward as we stand at the last check-in. I clench his arm. "Hey, I'm the one you had to grab to keep from jumping in the river—I'm telling you, brother, we are going home. By tonight we'll be nice and comfy in our bunks with clean sheets in a safe federal prison. What's to worry?"

"Oh, fuck off. I think I'm going to puke."

"Here, look what I have. Money! Come, let's spend the cash we have left in the duty-free shop."

A little shopping takes our minds off the still-grave situation. Richard finds a couple of dolls for his little girl. We both buy perfume for our mothers. We buy a fifth of VO whiskey for the plane ride.

Nothing unusual takes place boarding the airliner. What's unusual is the fact that I have stopped feeling hunted and frightened. But Richard is more nervous than I have seen him since we jumped.

The plane has assigned seating. Richard has the aisle. I'm in the middle of three. Next to the window sits a grandmotherly woman. When I sit next to her, she asks me sweetly: "Tu hablas Espanol?"

The plane takes off, but Richard is still nervous. As soon as it levels off, he opens the whiskey. The stewardess asks us to put the bottle away. She tells us that her drinks are free. Richard starts to say something to me, but he is cut off by an announcement: "This is the Captain, ladies and gentlemen! We have been ordered back to Bogota. We apologize for this inconvenience and thank you for your patience."

The plane begins to bank sharply.

Richard reaches for the barf bag tucked into the seat in front of him. "Fuck, I told you something's wrong! It's those goddamn visas." He pukes into the bag.

"What? The visas? What about the visas?"

"Blah. Blah," he barfs.

Trying to catch his breath and keep from barfing, he says, "They're in our own names! Remember the treaty thing that lady was telling us about?"

"Oh fuck that!" I quickly turn my head to the lady next to me, but she seems to not have heard the F word. I turn back to Richard. "Listen man, we have been like puppets guided by something unseen. I gotta tell you, R.B. Before I jumped off the wall, I looked back at the second floor—and we jumped a little farther than two stories, man—and I saw a glow I've only seen before on acid. I'm not worried, R.B. Whatever is guiding us isn't going to take us down now."

Richard: "Blah, blah" into the bag.

"Is that your answer, man? Blah?"

Now we are circling over some remote area outside of Bogota.

The kindly señora next to me asks in English, "Is your friend okay?"

Richard is looking dead ahead, bracing himself for the return to Bogota. "Ask her if she knows Lurigancho."

"Do you know about Lurigancho in your country, Señora?"

Her eyes get real wide. She says, "Oh, that is the casa de diablo! Many men have died in that very bad place. How you know this place?"

The loudspeaker comes on.

"This is your Captain. We will not be returning to Bogota. Our next stop will be Mexico City for a short stopover. We will be arriving in Los Angeles on time. Thank you. Enjoy your flight."

"See? Nothing! We're going home, Richard. Get used to it!"

Richard has somewhat pulled himself together. "Yeah, right. I can hear one of those goddamn DAS cops calling the immigration police in Mexico City. 'When they got off the plane, arrest them for having no passports. Then put them on a plane to Peru!'"

He gets up and goes to the latrine to wash his mouth and throw some water on his face.

The lady next to me says that she's going to Studio City to visit her daughter and her daughter's family.

"Oh, your daughter married an American?"

"Yes, and they have three children. I have three grandchildren."

When Richard sits down again, the Peruvian lady is showing me pictures of her grandkids.

The plane makes a smooth landing in Mexico City.

Nearly everyone gets off the plane.

The Peruvian lady tells Richard and me, "I will not get off the airplane. The last time I come to here, when I get back on the airplane they make me go through customs all over again."

"Why?"

"They tell to me that when I get off the plane, I come into Mexico. And now getting back on the plane, I am leaving Mexico. I think it is for the money they make when everyone pays for the visa. We have to make the visa form and pay some money because we are in the Mexico airport for an hour. Isn't that terrible?"

Richard says, "So we can just stay on the plane?"

"Oh yes! I ask the stewardess. She say we can stay on the plane if we are going on to Los Angeles."

"I'm not getting off!"

"Yeah, I've seen Mexico City."

We both feel in our gut that the immigration police are looking for us in the international terminal.

No immigration officials or cops board the plane. We take off again within forty minutes.

Coming into Los Angeles gives me a warm feeling inside. I know I'll find medical attention. I believe our government is not going to send me back to a place where there are no human rights.

"Richard, when we get to customs—whatever happens, brother— be thankful. Remember, Arthur is still there."

"Not much we can do about that from Terminal Island!"

"By the way, did I thank you for coming back for me?"

"Shit, I had to. You were making so much fucking noise."

Richard goes to one customs line, and me to another.

The lady at the customs booth asks me, "Did you purchase any items such as souvenirs or anything you wish to declare?"

"Lady! All I have is this broken foot and this cane. No passport or luggage."

"Do you have money?"

"No, I have no money."

The customs officer looks me in the eye and says in all sincerity: "I'm sorry, but it is illegal to come into the United States with no money."

She calls another agent, and three tall uniformed men come over to the counter. "What's your name, sir?" the oldest agent asks. The other two observe. One is a black man; the other two are white.

"My name is Edward James Padilla. I was born about ten miles from right here, officer. I'm home."

The female officer looks at the other three with a nod of her head that says take him away. The lead customs guy says, "Will you come with us, please?"

Just before I enter the door of a small office, which one of the men holds open for me, I can see Richard going into another small office with three other customs men.

Inside with my three escorts: "Mr. Padilla, could you please unwrap your bandages for us?"

"Sure I can. Something wrong, officers?"

"Not yet," says the black man.

Another says, "Not everyone who comes through here with something wrong necessarily has something wrong."

"What do you mean? Why would anyone fake an injury like this?" As I finish my sentence, I remove the last of the bandages and expose my foot.

"Holy Toledo, Bud, how the hell'd you manage that?"

"Hey, it wasn't easy!"

I am getting a strong hunch these guys are not going to take me into custody. They are simply doing their necessaries.

The black guy says, "Dude came through here last week from where you guys just came from, Bogota. He had a leg missing to the hip. His fake leg, his prosthesis, was filled with twenty pounds of cocaine."

The oldest officer says, "Well, you'd better get that foot taken care of, Bud! That's all we need. Just finish filling out that form. And if you can remember your passport number, put it down. How long you been out of the country anyway?"

"Just a couple weeks is all. Glad to be back home, though. Really need to get this foot looked at."

I walk out, leaving the agents in the office. There is Richard. He has just walked out of his office.

All that remains is for us to walk through the big double green doors hoping that no DEA or any kind of police are standing there waiting to nab us. We are limping up the long ramp, moving in the right-hand lane of a steady stream of people. "So, Eddie, what are you going to do now?" says Richard. He is grinning, focusing straight ahead.

We walk along for a while.

Then I touch his shoulder. When he looks at me, I tip my head to the right. "You want to stop over here for a minute?"

We move out of the stream of people. Instantly I re-experience the yard at Lurigancho, walking the circular track with all the other inmates, then stepping out to steal a private conversation.

I look at Richard and really see him. I see him as I remember him before we started this journey. I see him as he is now—much more carved out and damaged, everything that was hurt and reckless about him now shining deeply in his eyes. I also think that I can see several versions of his future.

He says, "What is it, man? Scared to go through the doors?"

"No, that's not it. I just want to answer your question before I do."

He looks over at the doors, people pushing through them, getting on with their business. Then he looks back at me. "So what's your answer?"

"All I can come up with is this—it isn't over."

For once, thank God, he doesn't say anything. He just looks at me like a mirror of the way I am looking at him. I say, "But the next part is going to be a lot harder."

"Right," he says. "Until now, we always knew where we were running to."

"And now we're there."

Afterword

As Richard and me were taking our leave from Pueblo Libre jail, Arthur was throwing up in the latrine. One cop had gone to get food, another was talking on the phone, and the last was behind the desk in the lobby reading the newspaper. Ten minutes after we left, Arthur returned to the cell and lay down on that crusty mattress, his head spinning from the whiskey.

Ten minutes later, Arthur began to clear up just enough to wonder what the hell Eddie and Richard might be doing.

He went to the open cell door. Looking into the hall, he saw one of the cops coming toward him carrying a cardboard box of barbecued chicken. Arthur said, "Hola. Ou! I drank too much the whiskey."

The cop was at the door of the cell. As he handed Arthur the box of food, he said, "Los otros gringos estan en el baño?"

Arthur did not believe that los otros gringos were in the toilet. A flash came over him, and he nearly puked.

The cop handed Arthur the box and quickly stepped over to the latrine and looked inside. The latrine was empty.

The cop understood.

He turned to Arthur and pulled his forty-five automatic from his side holster. He shoved Arthur back from the cell door, then slammed the cell door shut. Then the cop ran to the front yelling: "Se han escapado! Se han escapado! Los dos gringos se escapado! Cuja su madre! Hijos de la puta! Llama la guardia Sevil rapido! Rapido!

"Hey, what's up out there?" Arthur yelled through the bars.

No one answered. The action up front got louder. Men were yelling in Spanish, mostly cussing. Arthur could make out that they were yelling and screaming about Eddie and Richard. Then it hit him with the full force of reality. Eddie and Richard had gone.

"Oh fuck! Oh fuck! Shit! Those crazy-ass motherfuckers!"

Arthur was at the bars gripping tightly, trying to see down the hall. Within fifteen minutes the hall filled with armed soldiers, their boots loud on the tiled floor of the police station.

A high-ranking officer came to the cell door, uniformed from head to toe. He told one of the cops to open the door of the cell.

"Gringo, where are your friends?"

His eyes were mean and unforgiving.

Arthur suddenly realized that we had actually got away, and a smile spread across his face. The officer turned to the soldier standing directly in back of him and gave a gesture. The soldier used his rifle butt to smash Arthur square across the mouth and jaw. Blood splattered the wall.

Arthur fell to the right, hitting the wall with the back of his head, and bounced forward then down onto his right side. He landed with his face kissing the cement, blood flowing from his mouth.

The officer ordered the soldier to close the cell door. The soldier kicked Arthur back into the cell. Arthur's limp body moved a few inches with each swift blow from the soccer-playing soldier's steel-toed boot. In the distance, the World Cup game kept erupting with roars from the crowd. A vicious blow to his upturned hip. Another to his left arm. Then a hard one to his rib cage, a kick that pushed him just inside the threshold of the cell door, and then the soldier slammed the steel bars shut. The officer left, and a cop came to stand in the same position. He locked the door.

Arthur was left there to bleed.

When he regained consciousness, he thought he heard Richard

and me screaming in pain. Then he listened more intently. It was the cops screaming. They were being beaten by the soldiers. The officer who gave the okay to bust Arthur across the face was yelling for the cops to confess taking a bribe.

"No! No, no Jefe, no. Ahhhh!"

And the other two as well—all of this was happening in the office right next to the door from which we escaped.

The beating ended quickly. The ranking officer was satisfied that the gringos had received no assistance from anyone here. The soldiers found the spoon that had opened the door. They were convinced that we had made a clean getaway.

Arthur explored the inside of his mouth with his tongue, discovering missing teeth and broken ones. He saw three of his teeth on the floor, stuck in the blood. His face was swelling rapidly. But even in his intense state of pain, Arthur laughed to himself, hurting his face: *"You two bastards! I'll be praying for you guys. Son of a bitch! They really did it!"*

The next day a rep from the embassy came to the jail to talk to Arthur. "Who did this to you?"

Arthur mumbled the words, "The soldiers."

"I am arranging to have you taken to a hospital. But I'm afraid I can do nothing about them taking you back to the prison. Lurigancho."

Mumbling again: "I know the name of the fucking place."

"Do you know where your buddies are or are going?"

"Hope they go home! Don't you?"

"Tell you the truth? Yeah, I really do."

After two days at the military hospital, one wrist handcuffed to the steel frame of the bed the whole time, Arthur was transported to Lurigancho.

This time Arthur had an addition to his handcuffs—shackles around his ankles in matching silver. He rode with soldiers armed with automatic weapons. No bus rides for Arthur—he got his own brand-new Chevy Suburban for transport. A soldier told Arthur that the new Chevy was courtesy of the DEA.

At the prison the soldiers removed his shackles and turned Arthur over to four prison guards who were waiting to escort the gringo back to his old cell. The entire population knew what had happened. They knew that two gringos had escaped this fucking nightmare. The guards walked at the slow pace Arthur was taking. He was in pain not only from his mouth and jaw but also from the fact that he had to face everyone.

As Arthur and his escorts walked into the Big Hall, a roar of a cheer went off. It grew louder as they passed each cellblock, one after the next. It was a cheer to match a championship soccer crowd, a cheer that meant this crowd's team had just scored the winning goal. The cheering grew deeper as half of the population started pouring into the Big Hall, and the sound echoed throughout the prison and reverberated in the unending drumming of passion, of defiance, of the insane desire to live and to escape.

Arthur was a hero among men. He was a light in the darkness.

And René was cheering the loudest.

* * *

Richard Brewer was my friend. He died of pneumonia June 6, 2008. He was a father and grandfather.

I paddled his ashes out, me and two other men he called brothers, in a six-foot swell at sunset. His daughters, three grandchildren, and many others were gathered around a fire on the beach. R.B. left before I could tell him how much I loved him.

Arthur got a pardon not very long after we escaped. He is currently working on his health and spiritual development. I will always be grateful for the strength he showed and for the humor he could see in Hell.

The only other person from Lurigancho I later met was Oso. Went to the store for ice cream and there he was. Turned out we were neighbors in the little town of Fairfax in Marin County, California.

Not all our cellmates were as fortunate as Arthur. I would have not received a pardon. Doubtful R.B. would have, either. The head of the DEA was quite disturbed when R.B. and I called him a "turncoat pig" and refused to snitch off our brothers.

Murphy was still locked up inside Lurigancho when Arthur left. I have no idea what happened to him.

Jimmy never intended to help me escape. He told Diane that I had snitched him off. But Jimmy had made a deal with Del Gado and set up his own brother-in-law. Murphy and Diane were innocent of Jimmy's plan.

Murphy did snitch me off to the PIP and the DEA. He actually signed a confession naming me as the one who had set it up between him and Jimmy's brother-in-law.

Eventually Jimmy was gunned down in the street in front of his mother's house.

Diane gave birth to two of Jimmy's children, and they all moved to New Jersey near Diane's parents. Later Jimmy contacted me to ask if I had been seeing Diane when he was in Colombia. I replied that if I could find him I would kill him. Shortly after, Jimmy pistol-whipped Diane and knocked out all her front teeth. She was hospitalized for a month. Diane called me in 1996 and asked my forgiveness for abandoning and betraying me. She cried. In 2010 Diane's mother told me Diane had died a homeless junkie alone in a Puerto Rican Hospital.

Today I live with a very special woman, my wife Lorey. As of June 2013 we celebrate thirty-two years in love. Lorey is the inspiration for me to write this story out, the beginning of my healing process. For the last twenty-eight years I have been working as a therapist treating addiction.

Edward Padilla

Made in the USA
Las Vegas, NV
07 August 2021

27733883R00239